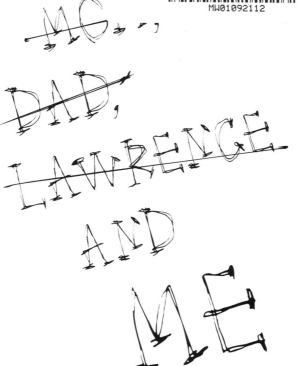

ME, DAD, LAWRENCE AND ME

DON HAUGEN

Some names have been changed in this book
to protect the privacy of certain individuals and families

ISBN: 1451513658
ISBN-13: 9781451513653
Library of Congress Control Number: 2010902959

DEDICATION

This memoir is dedicated to those who, through no fault of their own, have endured the most difficult childhood and adolescent situations one can imagine and against all odds have succeeded in making reasonably successful and happy lives as adults.

CONTENTS

PHOTOS

INTRODUCTION

The story I am about to tell you is a strange and unusual one, but I assure you it is true. It was my fate to be born the youngest son to Elling and Martha Haugen, my parents. I did not ask for them to be my parents, but given the opportunity I would have chosen differently. Some may believe God chose them for me. I think it was unexplainable fate that placed me in the position of being their child. I was born into my family by chance, and I was stuck there, for better or worse, pretty much forever. The two of them separately and together made life-altering choices, very bad ones many times, as it turned out. The consequences of their choices affected my life and many other lives profoundly. I struggled for years to overcome the damage my mother did to me emotionally. I struggled even more with the emotional problems my father caused for me. Surviving Mom and Dad was no mean trick.

MOM'S FAMILY

I was born in a house my parents rented in Minneota, Minnesota, during the Great Depression. My maternal grandmother, Emilie Blomme, served as midwife for my mother during my birth. It was in this place, with my mother and grandmother as witnesses, that I made my first crying screams on earth. By the time I came along, Grandma already had considerable experience as a midwife. She had assisted her daughters in the birthing of her grandchildren several times. It was a common occurrence at this time for Belgian mothers to assist their daughters when giving birth.

Both my maternal grandparents were devout Roman Catholics and had come from the Flanders region of Belgium. Emilie came from St. Laurens and Grandpa Gustav from Nevele. Each came from long established farm families in their respective communities.

Gustav and Emilie came to America through Ellis Island in 1906 on the ship *Red Starling*. Emilie was a month shy of her eighteenth birthday, and Gustav was twenty-one. They did not know each other in Belgium and did not meet on the ship. Still unknown to each other, they traveled to the same Belgian community in South Bend, Indiana, where they met, married and started a family. The first three of their six children, including my mother, were born in South Bend. They were, in order of birth, Mary, Martha, and Margaret. Martha was my mother. The remaining children, Rachel, Madeline, and Rene, were born during the family's migration through the Belgian communities in Kewanee and Moline, Illinois, and finally Minnesota.

They settled permanently by 1914 in rural Belgian community several miles north of Minneota, where they became tenant farmers. This was their livelihood until they retired in their sixties.

As Grandma became elderly and I became more interested in understanding the family, I took many opportunities to talk with her about her life in Belgium and America. She was especially talkative if we started off with a bottle of Grainbelt beer. She would swoon over the landscape of her native Belgium and the small community of St. Laurens, where she grew up. She told me how happy she was then and how pretty that area was. Indeed she was right. She knew I had been there, and that pleased her immensely. I had met her first cousin on one of my visits. She was in a nursing home too and close to ninety years of age, but she remembered Emilie. Among other things, she told me Grandma's name was not really Emilie, it was Marie and that she was a year older than she claimed to be. So I told Grandma this, and she looked at me with a puzzled wide-eyed expression before she confessed that her cousin was right. She was so pleased that her cousin remembered her after all these years. Grandma was about ninety at the time of this revelation.

She would often tell me that she never liked Minnesota. She said she hated it from the day they moved there. She called it a "Godforsaken land," flat and ugly. Grandpa had brought her out here when she was young with all those little kids. She liked Illinois much better; it was prettier. Then she would laugh, placing her hand over breast and say, "Oy yoi yoi yoi yoi," a Belgian expression and one of her favorites. It means something like, "Oh my God, I can't believe it," or "Wow, wow, wow."

Grandma was a happy woman, filled with laughter and tears, with a gift for talking. She had an expressive face that would sputter and spit with glee over the things that tickled her fancy. She was rather short, only five feet two inches, and kind of grandmotherly fat. She had false teeth, but they made her mouth sore so she often went without them. She couldn't hear worth a darn and had a hearing aid that didn't work well. So she would slap the middle of her very large breasts where the hearing aid lay hidden. She did this whenever I said something she didn't like, or if it was buzzing. The hearing aid buzzed a lot, so she was constantly slapping, muttering, and swearing at the device in Belgian. Then she would raise her large watery eyes toward heaven and ask forgiveness from God for her cursing and make the sign of the cross over her bosom. It was a unique and unforgettable pleasure to watch Grandma laughing, talking, sputtering, and spitting. Her rather generous lips would flop and flap around her toothless gums as she spun her stories in complete happiness.

Whenever I came to visit, I would knock on her usually open door and step into her room. When she saw me she would immediately make the sign of the cross and look up to heaven and utter some Belgian words of thankfulness. Then she'd say, "Donnie, Donnie, Donnie," and clutch me by the shoulders with both hands, look me in the eyes, and tell me how pleased she was to see me. This was followed by a big hug and tears of happiness tumbling down her generous Flemish face.

Soon we would sit down in her room with smuggled-in Grainbelt and get down to what she liked: me listening and Grandma talking. Oh, how she loved to talk. She told me over and over various stories about her and Grandpa making moonshine in their little farm house in the darkness of night. They would close all the windows and pull down the shades so the odor of the still and the kerosene lamplight wouldn't be seen or smelled from the road. She said it would get so hot in the kitchen from the still they could hardly breathe, and the sweat would pour off of them. "Oh, Grandpa and I would have fun—so much fun," she said.

She would tell her stories with the Belgian mixed with English rolling off her tongue. I heard many times how they could have been rich if Grandpa would have drunk less of the moonshine himself. Customers would come to buy and Grandpa would drink some to show how good it was. Over the course of several sales pitches he would get drunk and start giving the moonshine away. She told me the Feds came one evening and bought moonshine from Grandpa and then arrested him and took him to off to jail. And there she sat, no Grandpa and all those kids.

Grandma was right about the bleak landscape she found herself in. Minneota and the surrounding area were indeed unwelcoming. The vast area surrounding Minneota was flat prairie and essentially void of trees. Only the tough trees survive—large ones or little scrubby ones—because the winds are continual and often punishing. They start at sunrise and increase in strength as the sun gets higher in the sky. Only the setting sun slows the wind. One becomes thankful for nightfall to still the relentless wind.

My reward for spending so many young summers in Minnesota is a sensual one. I remember the smell of newly mown hay on moonlit nights with all the stars ablaze in that deep dome of a sky. Those summer evenings filled my sensual memory with that fragrance and that sky, which I recall with pleasure when I smell day old newly cut grass.

DAD'S FAMILY

My paternal great grandfather, Elling Knudson Haugen, was born in 1826 on the Haugen farm near Honefos, Norway. His wife, Gunhilde Viker, was born in 1830 on the Viker farm near Honefos. The two were married in April 1853 in the Norderov Lutheran Church south of Honefos. They signed out of that church the next day to set sail for the United States. They arrived in a Canadian port and somehow made their way to Wisconsin, probably by ship through the Great Lakes. Then they traveled overland to a Norwegian community in Eau Claire, Wisconsin. Gunhilde had several brothers and sisters, and many of them came to the United States. Most likely one or more were already settled in Eau Claire.

Gunhilde Viker was a descendant of the ancient kings of Norway, and facts and legends about her ancestors are recorded as far back as 100 BC. The history includes such characters as Harold the Fair Haired and Eric the Bloodaxe.

Great Grandpa Elling applied for citizenship in 1854. By that time he had begun tenant farming and had started a family in Eau Claire. Within a few years, the couple grew restless for better opportunities and migrated west, further into the great prairie, like so many Norwegians of the time. Their next stop was Mower County, Minnesota, where they settled in a tiny Norwegian settlement called Bear Creek, just south of Rochester, and began tenant farming once more.

By 1873 they had saved enough money to buy a large relinquished homestead north of Minneota, about two hundred miles northwest of Bear Creek. The family made the trip to their newly purchased land with oxen and wagon, walking all the way. After arriving on their new land, they built a sod house and settled in to till the soil. There they would spend the rest of their lives.

These young people married and began raising families, many of which expanded exponentially until it was hard to tell in that part of Minnesota who was a relative and who was not. The family prospered on their rich land. Some held local political office and were active in church and community affairs. Over time, their children acquired large parcels of land. Elling K. died from pneumonia in 1890. Gunhilde lived until 1918. Farming was still kind to the family until the stock market crash of 1929.

My paternal grandfather, Hans, and his wife, Helen, had six children—Sanford, Marie, Norman, Elling, Bertha and Harland. My father, Elling, named after his grandfather, was born in 1901. He spoke Norwegian at home, as did his siblings and parents. They went to a Norwegian-speaking Lutheran church in Minneota. His first real encounter with English was in the country schoolhouse near the farm. Before the Depression the family prospered on the farm. Dad was educated through eighth grade in the country school near their farm. After graduation he worked as a teacher's assistant at the school for three years. He was confirmed at Hope Lutheran Church in a fine-looking new suit and shiny boots at the age of twelve. Life was good. He worked on the family farm and apparently was doing well. The extended family members were all land owners and were well off compared to Gustav and Emilie, who were tenant farmers. Dad was a nice-looking young man about six feet tall. He drove a new car in 1929, and for a Lutheran, he was somewhat bold in that he went to barn dances and was known as a pretty good square-dance caller.

MY PARENTS

My mom and dad were neighbors. They grew up near one another a few miles north of Minneota and were two good looking young people. Mom was about five feet four inches tall with a nice figure. She was very pretty with large dimples in her cheeks when she smiled. She and Dad made a handsome couple.

Because they were neighbors, their families knew each other well. It was probably natural they would get together romantically. They went to the same dances together and probably went riding in Dad's new car too.

But they came from two separate communities. Mom was a devout Belgian Catholic and Dad a devout Norwegian Lutheran. Discrimination based on religion was a way of life. Minneota's shopkeepers were identified by their religious preference. Catholics shopped at the Catholic shops and Lutherans at the Lutheran ones. The lines were still clearly drawn when I was a young man in the 1950s. Harold Friend's saloon was for Lutherans; Catholics went to Joe Dero's. By and large, the Lutherans and the Catholics disliked each other.

Elling and Martha became involved romantically and planned to marry. An announcement appeared in the *Minneota Mascot* that the two well-known, popular young people were to be married. Somehow, my mother persuaded my father to convert to Catholicism, and they were married at Saint Edward's Roman Catholic Church in Minneota in 1930. There was angry family opposition to their marriage and hard feelings between the families that lasted for the next several decades. My older brother, Lawrence, was born in 1931, and I came along three years later. Both of us were baptized at St. Edward's. By the time I was born, Dad was in the terrible situation of being a poor Catholic man unable to find work to support his young family. There was no hope of any financial start from his now-poor relatives, to say nothing of the fact that he had left their Lutheran church. The good-looking man with sparkling blue eyes, who my mother and her family thought was rich, was now her poor husband.

MINNEOTA, MINNESOTA

I spent the first six years of my life in Minneota. In that short time, we lived in at least five different houses or apartments, maybe more. I don't know why we moved so much, but I think it was because Dad couldn't pay the rent, and we would be forced to move.

I remember four of the places very well, perhaps because of the things that happened to me in each one. Those experiences are fixed in my memory permanently. A lot of the memories are pleasant. We lived above Carl's restaurant. I must have been three years old. I got a little pink rubber truck for Christmas. At about the same time, my brother and I got identical outfits and matching hats. My mom took Lawrence and me to have a portrait taken together at a studio above Johnson's grocery store in those outfits.

We lived in a large house near Hope Lutheran Church. There, Dad pulled some of my baby teeth by tying a string around one tooth at a time and tying the other end of the long string to a doorknob, then he slammed the door shut. My snared tooth went flying out of my mouth with the slam of the door. It was very effective and made my brother and me laugh in shock and surprise. The teeth must have been really loose or I think I would remember the experience as painful. But I remember it as amazing.

When I was four or five, we lived south of the railroad tracks in a strange long duplex. I remember waking up in the night and no one was home. I had had a nightmare. I cried and screamed for what seemed like hours. Finally the neighbors came to see what was happening and comforted me. I had been dreaming about a really scary movie I had been taken to the day before. My parents and brother were summoned from somewhere and all became quiet again.

We lived in another house about a block south of St. Edwards. I must have been five years old by this time. I remember listening to the cops-and-robbers show *Gangbusters* on the radio. I remember playing in an old barn behind the house with my brother and other kids. We could also walk to the store and buy one-cent Baby Ruth candy bars.

Until recently, I had placed those childhood memories aside. Perhaps I chose to remember only the pleasant memories and forget the unpleasant ones. When I think of my childhood in Minneota it is always summertime. I recall little things that happened, like those mentioned above. Then if I spend much more time on the Minneota of my childhood, I begin to remember the other, unpleasant things.

CHAPTER 1

MEMORIES FROM CHILDHOOD

I don't remember when my mom started taking me with her to meet her boyfriends so she could have sex with them. It probably started before I was three years old. Or maybe it was when my brother, Lawrence, started school. One of the earliest times I remember probably happened when I was five. I recall it all too vividly, almost as if it were yesterday.

In my mind's eye, I can still see the small black dust-covered car turn into the driveway of a large field of tall corn and park. There we waited quietly for a while to see if other cars would be coming down this lonely narrow dirt road. None did. I remember that my mom and the man driving the car got out and climbed into the backseat. Mom told me to stay in the front seat and to lay down and go to sleep. I protested several times, but finally I did as she instructed. In the back seat Mom and the man took off some of their clothes. Soon the car began to rock. It was early afternoon on a cool sunny autumn day.

I laid in the front seat pretending to be asleep. Most of the time, I had my head buried in my arms trying not to hear or think anything. I had been instructed in this behavior many times before. I didn't like what I had to do, but I did it anyway.

My mother laid on her back in the back seat, naked from the waist down. The bottom of her skirt was pulled up around her waist; her breasts were bare and her legs were up in the air. Mom had a birthmark on the inside of her upper thigh; it looked like a large June bug. They sang a little tune about a June bug and joked about where the bug was heading. The man placed himself between her legs and put his belly against mom's belly. He was naked from the waist down. There was something wrong with one of his hairy legs. It was stiff or something. I know because I would peek over the back of the front seat to see what they were doing. They began to rub their bellies together. They made a lot of noise, grunting, groaning, breathing hard and giggling. They paid no attention to me peering over the front seat. Between peeks, I would lay down, shut my eyes, and put my hands over my ears.

When they finished rubbing bellies, the car stopped rocking. Mom said they should be quiet so as to not wake me. But I had been awake the entire time. I heard them open the car doors and get out. They talked softly. When they were outside the car I watched them pee and then put their clothes on. The man had a crippled leg and walked with a severe limp.

As far back as I can remember my Mom took me along when she met her boyfriends. I guess she couldn't afford a babysitter. The routine was always the same. They would park the car and Mom would put me in the front seat. Mom and her man would go into the back seat. She would tell me to go to sleep. If I protested she would get angry with me. I must have learned it was best if I pretended to be asleep. I don't think they cared; my pretending was good enough for them.

I don't recall how I learned to be so obedient; it must have happened over a considerable period of time. It is difficult to remember when she started these rendezvous or how many times she did this, but it was often. I recall hearing them in the backseat and standing up to watch them from over the top of the front seat. If my mom saw me, she would sometimes tell me to lay down and go to sleep. At times, I refused to stay down. I would lay down and then get up and tell them I wanted to go home. Mom would get angry and tell me to be good or she would spank me. Sometimes I think she threatened me with something worse. I know at times I was very scared.

The men were big, much bigger than me, and I was afraid of them. They laid on top of my mom, and they moaned and grunted. They were monsters to me, big hairy monsters. Generally they smelled like whiskey or beer and cigarettes. One of them dragged his leg when he walked.

Sometimes I thought my mom was getting hurt, and sometimes it sounded like she was having fun. When they finished rubbing bellies, Mom would wake me from my pretend sleep, hug me, and tell me what a good boy I was and how much she loved me. She would promise me candy or a present before we went home.

Mom didn't always rub bellies in a car. Sometimes she rubbed bellies with a man in a cabin by a lake. I remember watching the white painted guard posts along sweeping curves of the road on the way to the lakeside cabin. For some reason those posts have stuck in my mind. I also remember being locked out of the cabin much of the time and peeking through the windows. They must have been rubbing bellies.

Much later in my life when I began recalling these events, I tried to figure out where those cabins were. I think they were at Lake Benton, and the white guard posts along the curves in the road were south of Canby.

The men never took Mom and me home. They always let us out several blocks from our house. We would walk home, and I would get candy or a toy, usually from Johnson's store. On the way, Mom would make me promise not to tell Dad where we had been or who we had been with. She would warn me by shaking a finger in front of my face, if I told anyone our secrets she would not love me anymore or buy me anymore presents. We often stopped at her friend Lizzie's house on the way home. Mom would ask Lizzie to say we had been with her if my dad asked, and Lizzie would agree. I don't know why Lizzie would lie for us.

Dad usually asked us where we had been or what we had done during the day. Mom would lie and tell him I was with her and that he could ask me. If he did ask me I always performed the way I had been taught.

I loved my dad, but I was afraid of him. I knew Mom and I were doing something that was wrong. I don't know how I came to understand that, but I knew. I could feel it inside of me. There was something very bad about what we were doing. I have never been able to forget these men or the way I felt about them. I hated those men.

Because I had terrible secrets, I knew I had to be very careful about what I said. Sometimes I was afraid words would just pop out of my mouth by accident.

At times, I felt like I could just explode. I thought my mom, my dad, or one of the men would kill me if something just slipped out.

This fear became more real in regard to the cistern at the strange duplex. Dad went fishing with some his friends. They caught so many fish they didn't know what to do with them, so they put the fish down into the cistern. I was fascinated by the fish swimming in the cistern, so I would open the cover and look down at them swimming around. Dad said he would throw me into the cistern with the fish if I did not stop messing with them. I was not sure if he meant what he threatened to do. But I thought that if he did throw me into that deep hole, I would drown for sure.

Mom liked to play a game with me. It was "the how much do you love me" game. She would ask me how much I loved her, and I would stretch out my little arms to their limits. She would then ask me how much I loved my dad. I would show her the same amount for Dad. She could not accept this. I always needed to show her I loved her a little more. She would keep at the game until I reduced the amount of arm stretch for my dad. Mom had a way of always winning this game even though I wanted to show my dad I loved him just as much. She did it with humor somehow, making me giggle by teasing me and tickling me into showing her just a little more love in my outstretched arms. Dad would often be in the room with us when she played that game. I heard him say many times that she should not be making me play the game. But it was to no avail. She never stopped playing.

It seems that Mom rubbed bellies with many of the men we knew. They lived in and around Minneota and were friends of my parents. My brother and I played with their kids; we went as a family to their homes regularly. My folks would play cards, drink, talk, and laugh together with the man and his wife or other guests. This was difficult for me because I had all these secrets that my mom made me promise to never tell anyone.

In spite of our secrets, or maybe because of them, Mom and I were almost inseparable. I went everywhere with her, holding hands as we walked. She gave me lots of hugs and snuggled my face with hers, making me giggle, which made her giggle too. She frequently held me on her lap and told me how much she loved me. I felt very close to her. I loved and feared her. She was a wizard.

We had an old cook stove in the very long strange duplex across the tracks. It looked more like a barn than a home, lacking any windows in front for the inhabitants to see out of or be seen by passersby. It only had a front door, as I recall. In the winter, Mom often held me on her lap with her feet on the oven door warming them. I would extend my legs along with hers toward the heat. Together, we would go through her collection of mail order catalogues. She loved to look at them and pick out things for herself and for me. I always wanted a cowboy suit. I don't think she ever really ordered anything, and I never did get that cowboy suit. They were her wish books, but I don't think she could afford to buy anything.

Mom comforted me when I was hurt and doctored me when I was sick. Indeed, she nursed me on her breast until I was near three years old. I remember my Aunt Rachel scolding my mother for letting me nurse, so I must have been too old for it. A short time later, I remember Mom scolding me for eating dirt. I remember doing that, but I have no idea why I did it. I would make mud pies and eat them. Mom said when I had eaten a bushel of dirt I would die. "One bushel is all you get to eat in a lifetime," she would say. Grandma told me the same thing. Their continual reminders apparently deterred my appetite for mud pies, and I quit eating them.

I was undoubtedly my mother's favorite child. Lawrence was my dad's. Dad called him Sonny and played with him more than with me. That may have been because he was three years older and could do more. Lawrence and I slept in the same bed together at night. We played together in the house on rainy days. But generally he played with the older kids when it was nice outside. I played with the little kids in the neighborhood. I don't remember who they were anymore, but I do remember an older kid on a bicycle riding down the sidewalk and running right over me. No permanent damage was done to me, but I remember crying and screaming and running back to the house for my mom.

Often Mom and I would walk together from our strange duplex across the railroad tracks to downtown Minneota and the corner where the commodity truck came and parked. We pulled a little red wagon behind us. There we waited with a crowd of people until the truck came. Then Mom and the other people waiting would get groceries from the men on the back of the truck, things like flour, oatmeal, sugar, and raisins. These were relief groceries for the poor. We put our groceries in our little wagon and took them home. Then Mom would bake bread and oatmeal raisin cookies. I will never forget the cookies, the aroma of freshly baked bread, or the smell when my mom ironed clothes. They are pleasant reminders that not everything from my childhood was secretive and scary.

Mom didn't have a job; she stayed at home for the most part. I doubt if there would have been any work available for her. It was sometime in the late 1930s, and we must have been very poor. Dad worked for the WPA driving a truck. I remember him taking me for rides once in a while in what I think it was a big gravel truck.

The family went to St. Edward's Catholic Church on Sundays. Mom, Dad, Lawrence, and me. My maternal aunts, uncles, grandparents, and cousins all went to Catholic churches in the neighboring communities. Many of them went to church in Taunton, Ghent, or St. Leo. Generally on Sundays, regardless of what church we all went to, we'd go to Grandma's house for dinner and stay until evening. The men would drink beer and talk, the women would just talk. I would play outside with my brother and my many cousins.

The road north of town to Grandma's house was a long gravel one, with a bumpy bridge over a creek that finally led to a narrow lane and Grandma's farm. Closer to the house, the lane had white painted rocks spaced at regular intervals. There were patches of flowers planted everywhere around the large white house. There was a big red barn and a windmill, and usually a gigantic pile of corn cobs to play on. A creek meandered through the pasture in back of the barn. The water made large sweeping curves as it flowed gently downstream. There were deep pools in the curves. We used these pools for fishing holes and swimming pools.

Grandma's house was spotlessly clean. Dozens of lace doilies covered all the upholstered furniture and tables. Many shells from the ocean sat about on tables. "If you pick them up and listen you can hear the ocean," Grandma said. We would pick them up and listen. Sure enough, she was right.

Their home was full of Catholic things. Pictures of Jesus and Mary with immaculate hearts were prominently displayed. There were crucifixes in every room. There was a big radio in the parlor next to Grandpa's chair, which no one was allowed to sit in it except Grandpa.

Grandpa was about five feet eight inches tall, thin, muscular and wiry. He was rather quiet and gentle unless provoked by noisy grandchildren when he was trying to listen to Gabriel Heater and the news. Or unless he had too much beer. Then he became loud and sang Belgian songs while he danced a little jig of sorts. That made all of us laugh.

Except for the parlor, all the rooms in the house were obviously decorated by Grandma. The kitchen was her pride and joy. It was her workplace, and had also been the distillery. Her cook stove gleamed with shine and cleanliness. I watched, intently at times, as she cleaned the cooking surface of the great cook stove. She took some kind of wax paper and rubbed it across the entire hot surface until it would shine so you could see your face in it. The kitchen floor shined as well. I think she put wax on it too. Grandma's kitchen always smelled like homemade bread and roasted chicken. What a wonderful place to have a grandma.

Like my grandparents, my mom loved the Catholic Church and all the artifacts that went with it. The pictures of Jesus and Mary and the crucifixes always accompanied us as we moved from place to place in Minneota. I think Mom went to confession and communion most every Sunday. Mom admired the nuns; she thought they were so beautiful. She often said she always wanted to be a nun and could be if she were not married. She thought St. Edward's priest, Father Casey, was the most wonderful person in Minneota. Mom looked forward to the day I would grow up and become a priest too.

CHAPTER 2

AUNT RACHEL AND OTHER MEMORIES

My Uncle Henry and Aunt Rachel lived in Minneota too. Rachel was my mother's sister. She was sturdily built, taller than my mother and had huge breasts. She talked in a naturally loud voice, and she laughed loudly and frequently. Her face could easily flash from scolding me to laughing with me. Her house was filled with crucifixes and pictures of Mary and Jesus. The ever-present doilies rested on all her furniture. Her house always smelled of fresh bread and good things to eat. She had two children, Donnie Pete and Patty. Donnie Pete was a few months younger than me. There were three of us about the same age named Donald so each of us were called by our first and middle names.

Uncle Henry looked like Humphrey Bogart. He thought mostly of sex and fixing things that were broken. He could fix a clock or repair the engine of his car by himself. He liked to tease my mother by putting his hand up her skirt. She would pull away from him and ask Rachel how she could live with such a "dirty" man. Rachel would just say, "Sex is all Henry thinks about," and give him a sour look. Henry would laugh.

Donnie Pete was a skinny freckled faced kid about as tall as me. He lived in town too, so we played together a lot. One day, he and I put ten or so of his mother's nearly grown chickens into a hand-turned corn sheller. We shoved each chicken into the sheller intake hole one at a time. A corn sheller separates the kernels of corn from the cob. We separated the harder parts of the chickens from the softer parts. The juices ran out of the shelled corn hole at the bottom of the machine, and the harder parts came out through the end were the cobs were ejected. Feathers stuck to everything. And, of course, the chickens made a terrible frightened squawking noise as we ground them up.

Aunt Rachel heard the chickens pleading for their lives and caught us in the act of "shelling" them. She screamed at us and was absolutely furious. She spanked us both really hard until we were crying and screaming. In retrospect, I don't blame her. I don't know for the life of me why we did such a gruesome thing.

The house we lived in near St. Edward's was not far from Donnie Pete's house. I remember many things that happened while living there. I was five years old, going on six, and was to start the first grade in September. It was in this house that my brother and I came down with the measles at the same time. I remember laughing and giggling as we played and fought with each other in our darkened bedroom. We were not well supervised, and I went out into the bright sunlight many times while I was still sick. As a result, I seriously damaged my eyesight for the rest of my life.

My brother was a piece of work. Today they would label him hyperactive. One day he climbed on top of the porch roof while I was playing down below on the sidewalk. He hollered down at me to look up at him. I looked up to see what he was doing, and he urinated on my head. I learned that urine was salty, and Lawrence was not always to be looked up to.

We played with the neighbor kids in the barn behind the house. Sometimes we played upstairs in the old barn. The upstairs was really kind of like an old attic. It was our place to play "doctor." Our game was essentially a chasing game. At first, I was largely an unwilling participant in this game as were most of the girls. I had seen strange men take my mother panties off in the back seat of a car many times. I thought pulling down the girl's panties was bad. My brother and the other boys didn't seem to think so. They thought it was great fun. I remember being very uncomfortable with this type of play, probably because of the secrets I was keeping. I had never told anyone, including my brother, the secrets my mom had made me promise to keep. But with the Lawrence's encouragement, I joined in the game of pulling down panties too. And it was fun. There was a lot of running, chasing, laughing, and giggling.

It was the summer of 1940, and I had grown a lot. I was now able to tag along with my brother and literally run all over town. My Mom had stopped taking me with her to meet her boyfriends when Lawrence got out of school in the spring. I was free to play all over town as long as I was with my brother. It was a small town. We walked uptown to buy candy and pop if we had money or over to other kids' houses. We were always barefooted and seldom wore shirts. Shoes were for church only. Our feet were tough. Hot pavements and gravel roads didn't bother us in the least.

We had an old Coaster wagon, the old commodity wagon, and its wheels kept falling off. So we fastened them back on by putting a nail through the hole on the end of the axle and bending it. We road the wagon by putting one knee in it and pushing it with the other leg while placing one hand on the side of the wagon and steering the tongue with the other. We would go as fast as we could down the sidewalk then coast to a stop and do it again. It was murderous on the inside of my ankle because that bent nail would often catch me on the ankle bone and rip a hole in my skin. Another big problem was the uneven sidewalk sections. They were deadly on big toes. It was very easy to jam your toe into an upturned edge of the sidewalk. Repeatedly doing this led to an enormous bloody and painful stubbed big toe.

Our favorite games were cops and robbers, cowboys and Indians, and army games. We were well equipped. We each had cap pistols. I also had a spark firing Tommy gun, and my brother had a secondhand BB gun. I would try to set things on fire with my sparking gun, but I never was successful. Lawrence, however, was successful shooting my mother in the buttocks with a BB while she was bent over getting something out of the oven. He was eight years old and got a severe beating for that.

We listened to the radio a lot. My mother listened to her stories. Dad, Lawrence, and I listened to *Gangbusters* and the news. Finland was fighting the Soviet Union. They kept saying that "gorillas" were fighting the Soviets in Finland. When I was five, I didn't know the word *guerilla*, so it seemed odd that big hairy animals that lived in the jungle would be fighting with guns against the Soviets. I don't know if my mother could explain it either. I am sure I asked her. Maybe, she just thought that my confusion was kind of cute and let me continue puzzling over it.

You may have noticed that I haven't mentioned my dad's relatives. I haven't mentioned my paternal grandparents, aunts, uncles or cousins. That's because I do not remember ever visiting them or seeing them visit us. I believe the anger over my dad's marriage to my Catholic mother completely alienated us from my Lutheran relatives during those first six year of my life. My dad may have visited his people by himself. I do not know.

CHAPTER 3

FIRST GRADE, 1940

I started the first grade at St. Edward's Catholic School in September. It was about two blocks from my house. Sister Stella was my teacher. She was young and very pretty. I loved her. Mom said she looked like the Virgin Mary.

I was a poor student and could not do the work as well as the other kids. Sister Stella would put things on the blackboard at the front of the classroom. Students were expected to copy them in a workbook, but I could not do it. I sat about midway back in the first row of seats next to the large windows that covered the east wall of the room, and I had trouble seeing the blackboard. So Sister Stella moved me to a front seat.

Sister Stella must have thought that maybe I just couldn't see very well. She must have met with the other nuns and Father Casey about my problem. As a result, Father Casey took my mother and me to the doctor in Marshall, Minnesota, and I was fitted with a pair of very thick glasses. The world suddenly became bigger and brighter than it had been before. Sister Stella smiled at me a lot because suddenly my work improved.

I soon learned there were children at school who were called wallflowers, and there were others who were not. I was not. We teased the wallflowers and made them cry. I loved to play with other kids and was accustomed to the rough and tumble activities of my friends during recess. I learned the word *fuck* from other kids on the playground. I learned what fucking was and soon figured out that what my mom had been doing was fucking, not rubbing bellies.

One day long before I started school, a big black car with large red taillights came to our house. It was my Great Uncle Prosper and his wife. They had come from Illinois to visit us. Mom had said he was rich, as was everybody in Illinois. His car looked like it. We had a car, but it did not look like Uncle Prosper's. I heard Prosper talking to my folks about maybe moving to Illinois. But we did not move, and I must have forgotten about it.

But then after it had become much colder outside, probably middle October 1940, my parents gathered all their belongings and put them in the car. We left Minneota in the dark of early morning, my brother and I bundled up under blankets with our household goods in the back seat. We moved that day to Illinois, where all the rich people lived.

Sister Stella and St. Edwards Catholic School became a part of my past, and I never returned to a school of any kind in Minneota.

We moved south of Cambridge, Illinois, to a farm that belonged to Grandma's nephew, Eddie Roman. Prosper had arranged it. It was a nice farm with a big white house and big red barn. There were a lot of trees around and a large creek down the road. Like most farms in the early 1940s, this one had no electricity or running water. The toilet was an outhouse. Water came from a well with a hand pump. Our waste water disposal was a "slop pail" hidden under the sink. Baths were taken in a metal tub. Our lights at night were kerosene lamps.

Within a few days of moving in, my brother and I were covered with itchy welts all over our bodies. Mom took us to the doctor thinking we were allergic to something in our new environment. We were. We had moved into a house full of fleas, and the fleas loved little kids. The house had to be fumigated, and my brother and I were bathed in kerosene. Mom said she had never heard of fleas biting people.

My new school was a white one-room building about a mile east, the opposite direction from the creek. This school was very different from the large brick school I attended in Minneota. It was called Red Oak Hollow. Grades one through eight were all in the single room together. In my old school, there were only first graders in my room. I was six years old and it was middle October.

The kids at school teased me about my thick glasses, and my teacher was concerned about my eyesight. She apparently talked to the appropriate county people, and soon they were considering sending me to a school for the blind. They talked with my parents and me. My mother was determined that I should not be sent there, and the school authorities agreed to wait and see if my eyesight deteriorated further. If it worsened, then I would go. I remained at the little white schoolhouse.

Soon I was having fun with my new friends. They were kids from about six to about fourteen years old and maybe thirty in number. Halloween came quickly, and we had a party at school. I remember it well because we got to dress up in scary costumes.

After I had gotten dressed in my scary outfit, Mom and Lawrence painted my face. I wanted to see how scary I was, so I climbed on the kitchen sink to see myself in the mirror. Below the sink was a cabinet with an oval shaped knob for a door handle to access the slop pail. I slipped and fell and caught that knob under my kneecap. There my knee stuck. The knob punctured the skin and lodged under my kneecap and held me fast. Mom got me loose while I cried and screamed. She put iodine on the wound and bandaged it up. Now, iodine makes a six-year-old cry too. It hurts like the devil. There were no stitches, no doctor; I just dried my tears and was off to the Halloween party. I still have that scar today to remind me of my first school party.

At Thanksgiving we cut out paper turkeys and pilgrims, colored them and then pasted them on the school windows. The effect was something like stained-glass windows. That night there was a party at school. Mom, Dad, Lawrence, and I went to the party together.

I liked school. With the aid of my new thick glasses, I learned quickly to read. I was fascinated with books and stories. I soon read at a level far beyond the first grade. A whole new fascinating and truly wonderful ability became mine. I read everything I could get my hands on. I loved all kinds of reading material, especially comic books. In the first grade I was reading several comic books everyday, stacks of them every week. My brother and I would trade them with other kids by the stack whenever we could. One school book I really loved was an illustrated one about the cat and the fiddle and the cow jumping over the moon. I stole that book from our little school library because I loved it so much.

A music teacher came at least once a week and gave us music lessons. She taught us by having us sing songs. The entire school would sing, all thirty or so of us. She taught us a number of Stephen Foster songs. I remember in particular "Old Black Joe" for some reason. We learned patriotic songs like "America the Beautiful" and "God Bless America."

We had recess every morning and afternoon and a long lunch period. During these breaks we went outside to play. We played fox and goose when we had fresh snow and built snow forts. Once we had our forts built we would play war and throw snowballs at each other. It seems that allowing that many kids of different ages to play together would not work well, but it did.

I was growing closer to my dad now that we lived in Illinois. He was home everyday doing farm work, so I would see him all the time. He let Larry and me help him repair the fences, pull weeds and help with the garden. We had to be careful for snakes, though. Dad said there were a lot of poisonous snakes. I really took him seriously, so whenever I needed to crawl under a fence, I would have my dad check for snakes. He did, and if he felt it was safe I could crawl under. He taught me that the birds I thought were wild canaries were actually goldfinches, and he taught other things of which I am still skeptical.

For example, he said there was a snake called a blue racer. It was blue and quite long. That part was true. He also said that when it chased you, it would take its tail into its mouth and make a wheel. In this wheel shape the blue racer could out run anyone. I was very afraid of them, although I had never seen one. My brother and I began to call it the "blue eraser" because if it caught you, you were just erased.

Dad once pointed out what he said was a rattlesnake warming itself on the cow path. Sure enough, it was a rattlesnake, complete with rattles, a fanged, hissing mouth, and a darting tongue. I think he told both fact and fiction. But it was hard to decide what was true and what wasn't.

Dad gave us many pearls of wisdom that first summer we were all together. He said that hedge apples were poisonous, and we should not eat them. Hedge apples are big round green "nubbly" balls. We took his word for it. So we just threw them at each other. He instructed us on how fish and frogs got into all the ponds and lakes. We had been asking about that for sometime, because it didn't seem possible that fish could be in every pond and lake.

He said the sun draws up water, and you can see that. On this day there were rays of light coming through the clouds down toward the earth. He said those rays were actual evidence of the sun drawing up the water, and in that water were fish and frogs. They were being drawn up into the sky. When it rains, those fish and frogs come down with the rain and get distributed to all the ponds and lakes. It made sense, but Lawrence and I had never seen it rain fish and frogs. He said he only saw it once. When he was a boy on his dad's farm, it rained fish and frogs for hours. There were so many fish and frogs falling from the sky that when he and his brothers went out to do chores, they could not stand up for slipping on the slippery fish. Dad's face was very serious during his entire lecture.

He explained thunder and lightening to us too. He said when we hear thunder, it is the gods up in heaven rolling enormous logs at one another. Sometimes they'd get mad at each other and throw huge bolts of lightning. Since the lightening bolts always missed the intended god they were hurled at, they would come crashing down to earth. Hey, simple enough! Thanks, Dad.

Lawrence and I were always full of questions. One of them was if there was really a devil. I suppose we got some of our curiosity from church. Dad said there most certainly was. He saw the devil once at a dance hall in Lynd, Minnesota. It was during a thunderstorm and the devil, all red with a long arrow-pointed tail, came swinging down from the rafters high in the ceiling to the very floor he was dancing on. The horned devil snapped his tail and bolts of lightning went crashing across the dance hall. Many people were injured. The devil jumped from the dance floor, soared through the air, landed on the ceiling's bared joists, and escaped right through the roof. Sure, Dad. Yup!

Lawrence's favorite pastime for as long as I can remember was beating the crap out of me. I think it was his cure for boredom. After being beaten to the point of being hurt, I would go crying and screaming for my mom or dad. I wanted them to make him stop and to punish him. Both of them had heard me crying and screaming many times and were shouting at my brother much of the time to leave me alone. But their intervention was usually only good for a few minutes.

One day I think Dad thought it was time to teach me something about defending myself against someone bigger than me. After all, he probably learned this in his own family of several brothers. He decided to teach me how to box. He should have taught me wrestling too. Dad scheduled boxing lessons for me every night for a while. He was the referee, and we would have a bell to start and end each round. We didn't have boxing gloves, so we tied each of our hands in towels held with string. Dad taught me a lot during these lessons. He coached me on how to protect myself from my brother. I couldn't turn my back on my brother and let him just pound the crap out of me. I had to face him, as frightening as it was, and I would do much better. I had to throw as many punches as I could right at his face. Dad was right. I put these lessons to good use many times in the next several years against my brother and other kids.

We were a family now; Mom was home all the time and so was Dad. I guess my folks sensed this too and Mom arranged to have a family portrait taken of us in our living room. We sat together very handsomely against the living room wall right below a small cuckoo clock.

The neighbors down the road by the creek had a bunch of kids. They often invited Lawrence and me to swim in their swimming hole. They had made it deep and complete with a long mudslide. We would all strip down naked and slide down the slippery blue mud bank in to the refreshingly cool water. The older kids teased Lawrence and I because we only had "peach fuzz." I didn't know what they were talking about at first, but I caught on in a moment because the older boys had pubic hair.

These boys introduced Lawrence and me to smoking. First we learned to smoke dried corn silk rolled up in catalogue paper. That is a very powerful cigarette for a six year old. Then we graduated to real cigarettes. We always went in the trees behind the corncrib to smoke. Maybe we introduced them to the chasing game, or maybe they already knew about it. But in the evening when the adults were together, we played our old favorite game: chasing the girls and pulling their panties down. Maybe that was a universal game played by kids everywhere.

Mom and Dad made friends with the neighbors in the area. All of them had children around our age. The Byers family lived to the south of us and the Mott family to the north. We went over to the Byers' farm a lot. They had a daughter my age named Debra. She became my first girlfriend. She and I would play in her dad's barn. We would play the chasing game: I would try to take her panties off, and she would try to take my shorts off. We would kiss each other, and sometimes I would put my finger in her vagina. She liked me to do this. I am embarrassed to even tell you about this behavior. I don't know how I ever got the idea in my head to be so sexual. The only thing I can think of now is that I must have seen my mom let her boyfriends do that. I don't think six year olds are ordinarily that sexual.

It did not take too long for Mr. Byers or Mr. Mott to show interest in my mom, and it wasn't long before they would come to visit when my dad was gone. Mom would tell me and Lawrence to go outside and play while she talked with her guest. Then she locked the doors, and we couldn't get back in the house until the man was ready to leave. I think we each thought that mom was having affairs again, but we never said that to each other. I don't know why. I guess she had taught both of us about secrets, so we honored the trust she put in us. It was only decades later that Lawrence and I discussed what Mom was doing and the secrets we both had been keeping for decades.

Mr. Byers was a big friendly man who liked my brother and me. We often walked over to his farm. It was about a mile away. In the summer, he would sometimes need to drive into Bishop Hill to get something, and he would invite us to come along. He always took us to a café where they served ice cream and malted milks, and he'd buy us whatever we wanted. Mr. Byers had many interesting things in his house. He had a player piano, the kind that played itself. You put a big role of paper in it with holes punched in it, and it would start playing. He had a device with which you could look at pictures, and it would make them three-dimensional. And George liked dirty stories, like my folks. When they were together they would drink beer and tell dirty stories right in front of us kids. I can't believe they didn't know we knew what they were talking about. Perhaps they were just crude.

Mr. Mott, a short heavy-set man with a red face, was the most frequent visitor to my mom. He and his wife and kids had an interesting device in their house too: a hand-cranked machine that generated electricity. At parties they would bring it out, and all of us would form a kind of U-shaped circle and hold hands. The person on each end of the U-shape would hold a handle. The handle was attached by wires to the electricity-making machine. Someone turned the crank and an electrical shock would flow through each one of us while we held hands. The harder the machine was turned by its hand crank the greater the shock that went through us all. The first one to let go of someone's hand because they could not tolerate the intensity of the shock was the loser.

We went to a large picnic with the Motts and many other families one Sunday during the summer. Mr. Mott was talking to my mother and dad. My brother and some other kids were around too. For some reason unknown to me, Mr. Mott asked my mom if he could take me in his rowboat across the lake. I wanted no part of this; I couldn't swim a lick. I was only six, and I thought Mr. Mott was a monster, one of my mother's monsters. I didn't like him. But mom said that would be a splendid idea. I began to try and weasel my way out of the ride but to no avail. Mom was making fun of my fear. I would have looked like

a real "chicken" if I refused any longer. So, I got in the boat and he rowed us out into the middle of the lake. I was sure he was going to throw me overboard, and I would drown. But he didn't. I am still not sure why he just wanted to take me and not my brother too.

We went to the Catholic church in Cambridge on Sundays. It was a big stone church filled with the statues and candles. These artifacts of the church were comforting to me. There was a priest and nuns, and it was a lot like St. Edward's.

CHAPTER 4

SECOND GRADE, 1941

For some reason, probably economic, we moved during the fall, just after I started the second grade. We moved from the Eddie Roman farm to the Merle Nystrom farm, about three miles away. At first we were allowed to continue school at Red Oak Hollow, but before winter set in we had to transfer to another school just north of Bishop Hill, called Swamp College. It was a long walk to the new school, about three miles. We always walked both ways.

One day Lawrence and I killed an opossum on our way home from school. It was crossing the road right in front of us, so we hit with a big stick we found. We put him in our large lunch box. Our lunch box was a large slightly used syrup pail complete with press down lid. We took the opossum home and laid it on the porch. We went to get Dad to show him what we had caught. But when we returned with Dad, the opossum was gone. We had killed him, and he came back to life. Dad said opossums could do that. I thought it was amazing.

As I recall the contents of our syrup pail lunch box, it allows me to consider the extent of our poverty and the way my folks fed us kids. We had homemade bread sandwiches smeared with homemade lard. Sometimes the lard had brown sugar on it. At other times, there was a piece of pork chop or head cheese on the lard. At home we often ate bread that had become a bit stale by putting cream that had soured on it and brown sugar. I liked that, but I always hated head cheese.

I began to understand how Dad was paid for his work on this farm, probably because Lawrence and I were asking questions about why we had to move again.

We didn't like changing schools. Dad was being hired by the month to work the farm. His salary was $100 a month. He got two pigs a year to butcher for his family. We could have a cow and some chickens. We could also have a garden, and of course we got to live in the house.

Our new farmhouse had electricity, and my mom got an electric refrigerator, the first one she had ever had. She went berserk with it. She made ice cream in the ice cube trays. It tasted pretty bad. But the homemade popsicles made with Kool-Aid were very good. We were getting rich in Illinois.

My Aunt Rachel, Uncle Henry, and their kids, Donnie Pete and Patty, moved to Illinois that fall. In December, the Japanese bombed Pearl Harbor. We were all over at my Uncle Prosper's in Moline when we heard the news.

Nearly every Saturday night we went into Cambridge. Before we went to town, my brother and I would get a bath in a square galvanized tub, usually with the same water for both of us. We were generally dirty and needed that bath, which my mother supervised. We still never wore shoes in the summer. In Cambridge, Lawrence and I would always go to the movies. Sometimes Mom and Dad went with us, and sometimes they went to the saloon and visited with friends. In those days the saloons were more like English pubs; families went to eat meals as well as drink.

Dad gave me and Lawrence a runt pig to raise. She loved to have her belly scratched and come in the house. She did well with our loving care. When she had grown large enough to go to market, we went with dad and sold her. He gave us the money for her. We took turns riding her down the slaughterhouse chute. Farm kids think they understand this kind of thing early on.

We were not permitted to watch the butchering of hogs for our own eating purposes. I think they thought it was too gruesome for us. But the butchering of chickens for Sunday supper was a weekly occurrence. My mother was an expert at it. She had a short piece of tree trunk about eighteen inches in diameter, which she had set on its end, and a sharp hatchet. She would hold the chicken by the legs and pull the wings down around the legs and secure them under fingers. She then would lay the chicken's head and neck across the stump and with a single chop the head would come off, and she would throw the chicken to the side. The chicken would jump and flop with blood spurting everywhere from its headless body until it died. It was a gruesome site to behold, especially if you were imaginative enough to think that your neck could be on the block. The feathers were loosened by dipping the whole chicken in hot water. Lawrence and I would pluck the feathers off. Mom would fry or roast it and serve it to us the same day.

One evening the Byers family came over to have a chicken dinner with us. We kids were playing and having fun while the adults were visiting before coming to the dinner table. For some reason, I got behind Mr. Byers chair and just as he was to sit down at the table, I quickly pulled the chair out from under him. He fell to the floor like a ton of bricks. He was a very big man. I thought I was doing something funny. But my dad was up in a flash, mad as hell trying to catch me. He threatened to beat me, which he had never done before in his life. But this time I was terrified, and I hid under the sewing machine in the dining room in plain sight. My dad was pulling on my arm to get me from under there, but I was hanging on to the sewing machine treadle with both hands. Suddenly my mother appeared with a man sized stove poker in her hand.

"Elling," she said, "if you hit that kid, I'll kill you with this poker."

She meant it. Dad backed off, and Mom got me out from under the sewing machine. Of course, I was crying. She dried my tears, and then told me I must apologize to Mr. Byers, which I did as soon as I stopped sobbing and became calm again.

Our farm house was heated by a large pot-bellied coal-burning stove. It sat in the middle of the living room like a king on a throne. It was a beautiful centerpiece, large chrome rings around the top and bottom of the belly part, and short curved chrome legs. It had a chrome door with an isinglass window so you could see the fire inside its belly. All the chrome was covered with fancy engraving. On the top of the stove was a place for a pot of water. We would build such a fire in the stove that it would glow red hot around its belly at night. On cold nights we huddled quite close to it. However, we were very careful because it could fry you in an instant if you fell against it. My brother and I slept upstairs in an unheated room. The only heat upstairs was the heat that rose to the ceiling of the room with the stove. A register in the upstairs hallway floor allowed some heat to escape into our room. Our moist breath enabled

Jack Frost to come to our windows every night in winter, always leaving thick leafy, icy white patterns on the inside of the panes. It gets very cold in northern Illinois in the winter.

Whenever it snowed that winter, we took our sled across the road to a large hilly forested area where we would slide down the hill until dark. We only had one sled, so usually my brother would lay on the sled face forward so he could steer, and I would lay on top of him. We liked to choose steep downhill runs with trees so we could go really fast and were forced to dodge trees on the way down. Generally we ended up tipped over when Lawrence made a sharp turn to avoid a tree. Then we would lay there laughing covered in snow, joyful over our near miss. We knew better than to bang into trees head first.

At night, sometimes coon hunters would comb the wood for raccoons. Their baying hounds, bright flashlights and gunshots would let us know when they were successful.

When there were leaves on the trees, my brother and I could scare ourselves silly by imagining ghosts and monsters in the forest. We could see the outline of trees and imagine shapes as huge hulking beasts. There was a large old cemetery just west of our forest that was a great inspiration to our imaginations.

Trudging off to Swamp College was a long trek everyday. My good brother would often walk in front of me on the way home to break the force of the wind, which was very cold during the winter. He was a good windbreak because he was twice as big as me.

We both hated the school, but what could we do? We did our work, and we did well. I could now read at the eighth-grade level, and the teacher let me read aloud short stories that she would choose for us. It was kind of a competition. You'd read until you made a mistake, and then another person would start reading. It was a fun way to learn to do your best. I think my reading ability came from reading so many comic books. We were still reading huge stacks of them every week and trading with other kids.

One of my favorite comic books was Red Ryder and Little Beaver. They always advertised the Red Ryder lever action five-hundred shot BB gun with a compass in the stock. I wanted one so bad and got one for Christmas. I plinked a lot of tin cans and birds with it. But I caught hell if my dad saw me killing song birds. Pigeons were okay, though.

Our neighbors had a large number of beehives on the other side of the forest. One day in the summer of 1942, Lawrence and my cousin, Donnie Pete, maliciously tipped all the beehives over. The honey bees came out with vengeance on their minds, and they got it. They went into our clothes and hair and stung us on every part of our bodies. We were in such distress we ran down the road tearing all our clothes off. We ran towards the house of the farmer who owned the bees. The farmer's wife came out to see what was happening. She was very concerned for us, and soon all three of us stood naked in the farmer's kitchen while his wife applied baking soda and water paste to our hundreds of stings.

CHAPTER 5

THIRD GRADE, AUTUMN 1942

Soon summer was over, and we moved again. This time we moved to the John Kewish farm, about three miles north of Galva. The farm was on the east side of a gravel road that paralleled railroad tracks running north and south from Galva to Kewanee. The farm had an enormous house with a huge back porch. But there was no electricity, so my mother's refrigerator was useless. And of course there was no running water in the house. There was a large barn, a windmill, and some other out buildings.

I have no idea why we moved again. I remember asking, but I don't recall any answer. My mother was furious with the move, and she let my dad know how she felt almost daily over the next several months. They began to have terrible verbal battles, but they never hit one another. My mother was the aggressor, and she bested my father on every occasion, not only with the number of words but with loudness and her capacity to swear. Her final death-blow sentence usually contained the words "you fool," which really hurt my dad's feelings. Dad was a quiet man; he made Gary Cooper seem verbally hyperactive. He seldom used swear words. He never got drunk or smoked cigarettes, though he chewed tobacco and snuff. He was no match for my hot-blooded verbal mother.

We had a lot of cows on this farm, a few geese, and a gasoline-powered washing machine that sat prominently on the enormous porch, which covered the width of the house. The machine's engine made a tremendous noise and gave off a smoky exhaust, but Mom loved it. Washing clothes was hard work for her. She had to pump the water by hand, heat it up, start up the engine, put the thing in gear, let the machine thrash the clothes around for a while, take it out of gear, run the clothes through the wringer and into rinse water, then out of the rinse water, through the ringer again into a basket, and then take and hang them out on the clothesline to dry. That was just for the white clothes; then she had colored clothes to do too. My brother and I often helped her with this job.

In the evening Lawrence and I would walk out to the pasture, gather the cows, and bring them to the barn for Dad to milk by hand. The trip to and from the pasture in bare feet was often an obstacle course of cow pies, fresh and otherwise. The fresh ones would squish between your toes like warm pudding. You get use to it. The hard ones we used as sailing discs. That may be how the Frisbee was conceived. There were snakes to avoid out there too. The cows instinctively knew to avoid snakes, so if you just watched them you knew when to be careful.

The geese were a constant target of torment for my brother and me. We would chase them, and sometimes they would chase us. Big ganders are formidable opponents. Ours could beat the crap out of us with their wings and bite with their hook-tipped beaks. Mom had a way of taking care of the geese. Every few Sundays we would have Auntie Rachel and her family over for a roasted goose dinner.

We started school in another one-room school house. It was located directly across the road and railroad tracks and to the west about a mile. We always took the shortest route to school. We just crossed the road, went down into the ditch and then up over the double set of tracks and through the ditch on the other side, then back up onto the road that led to the school. We were supposed to walk up the road and cross the tracks at the proper intersection for our own safety. But that added another quarter-mile to the walk. Dad said it was very dangerous to cross the tracks the way we were doing it, but we were not afraid of the trains. If a train was stopped on the tracks, we would crawl under it to get to the other side. We were fascinated by trains. We frequently sat in front of our house and counted the cars as we watched them go by.

The trains that went by the old farm house shook the windows. Some were very long freight trains, others were sleek, fast-moving passenger trains. Sometimes there would be more than one hundred cars in a freight train, and often they carried military equipment. Dad said that the silver colored passenger trains were going sixty miles per hour or more when they went by the house. According to him they were the Silver Streak and the Rock Island Rocket. We definitely could not outrun them.

I was in the third grade and my brother was in the fifth. He had been held back a year while at St. Edward's. We had a male teacher, which seemed unusual, but we got used to him. There were the usual new kid fights. At every new school, the kids that had been there always tested us on the playground battlefield. Because my brother and I had been fighting with each other since I was born, and as the new kids at several schools already, we quickly established ourselves high up in the playground pecking order.

We started playing tackle football in the fall during recess and the noon hour. I was very good at carrying the ball without getting tackled, so I got to carry the ball a lot. One day some one tackled me and I fell hard with the football jammed against my chest. It knocked the wind out of me. I was sure I was going to die. But after awhile I was able to breathe again. It was a miracle.

Our school had an outdoor well with a big old iron pump and a large handle. When winter came I made the mistake of putting my wet hands on the ice cold iron water pump handle. My hands froze solidly to it in an instant. Someone got some warm water from inside the school and poured it over my hands and the pump handle. Miraculously, I was freed with no loss of skin.

During the spring, the school put on a talent program and brother sang a solo. He was a very good singer. He sang, "When My Blue Moon Turns to Gold." My mother was so pleased and moved by his performance that she cried.

Mom was a good singer too. She would often sing as she did her the ironing or cooking. She sang songs like "You Are My Sunshine," "Clementine," "Home on the Range," and something about "slide down my cellar door." She especially liked the music of Gene Autry and Roy Rogers and would sing along with them on the car radio when we went somewhere in the evening.

Mom and Dad both liked music, and they liked to go to dances. We had been going to dances as a family since I was very young. Often they were house dances or at a pavilion. Lawrence and I were always taken along. When I was too little to dance I would get tired and be put on the bed where everyone stashed the coats for the evening. We must have gone to dances mainly in the winter. I would fall asleep among the coats and would wake up the next morning at home in my bed, never remembering how I got there. As I became older, my mom would have me stand in my stocking feet on her feet, and she would dance around the floor with me. Then older girls began to teach me how to dance, and I would dance the night away along with my brother and parents. These dances were a lot of fun for all of us.

After moving to the Kewish farm, we started to go to the movies in Galva on Saturday nights, just like we had in Cambridge. I loved the movies and the cartoons that preceded them. Bambi came to the theater that year. I thought it was a little scary, but I really liked it. My parents often went to the saloon while we were at the movies. They would meet Uncle Henry and Aunt Rachel and other friends and spend the evening talking, eating, and drinking, though they never got drunk.

We started to go to the Catholic church in Galva. I had become fascinated with Catholicism. The Latin mass, which I could not understand, always seemed mystical and important. The priest's vestments, stain-glassed windows, candles, incense, statues of the Virgin Mary, and the Stations of the Cross were in every Catholic church I had ever been to. They were always familiar. The nuns were always so graceful in their flowing black habits with their faces framed in white cloth. No matter where we moved, these symbols were comforting.

I soon began catechism classes so that I could make my first communion, which I was eager to do. My brother was an altar boy, and I thought that was really a good thing to be. But you had to have made your first communion. I wondered how Lawrence could be an altar boy because he sinned a lot.

The nuns taught me that God knew me and everybody else in the world personally. He knew everything that all of us had ever done, even the Protestants. I learned about sin—original, venial and mortal. I was instructed about the Ten Commandments and learned that I was not to break any of them because if I did, God would know. To cleanse my soul in the eyes and mind of God, I had to go to confession and tell my sins to a priest. The priest would talk to God about me, and through the priest, God would forgive me if I was truly sorry. I could not receive Holy Communion unless I had gone to confession. I must not lie to the priest, because God would know it immediately. I was swallowing God when I received communion, so I should not bite the wafer, because God was in it.

I took it all in without question. I learned my catechism, and I made my first confession and communion. I did not tell the priest about the secrets I was keeping for my mother. I was more afraid of mom than of the priest. I was afraid of God too, but I thought he already knew. Somehow I had screwed with my little mind so that I thought my mom was really more powerful than God, even though God was omnipotent.

I learned too that I had a guardian angel who had been with me every moment since I was born. The angel looked out for me, and I should always leave room for my angel on my chair when I sat down. I should always leave a little food on my plate at each meal for my angel too. I was impressed that God knew everything and that I had my own personal angel, and I followed my angel instructions faithfully.

Sundays after church, we usually visited with Aunt Rachel's family, either at her house or ours. Some old friends of my parents from Minneota had moved to Illinois too. They were also a Catholic family and were included in our family Sunday dinners. They had a girl my age, and we became boyfriend and girlfriend, whatever that means when you are eight years old. I saw her frequently, and we played together. Sometimes she and I would find a place in her barn (she lived on a farm too) or mine, and we would kiss and I would put my finger in her vagina.

One day my girlfriend's mother was talking to my mom, and she said she feared someone was pregnant. I thought she was saying her daughter—my girlfriend—was pregnant. I thought "Uh oh! I should not have put my finger where I did." Fortunately I had misunderstood what they were talking about.

Sometimes we went to Uncle Prosper's on Sunday. Prosper was a very big man, not fat, just big. He was loud and boastful when he drank, which he always did when we were at his house. He would become the center of attention by telling elaborate stories that were frequently dirty ones. Uncle Prosper also raised and raced pigeons. They were his hobby, and he loved them dearly. They were his pride and joy. Unfortunately, Donnie Pete, my brother and I did not appreciate the value of the pigeons.

One Sunday there was a big party at Prosper's with lots of people attending. Fascinated by Uncle Prosper's large elevated pigeon coop, we climbed the stairs and entered the large coop where pigeons lived. I don't know what got into us, but it was destructive and devilish. We began taking his prized pigeons eggs from their nests and throwing them at each other. We broke dozens of eggs. When we ran out of eggs, we began chasing the pigeons in the coop. It scared the hell out them and they made a lot of noise as a consequence. Uncle Prosper heard the commotion in the coop. He came up the stairs and saw what we were doing. He was absolutely crazy with fury. He tried to catch us, but we escaped and ran down the stairs and into the crowd of people gathered to see what was happening. Prosper was screaming that he would kill us as he chased us. We ran directly to our moms and dads for protection. If it had not been for our parents' intervention, I think he would have killed us. I believe my dad and Uncle Henry had to pay Uncle Prosper for the damage we had done. All three of us kids were spanked. My mother spanked Lawrence and me.

A boy of about sixteen years old lived on a farm just down the road and to the east of our farmhouse. He had an enormous German shepherd dog and a .22 caliber rifle. He liked to go rabbit hunting with his dog. I see this dog in my memory as having had a huge head with very mean looking eyes. When he snarled he twisted up his nose and showed his bared front teeth and huge white curved fangs. Saliva drool hung from the corners of his mouth. I was afraid of this dog.

My brother wanted to go rabbit hunting with the boy, and I tagged along. We went to the field just across the road from our farm house. As we walked all three abreast with the dog, a rabbit jumped up from the grass a short distance in front of us. The boy lifted his rifle to his shoulder and shot. He hit the rabbit. I ran to pick it up. As I did, I heard the dog running too. I heard his breath and the beat of his feet against the ground. I arrived at the bloody dying rabbit an instant before the dog. The dog jumped on me biting and growling. He grabbed my upper arm and bit through my clothes. His teeth sank into my flesh as he picked me up and shook me with short violent movements of his head. I instinctively curled up into a ball to protect my throat and belly. He turned and twisted menacingly over me biting and tearing at my arms, legs, back and head. I thought he was killing me. The boy tried to call his dog off of me, but the dog would not sop. He beat his dog with the stock of his rifle until both the dog, the rabbit and I lie bloody in the dirt. I was full of holes. My brother and the boy carried me the short distance home. I was crying and screaming.

By the time we got home, I felt very weak. My head was spinning, and I was trembling all over. I was in shock. Mom and Dad put me in the car and took me to a doctor in Galva. He cleaned, stitched, and dressed my wounds and sent us home with instructions that I should be kept warm and quiet for the next few days. There were probably a lot of other instructions too but I don't remember.

I was very frightened. I knew I was going to die, and I began to think strange things. I thought that my mom was going to just let me die. Then she would not have to worry about me telling her secrets. I thought maybe God was going to take me because I was so full of sin. Maybe God had sent the dog to kill me.

A few days later I was playing in the hayloft of the barn, jumping into the hay and something stabbed me and made two small holes in the calf of my leg. I thought maybe a poisonous snake had bitten me. I ran to the house crying and screaming that a snake had bitten me. Mom said, "That does not look like a snake bite." Dad said it did not look like a snake bite. But I insisted it might be, and I wanted Dad to suck the poison out of the bite. Dad had told me long ago that if you get bit by a snake someone needs to suck the venom out. You couldn't swallow it but had to spit it out.

Dad sucked the venom from my leg. Larry laughed at me for being such a big baby. Mom said I was acting crazy. Dad said that maybe a snake had bitten me, but I would be alright; he had gotten all the venom out. In my mind, I was wondering if God had sent a snake to kill me since the dog had failed. I knew that God knew all the bad sinful things that I had ever done, and maybe he was after me.

I was very ashamed of myself for being so frightened and such a crybaby. But I felt like I was just full of sins. I felt dirty. I knew I had germs on my hands. I insisted on washing them all the time. This soon drove Mom to even more anger and intolerance. She said I was acting crazy and to stop it. But I couldn't.

I prayed and prayed to Jesus to let me stay with my family. I prayed on my knees because I thought that was better. Maybe God would listen if I suffered more while praying. Finally, after a few weeks my obsessive-compulsive need to cleanse myself lessened. My wounds were pretty well healed, and I began to return to being somewhat normal.

Mom and Dad continued to argue. Mom accused Dad of burying or hoarding some of the money he was earning. She was sure he was burying his extra money in a Prince Albert tobacco can somewhere in the yard. Lawrence and I spent a lot of time looking for Dad's alleged buried treasure but never found it. Mom remained convinced that Dad was not sharing all his money with her.

Arguments continued over money and adulterous behavior. Dad accused Mom of being a tramp and sleeping with every man she had ever met. She accused him of the same thing with women. They seemed to hate each other, and I was worried that they might get the divorce they threatened each other with.

Because he was older, my brother had always been bigger and stronger than me. When we fought, which was nearly every day, I would usually get the worst of it. At this stage of our young lives we were into wrestling, boxing, kicking, bows and arrows, BB guns, slingshots, stick fighting, and rock throwing. I got pretty good at hurling rocks at him after he would pummel me. I was smart enough to realize that rock throwing was only effective from certain distances or advantages. I would throw rocks from a distance, which would enable me to run to my mom to protect me. One day I made a really good throw and hit him with big stone right in the forehead. Blood came gushing out of the wound, and he began to cry and went screaming for Mom. I felt very bad about making him bleed and began to cry too. I thought he might die. He didn't. He healed, and we were right back to arguing and fighting in a day or two.

Lawrence and I had slept in the same bed at night since I was an infant. I think we were too poor to afford a house a bedroom or even a bed for each of us. Or maybe Mom and Dad just did not think it was necessary for us to sleep separately.

As we grew older we always had an imaginary line drawn down the middle of the bed. We each had a half. If anyone crossed the line, he would get hit by the other. We teased each other constantly by putting a hand or foot over the line, and that would lead to fighting and giggling. Soon we would hear Mom tell Dad to "go in there and make those kids shut up." Dad would dutifully get out of bed, get his razor strap, come into our bedroom and wallop the bed with the strap. My brother and I would cuddle together, pull the covers over us for protection and giggle. Dad never hit us. He just hit the bed. But we would be very quiet after he gave the bed a few good whacks, just in case he changed his mind and actually hit us. When he would leave the room, we would start giggling and begin the game all over again until we fell asleep. Usually we fell asleep with our arms and legs entangled with one another in some kind of cuddling position. I think we cuddled because we really did love and need each other.

CHAPTER 6

FOURTH GRADE, AUTUMN 1943

Sometime in October, we moved again, this time to a farm near Atkinson, about thirty miles north of Galva. I had turned nine years old in August. The farm belonged to a man who had a German last name. The house was nearly new and freshly painted, as were all the other farm buildings. Dad said the farm buildings had been recently painted because someone had painted yellow swastikas on them. Some people in the area thought the owner was pro-Nazi. I don't know if he was or not. The house was very modern. It had hot and cold running water, a bathtub, inside flush toilet, electricity and a refrigerator— a big step up in convenience for all of us, especially my mom.

I went to the toilet real often, flushed it, and watched with the fascination as stuff disappeared down the hole with the swirling water. I had seen this before at school and other people's houses, but not in ours. It was the first time that I could remember ever living in a house with a flush toilet.

I took a hot bath everyday. I think my mother insisted on it. I had accumulated nine years of dirt on my little body, and she and I thought I needed a good scrubbing. It was the first time we had a real bathtub with faucets. Our bath before had always been a square galvanized tub filled with buckets of stove-heated water. With this new tub, I was squeaky clean and red from a good scrubbing everyday. Maybe I took a bath everyday because of the novelty of the new beautiful tub or maybe because of my mom. Or maybe it was because I was still trying to wash away the germs on my body or the many sins on my soul. Lawrence was still teasing me about how I acted when the dog attacked me. I didn't tell him I was still afraid of germs. I felt ashamed and didn't like being teased.

It was about a mile to school, and I walked it myself each day. Lawrence was going to a different school for some reason. My school was in a one-room building with about a dozen kids. I was the only one in the fourth grade. The teacher was very kind to me and let me learn more as less as I wanted. I was not restricted to fourth-grade studies. I was an able student, and I did fine with my school work. I don't recall making any friends there. I missed being with the kids from the last school, and the school before that, and the one before that, and the one before that.

Winter came and was on its way out, but with the Ides of March in 1944 we moved again. The fifteenth of March and the first of October seemed to be the dates that farmers like my dad changed farms to work on. "Beware the Ides of March" had real meaning to me. I had already attended five schools and was on my way to the sixth.

I didn't know at the time why we moved from that nice farm so soon. Lawrence told me it was because Mom was messing around with the man who owned the farm, and his wife wanted us out of there. At any rate, we moved to 338 Helmer Street in Kewanee, Illinois. It was a large gray house on a corner with inside hot and cold water, a bathtub, and a toilet.

Dad got a job at a factory and Mom stayed home for a while. She and Dad were trying to figure out if she should go to work. She had never had a job before in her life. After a very short time Mom took a job at the Boss

Glove factory. I remember it well. They made those chocolate-colored cloth gloves. I was disappointed she was not making something to win the war, like guns or tanks. But she didn't stay at the factory long and soon took another job at a downtown hotel restaurant as a waitress.

A few blocks away, a new school awaited my brother and me. It was still March, so Mom enrolled us in St. Mary's Catholic School for me to finish the fourth grade and Lawrence the sixth. St. Mary's was in a large brick building, much larger than any school I had been to since the beginning of the first grade. I was used to the little one-room schoolhouses, and I liked them. I didn't like St. Mary's. It was too big and there were too many kids. There were at least thirty in my class alone, and there may have been more than one fourth-grade classroom. I received little individual attention, and all the kids were strangers.

On our first day walking home from school, some kids about my size started to tease me about my thick glasses. They called me "four eyes," "goggle eyes," and other things like "sissy face." Those were fighting words, and the adrenaline began to pump inside of me. I had been here many times before. So I asked them if they wanted to fight. Two of them said they did but they were not supposed to hit a sissy wearing glasses. That was all it took. I took my glasses off, handed them to my brother, and started punching them one at a time as hard as I could in the face. Each one got several smashing blows to the face. It was over in a couple of minutes. They had bloody noses and lips and were crying.

I liked fighting. I could feel my heart thumping in my chest with fear and excitement before each fight, and I felt very calm when they were over. As we walked the rest of the way home, my brother and I laughed at those dumb kids for picking on me. I, a flyweight, had been fighting a heavyweight, my brother, nearly everyday of my life. Kids my size were no match for me. I had several other fights with kids both on and off the playground over the next several weeks. I won them all, and I got the respect of the other boys at school.

It was mostly kids teasing me about my thick glasses that led to the fights. My glasses were a constant problem for me no matter what school I went to. I kept breaking them too, and that made my parents angry because they cost a lot of money to replace. Lawrence was lucky; he didn't wear glasses. He did not get any fights that I recall, except with me.

The school was next door to St. Mary's Catholic Church. We began going to church there on Sundays, and Lawrence became an altar boy again. I went to confession on Saturday and communion on Sunday, being careful not to bite the wafer containing God. That was a difficult trick because as soon as the priest would put the wafer on my tongue, my tongue would shove it to the roof of my mouth, where it would stick like it was glued there. Then it took considerable effort to break God loose and not bite him. It usually took several minutes, all the while with my head bowed in solemn prayer and my eyes rolling in my head in unison with the tongue in my mouth. I was a good Catholic boy. I said my prayers before and after meals and before bed everyday. It was an obsession to gain the grace of God, and I was encouraged in it both at school and in church.

As the weather got warmer we began playing marbles on the playground during recess and after school. Marbles became our passion. I usually walked around with my pockets full of marbles and my hands clutching a comic book or two. Lawrence and I were always looking for a game or to trade comic books.

Our comic books were generally about super heroes—Captain America, Captain Marvel, Superman, Plasticman, Submariner, the Green Hornet, and others. They were all busy beating up or killing Germans and Japanese. They always depicted our enemies as mean and ugly. The comics were excellent propaganda tools. I grew up actually believing Japanese were small, mean, and wore thick glasses. Germans were big, ugly, and dumb. I had read this material nearly every day since 1942.

We were kept well abreast of the war, even children like me, with the newsreels at the movies, the radio, and newspapers. The war was uppermost on everybody's mind. Each movie began with a newsreel. Generally it was Paramount News, "the eyes and ears of the world." And the eyes and ears were on the war on every front. There were many war movies, like the one about the Bataan Death March.

My brother and I were big on airplane movies, especially those with fighter planes. There were many movies made with realistic airplane dog fights and our bombers being attacked by German fighter planes or Japanese Zeros. We learned about tail and turret gunners. We knew a P-38 from a P-51, and a B-25 from a B-29. There were snipers, hand grenades, machine guns and flame throwers. We ate that stuff up. We bought toy weapons that looked like the real thing, and then we would play war. We couldn't wait until we were old enough to go kill Japs and Germans.

Lawrence and I were busy with the war effort. We collected used newspapers and sold them by the pound. We went to surrounding neighborhoods and asked people for their old newspapers and carted them off in our big red wagon. We collected used pop bottles and sold them too. We each got paper routes for the Kewanee Star Courier and delivered newspapers. We earned a lot of spending money doing these things. And we bought mostly candy, soda pop, movie tickets, and toys with our money. Occasionally we would get a pack of cigarettes. Mom and Dad bought us our clothes.

One day while my dad was gone, Mr. Mott came to the house while my mother was home. My brother and I were surprised to see him. We had not seen him since the Red Oak Hollow School days, back near Cambridge. After they talked for a while, mom gave us some money to go to the store and buy some candy and soda pop. She locked the doors while we were gone. They were still locked when we came home. We pounded on the door, and Mom let us in. Mr. Mott left.

CHAPTER 7

SUMMER, 1944

We moved again after school in the spring, this time to a house Mom and Dad bought on Dewey Avenue, in the southwest corner of Kewanee. The factory Dad worked at and the railroad tracks were only about two blocks west. The house was a small white cottage-like thing among a wide variety of shanties and empty lots in an area sometimes referred to as Shanty Town. We were a couple of blocks south of Chautauqua Park. A little further south were farms. We were on the very edge of town.

The house did not have an inside toilet, bathtub, or hot or cold running water. There was a sink in the kitchen with a cold water faucet, so it must have had its own well. There was no sewer hookup, so we collected dishwater in a slop pail under the sink and emptied it in the backyard. Our little two-hole white outhouse was about fifty feet in back of the house just on the other side and to the left of where we emptied the slop pail. For baths, we returned to the old square galvanized tub, which was placed in the garage on bath days. Mom still supervised our Saturday baths if she was around. If she wasn't, we didn't take a bath.

Soon after school let out, Aunt Rachel, Donnie Pete, Patty, Mom, Lawrence, and me took a train to Minneota. None of us kids had ever been on a train before, so it was very exciting. We soon figured out how to open the windows and stick our heads out to see what was coming. Usually what were coming were little pieces of cinder that hit us in the face. Passing trains and bridges proved to be a real hazard to keeping our heads attached to our bodies.

Mom told us if we didn't keep our heads inside the train, we would get them knocked off.

We visited relatives in Minnesota. We went to Grandma Blomme's farm, Aunt Margaret's farm, Aunt Mary's country store and gas station, and Aunt Madeline's farm. Rene was still at home with Grandma and Grandpa. Grandma's house was like I remembered it. The white rocks still lined the lane and the living room tables still had the shells from the ocean. My favorite place was Aunt Mary's because they had a lot of kids near my age, as well as free ice cream and soda pop in their store.

We went to Dad's sister Bertha's house too. I had never been there before because when we lived in Minneota, we were being shunned by them for being Catholic. It didn't seem to make any difference now. She had three kids. The oldest one was Dickie, who was close to my age. We stayed there for a couple of days, played with the kids and ate Vienna torte.

Mom took us to Grandma and Grandpa Haugen's farm. It was the first time I had ever been there too. I was scared into a terrible fright before we even arrived. Mom had over the years filled us with stories on how terrible the Haugens were. They had a big brown curly haired dog that was not used to kids. He was the first to greet us when we drove up to the house. He growled at us and tried to bite us, but Grandma came out and tied him up, and we went into the house. The house was filthy and smelled like sulfur. I thought it smelled like a witch lived there (too many movies). Grandma was old gray, big, tall and covered with age spots. I thought her arms looked like slabs of lefse, the soft, freckled potato flatbread much loved by Norwegians. Grandpa was a very skinny little old man with hollow cheeks and large cheek bones. He was paralyzed from a stroke and couldn't talk, stand, or sit. He just lay in bed making weird sounds that scared Larry and me. We didn't understand anything about stroke victims. Grandma was very nice to us and offered us food. Mom tried to talk to Grandpa, and he seemed to know who she was. Mom said she had always gotten along with Grandpa.

Lawrence and I looked at her. "You said they didn't like you." She replied that Grandpa had always liked her. I left Grandma's house confused by their situation. But I still believed the original stories my mother had told me about the weird Lutheran Haugen family. The house did smell like a witch's house, and Grandpa was definitely scary. Their dog was devil-like. And neither Lawrence nor I wanted to eat anything there because the kitchen was so dirty, just like mom had said.

We returned on the train after a couple of weeks. On the way back there were a number of soldiers on the train. My mother went to the back of the train car where they were sitting and made friends with some of them. She spent most of her time back there. Rachel became upset with her because she had to look after her kids as well as Lawrence and me. Soon we arrived in Owatonna, Minnesota, where we had a four-hour layover. Rachel, her kids, Lawrence and I went to a nearby park and passed the time by playing and sitting around. Mom went with the soldiers somewhere. When she came back she smelled and acted like she had been drinking. Rachel was furious with her and asked her how she could behave like that.

"Go off with those soldiers right in front of your kids, you should be ashamed of yourself. You will pay for that someday," she said. Mom just brushed her off, and we boarded the train. Once we were on the train, Mom went back and sat with the soldiers again.

When we returned from our vacation, Lawrence and I continued our paper routes, and we began a new job. He got a job setting pins at a bowling alley downtown and he got one for me there too. He was big enough so he could set two alleys at a time. I was only able to set one alley at a time. I could only pick up three pins at a time because my hands were small, he could pick up four and could fill the rack much quicker than me. I didn't weigh very much, so I struggled some to pull the rack down and set the pins, but I could do it. The guy who ran the bowling alley liked me and was afraid a bowler throwing his second ball down the alley while I was pick-ing up the pins from his first ball might kill me in the pit. He often put me in the elevated crow's nest that overlooked the foul lines of the ten alleys. My job in the nest was to observe the foul line and press the foul button if someone went over the line while throwing a ball. I usually did well at this unless I fell asleep, which I did often because it was boring. Then the bowlers would holler up unpleasant words at me, and I would wake up. The owner said Lawrence and I needed to get Social Security cards if we were going to work there. So at the age of nine, I got a Social Security card with Dad's help.

The bowling alley, the other pin setters, and the boys in our shanty town neighborhood were probably not good influences on us. We began hanging out with kids that smoked cigarettes and just kind of roamed the streets at night. We hung out in our neighborhood, and uptown around the bowling alley and the YMCA across the street. On my tenth birthday I bought a carton of cigarettes for myself. I spent most of the day smoking and drinking coffee. I think I thought I was Humphrey Bogart.

There were some boys who lived near the park whose dad was in the Navy. He had left a .45 caliber pistol at home for some reason. These boys frequently had the gun with them when we ran around at night. Lawrence and I had discovered that our dad had a .38 caliber pistol in the house, and we often took it with us. But Dad was smart enough to usually take the revolving chamber that held the bullets out of the gun, so it was quite useless. Lawrence had a .22 caliber rifle, but we didn't carry that around town. We used it hunt rabbits. One day when one of my friends came over to play cards, some other boys I didn't like came onto our yard. So I went into my bedroom and took my brothers .22 out from under the bed. I went into the front yard and pointed the rifle at the uninvited kids. I threatened to shoot them if they didn't leave. Of course they ran like hell to get away. I calmly turned around and walked back through the front door. As I entered our living room, I tripped over my own feet and my finger accidentally pulled the trigger. The rifle fired a shot with a tremendous bang right into the hardwood floor. I didn't know the rifle was loaded. I was so scared, I just trembled. I could have killed somebody. My friend agreed, and I put the rifle back under our bed. But I needed to cover up the bullet hole in the floor, or I was sure to catch it from somebody, most likely Lawrence. We moved the furniture in the room, pulled the carpet over the hole and then put the furniture back. No one ever discovered the bullet hole in the floor.

Dad began to work two shifts at the factory and Mom started working nights at the restaurant by late summer. Mom had pretty clothes now. She wore lace dickeys on her bosom with nice skirts and jackets, and she loved high heeled shoes. She wore a lot of perfume. Neither one of them was home with us very often during the day or evening, except for weekends. This left Lawrence and me responsible for our own meals. These meals usually consisted of breakfast cereal, milk, Campbell's soup, hot dogs, and ketchup.

CHAPTER 8

FIFTH GRADE, AUTUMN 1944 TO SPRING 1945

I began the fifth grade in a new school again. Lawrence and I attended a one-room country school a little over a mile southwest of our new house. There were the usual fights followed by friendships, and then we settled in. I liked our new school very much because it was small, and I received a lot of attention. I learned the Palmer Penmanship method of writing. I was so good at not making inkblots with my straight pen that I won the privilege of writing a letter to Washington, D.C., to obtain information on dinosaurs for the school.

I acquired a new girlfriend, Marilyn, and I was thrilled when she and I were selected to play Mary and Joseph in our Christmas play. Marilyn, her brother, and some other kids always walked home together with Lawrence and me. It was so much fun. One day as we were walking, an airplane landed in an open field next to the road. We went over to the plane to admire it, and the pilot generously let us each take turns sitting inside it. I wanted to be a pilot before, but now I was really hooked.

I learned many things in Shanty Town. The neighbor boys, who were older than us, called me and Lawrence over one day to where they were huddled around their dog in their garage. We went to see what they wanted. They were "jacking off" their dog and then letting him run around their yard spurting semen out his penis. They all laughed as the dog went humping around the yard. I was embarrassed and really didn't know if I should laugh or what.

I learned from a nearby farmer that peanuts grew under the ground and you had to dig them up like potatoes. I found that incredible. A neighbor girl taught me how to play "Doctor Doctor" on the piano and between lessons taught me how to French kiss. We played the chasing game at night sometimes, the same way we had before, but now it was catch the girls and hide and "neck" with them. We spent a lot of time in Chautauqua Park playing softball. They were just pick-up games without coaches, but fun. We went looking for "fucking rubbers" in the park. For some reason the older boys thought this was great fun, and we usually found a lot of them. They bought rubbers too, which we filled with water and threw at each other. They made great water bombs.

Mom's girlfriend, Betty had an illegitimate baby. I went with Mom to the neighbors to see it. There was a used rubber lying near the kitchen sink. They saw me looking at it.

"Do you know what that is Donnie?" Mom asked.

I said no, and they just laughed. Of course, I knew, but I was embarrassed.

One day my mom made arrangements for Lawrence and me to go to her friend's house after we finished at the bowling alley. We did as she said, but when we had walked to her friend's house about eleven o'clock that night, no one came to the door when we knocked. The door was locked, so we began shouting the woman's name. No one came to the door. We waited and waited, and no one came to the door or to the house. It was cold outside, and there was snow on the ground. It was so far to walk to our house, we decided to just wait until someone came home. No one did. We sat on her porch all night in the cold, shivering, waiting. Finally in the morning, we walked the couple of miles home cursing Mom and the lady who wasn't there.

Our furnace blew up later that spring and burned our house down. We lost all our family pictures and furniture. Fortunately, Dad, Lawrence and me escaped without injury. Dad accused Mom of putting something in the coal to cause the explosion. She was not home when it happened and later denied doing anything.

So we had to move again. This time we moved to the other side of town to 219 South Vine Street. This was a house that was divided into four apartments. We moved into the right hand upstairs apartment. You could get to our apartment by entering the front door and going upstairs, or by going to the back of the house and up an outside stairway.

Lawrence and I got a puppy we named Spike. Spike's brother went to Uncle Henry, who named his dog Puppy. One day when we came home from school, Spike had fallen off the second floor outside stairway landing, where he had been tied, and had hung himself. We found him when we came home from school hanging and very dead. It was a painful lesson in loss for both of us and perhaps a bad omen.

President Roosevelt died suddenly in April at the "Little White House" in Warm Springs, Georgia. The nation mourned, as did our city, our school, and my family. Dad was a Socialist and belonged to a union and the Socialist Labor Party. But he loved President Roosevelt, as did my Mom, Lawrence, and me. Ernie Pyle, the war correspondent was killed that spring by a Japanese machine gun, and the war in Europe was certain to end soon. Van Johnson starred in nearly all the movies, but Huntz Hall and the Bowery Boys were our favorites.

Lawrence and I finished out the school year at our little country school, which we reached by taking a bus to the end of the bus line. We would get on the bus with our bicycle. At the end of the bus line, we would take the bike and ourselves off the bus, and I would sit on the cross bar or on the handle bars, and we would finish the trip to school. These bicycle trips were often scary but great fun.

Soon my dad decided he could save some money if he bought a bike and rode it to the factory instead of using the car. His enthusiasm for the bike soon waned, and I inherited his man-sized bike with its crotch-crushing crossbar. The trouble was my legs were too short to reach the pedals no matter how much the seat was lowered. With the help of my brother, I learned to ride this bike by tipping it sideways, putting my right leg under the crossbar and to the right side pedal, push off with my left leg and then put my left foot on the left pedal and begin pedaling. And thus I would go. In this odd slanted sideways fashion, I soon was traveling all over town on my full sized man's bike, following my brother around on his.

CHAPTER 9

SUMMER, 1945

I spent two weeks of the summer with my Aunt Rachel, Uncle Henry, and my cousins on their farm near Atkinson. I loved my Aunt Rachel because she had always treated me like her own son. She was very demonstrative with her affection and praise, and she could bake and cook up a storm. Her house was much larger than the one she had in Minneota, but it still had all the lace doilies, crucifixes, and Catholic pictures like long ago. Her house was big, clean, and comfortable, with all the amenities, even a guest bedroom for me. The only thing it lacked was an indoor toilet.

One day Donnie Pete and I caught a woodchuck on the way home from fishing in the nearby canal. We wrapped him up in our minnow net and took him home. Rachel saw the woodchuck and told us to let him go. We agreed, but we didn't want him to run away. For some reason we thought the outdoor toilet was good place to put him for safe keeping. That was a big mistake because the first thing the woodchuck did was crawl up on the bench and down through one of the sit down holes into the shit below. We tried to get him out but the smell and mess soon discouraged us. It wasn't long before Rachel had to use the outhouse. In she went and sat down on a hole. The woodchuck must have become frightened and jumped up with his shit-covered body against Aunt Rachel's butt. That scared the bejesus out of her and she came running out of the toilet screaming. She knew immediately what we had done. She gave us a terrible scolding, but she did not spank us. She said to leave the woodchuck alone and that Henry would get it out, which he did without our help when he came home.

There are many things for boys to do on a farm, especially if you have an imagination. We would take Donnie Pete's pony out for rides and try and chase down the young cattle and lasso them. Fortunately, we were unsuccessful at this, or we may have been killed. The young cattle in the pasture were big. So we tried some smaller bull calves that were in the barn. We tested our skill at "bulldogging"—wrestling the calves to the ground. We did this so much that they became sick. Uncle Henry suspected that we had been messing with his calves and told us we needed to stop doing that because we were killing them. They were getting kind of wobbly when they walked. They were too young for bulldogging. He suggested we try some of the bigger ones in the pasture. We knew better than to try that.

The fun and good food soon ended, and I had to go back home to a summer of setting pins at the bowling alley, going to movies, eating Dairy Queens, and hanging out at the municipal swimming pool. The swimming pool was quite a walk from the house, but there was a Dairy Queen on the way, and we always stopped for a cone.

There were two grocery stores on our block, one at each end. We went to the store most every day to buy groceries and charge them to Dad's account. We would buy bottles of pop and a bag of peanuts with our own money, because Dad didn't like us to charge candy or pop. We took our salted peanuts and put them in the soda and shook the pop up with our thumb over the top of the bottle. Then we would slowly release our thumb and open up a little hole on the edge our thumb and let the pop fizz up into our mouths. It was so much fun. The Coke-soaked peanuts at the bottom of the bottle were a tasty treat.

My brother thought I was a really good boxer. So one day he got the bright idea that we could make some money by putting on a fight in our backyard with me as the star attraction. We would use real boxing gloves and have two three-minute rounds. We would charge admission to view the fights. He got a big tent from somewhere, and the fights were to be held inside so kids would have to pay to see them. I would take on all comers near my body weight. We put up flyers at the grocery stores saying, "Killer Don will take on all comers (in his weight class) in the sport of boxing," with our address and the scheduled time of the bouts. Quite a few kids showed up, and I had to fight about four or five of them.

I got some bruises, and I gave out some too. It was a novel but hard way to make money. After fight day, whenever I went to one of the stores, the owner would call me "Killer Don." I probably weighed seventy-five pounds, and I wore thick glasses. I looked more like a little professor than a boxer.

My brother and I had a ravenous appetite for green apples. We would search nearby neighborhoods for apple trees with green apples, salt shaker in hand. We collected them in a paper bag, and when we had stolen enough to satisfy our needs, we would find a curb or stoop, sit down and eat them all, generously sprinkling each prospective bite with salt. They were absolutely indescribably good. Dad said we would get sick eating so many green apples.

He said, "You will get the colored marbles from eating so many of them."

"What are the colored marbles, Dad?" I asked

"You'll find out when you get them."

We never did get sick from all those green apples. They just satisfied a craving we had.

The war was over in Europe that summer, and around my eleventh birthday, the two atomic bombs were dropped on Japan, ending the war in the Pacific. There was a big celebration downtown, and a kid fell off the back of a truck and was run over and killed. My friend Joe Swan dived into shallow water while swimming and broke his neck that summer. He died. Billy Redmon, a kid from the bowling alley, was accidentally shot and killed. Kids were getting polio all over the country. They were dying and becoming crippled.

Summer was soon over and we started back to school.

CHAPTER 10

SIXTH GRADE, AUTUMN 1945

Although we had moved, Lawrence and I wanted to return to our country school. So we didn't tell the school we had moved out of their district. We made the journey like we did before, taking the bus to the end of the line and then Lawrence's bike, with me riding with him. It was a great autumn at our school. All our old friends were still there. The highlight for me was the softball game we started in October. We chose up sides for two teams, and every noon hour and recess we played the Tigers against the Cubs. I don't really remember who won the real World Series that year, but we had such fun ourselves it doesn't matter.

By late fall, someone had informed the school district that our house had burned down, and we had moved out of the district. They made us find another school. Lawrence and I were very unhappy because we loved that school.

Lawrence decided to go to Kewanee Central Junior High for the remainder of the eighth grade, and I decided to return to St. Mary's Catholic School to finish the sixth grade. I was in constant trouble at the Catholic school right away. I got into many fist fights, some right in the classroom. I was frequently sent to be disciplined by Mother Superior. I hated it there and skipped school often. I would just write out an excuse for myself and sign my mom's name and that was it. No one ever questioned it, and no one at home knew I was skipping because no one was there to notice. If anyone did know, they never said anything. I began to steal things from stores that I wanted, toys, candy and knives mostly. Sometimes I would try to sell them to other kids. I took to stealing paring knives, and I frequently carried one in a little holster. I carried a pocket knife and wondered if I would really stab someone in a fight.

I began to think I was ugly to look at and not handsome at all. I didn't like my thick glasses. I wanted to be handsome and not have to wear them. I wanted to look like my brother or my dad. They were tall and good looking. The reflection I saw in the mirror of myself was that of a short, sad, ugly kid. So I practiced smiling in the mirror. I thought I looked better smiling, so when ever I came out of the bathroom I wore a big smile. The other kids must have thought I was a nut.

Lawrence and I cooked, if you can call it that, our own meals. We ate cereal, Campbell's soup, pork and beans, hot dogs, ketchup, candy bars, and soda pop. The only time we ate a decent meal was when we went to Aunt Rachel's, which we did on most Sundays. My mom would always show up at home so we could go to church. Our trek to St. Mary's Church on Sunday morning was followed by a trip to Aunt Rachel's for Sunday dinner. Her home had become an oasis for me, and I wished she was my mother.

I still had to go to confession every Saturday. I didn't like confessing my sins and didn't like the penance I would get from the priest. I did not like it if I would get about twenty Hail Mary's, twenty Our Fathers, and an Act of Contrition for penance. I hated it if I had to say the entire Rosary for penance. That was cruel and unusual punishment. I hated kneeling and praying. It hurt my knees. And I was beginning to think God was not listening to my prayers. I wanted him to make my parents stop fighting, for them to be happy and not get a divorce. I wanted him to make me tall, handsome, and not need glasses. My prayers were being ignored, but I still believed in God. Maybe I only had to try harder to be good, and then he would start doing something for me. I also had to learn all my prayers and catechism answers so I could be confirmed as a soldier of God soon.

Dad was starting to go out by himself on weekend nights. He would get all dressed up in his suit with a shirt, tie and hat. He often put his .38 cali-ber snub-nosed revolver in his pocket. I asked him why he was carrying it. He would always say there could be trouble where he was going. I would ask, "Where are you going, Dad?" He usually said he was going to the Eagles Club or a dance somewhere. He was a handsome man. He looked like a cross between

Gregory Peck and Errol Flynn. Tall, thin, blue eyed, with thick black hair that always stayed in place. I was an average sized, skinny blond sixty-five-pound eleven-year-old. I had no hope of ever looking like Dad. I could not understand why my mother, who was not as pretty as he was handsome, didn't like him.

During the spring of 1946 Mom's failure to come home at night became more frequent. She would disappear for days at a time. When I did see her, she was usually getting dressed to go to work or go out. We didn't have much modesty in our apartment. I often saw her nude. Sponge baths at the kitchen sink were the way we bathed. Nudity was common. I saw the birthmark on her thigh again. It reminded me of my days as a child peering at her in the back seat in the arms of her lover. They were not pleasant memories for me. On a couple occasions while I was home during the day skipping school, strange men would come to the apartment asking for her. I only knew one of them, a local prize fighter. My mother had given me tickets some weeks before to see him fight. She knew I liked boxing. But I wondered how she got those tickets.

Our apartment only consisted of three rooms, a kitchen, bedroom, and a living room. All the rooms were in a row along a short hallway. There were no doors separating them. Lawrence and I slept on a hideaway bed in the living room next to the radio. The toilet was out in the hall at the top of the stairs, outside of our apartment. We shared it with the other upstairs apartment. There was no bathtub or shower.

The toilet in the hall was in a very small room. I could sit on the stool and write on the wall. One day I wrote "Mom, Dad, Lawrence, and me." I really don't know why. For some reason, our names on that toilet wall have stayed in my memory all of my life. I can see them plainly now.

March rolled around, and I was confirmed into the Roman Catholic Church along with about a hundred other kids. Someone took a picture of Mom, Dad, Lawrence, and me plus my Aunt Rachel, Uncle Henry, and Donnie Pete and Patty. Lawrence and I had on two-toned suits that were too small, with buttons obviously missing on each of our suit jackets. I didn't notice the missing buttons, but many years later, Aunt Rachel gave me the picture, and I was shocked to see how badly we were dressed that day. About the same time, another Aunt, my dad's sister, Marie, gave me a picture of my dad on his confirmation day. He was dressed in a nice suit and wore a tie. His feet were shod in shiny boots. There were no buttons missing on his clothes. Seeing his confirmation picture made me furious and then sad. I wondered why my parents had neglected my brother and me so badly when they themselves had not been.

On June 6, 1946, my grandpa, Hans Haugen, died after being paralyzed and bedridden for ten years. My dad said it was a blessing. He immediately made plans for us to travel to Minneota for Grandpa's funeral at the Hope Lutheran Church. Mom was nowhere to be found, so Dad said we would go without her. We loaded ourselves into Dad's 1942 Plymouth, and off we went, just the three of us. It took a very long day traveling the 550 miles.

It was a big funeral, with many of Grandpa's brothers in attendance, as well as his children, grandchildren, and a lifetime of friends. I had never seen a dead person before, and it was scary to see him lying all stiff in the open casket. I wondered what it felt like to be dead. I had neither met any of Grandpa's brothers before, nor had I seen any of my uncles or aunts, except for Bertha and her husband. They all seemed very nice; none of them acted like witches or devils.

There was one relative to whom I took a particular liking: George Peterson from Grand Meadow, a small town just a stone's throw from Bear Creek, Minnesota, where the Haugen family had first settled back in the 1850s. George was Grandpa Haugen's older sister's son. He was a kindly gentle older man who was good at talking to kids. I learned that his mother, Gurinne Thompson, died following his birth, and George had been adopted by one of Grandpa's other sisters who had married a man named Peterson. Thus, his last name. Gurinne Thompson had given birth to several children, but George was the only one who had been adopted.

George invited us to stop at his house on the way back to Illinois and to stop at his brother's farm near Spring Valley, Minnesota. My dad said he would love to do that. He told Lawrence and me he had known George and George's brother, Albert Thompson, his wife Olive, and their daughter Dorothy since he was a very young. He said that Albert was his first cousin. Dad said he would also like to visit some other relatives around Spring Valley on the way home. Lawrence and I didn't want to stop; we didn't think it would be any fun, but we agreed. They were all friendly at the funeral and really very nice, but these people were all Lutherans. Their church was weird and their minister spoke in English. We understood every word. There was no smoke, incense, or tinkling bells. My brother and I just wanted to get back to Kewanee to be with our friends. After a few days of getting acquainted with Dad's brothers Harland, Norman, and Sanford, and his sister Marie, plus a myriad of cousins, we were on our way to Grand Meadow and Spring Valley.

George had a nice home, much better than ours in Kewanee. We stayed there for a couple of days, and my brother and I were treated with great attention and affection. We then went to the Hardecoff farm—more relatives with a lot of kids. Some of them were girls about our age. We became so friendly within a couple of days that my brother and I found ourselves being kissed by our newfound girl distant cousins. They were pretty too. Then we were off to the Thompson farm.

The Thompson farm was located about a mile west of the south end of town. We turned west at the end of the baseball park, drove about a mile over a little rise in the road and the railroad tracks, and a dark green grove of tall arborvitae trees. And there on my right was as pretty a little farm as one could imagine. The house and yard were enclosed by a white picket fence. It joined the arborvitae on the east and then went straight west for about a hundred feet, and north about another hundred feet to a little red garage.

The house was a stucco cottage with wooden shingles. The front of the house had one large window on each side of the door. On the west side the picket fence was interrupted by a large over arching white picket entry and gate. From there a sidewalk led to a pump house, woodshed and an outhouse, or straight ahead to a door that took you inside a large screened-in porch that was the nearly the full length of the house. From inside the porch you entered into the kitchen then a dining room; to the left was a living room and a left again into the master bedroom. There were two bedrooms upstairs. One was Dorothy's and the other was a small room, half of it used for storage. There were no doors on the bedrooms only one at the bottom of the stairs. We stayed in the small room, where the three of us slept in a full size hide a bed for a couple of days.

Outside was a very nice red barn with a lean-to on the east and west sides of it. A large haymow door was located on the second floor front of the barn complete with peak and hay fork track. The barn had a cupola and weather vane. There was a chicken house with many chickens walking around in front of it scratching in the dirt, searching for things to eat. The east lean-to contained to giant horses. The west was home to four cows. A grove of splendid pines protected the farm place from the wind to the north and the west. The south side of the farm yard was open to the road, the south winds, and the sun. The entire farm covered twenty acres.

It was a place that made me think perhaps they made gingerbread men here. It looked like a storybook farm.

Albert was only about five feet seven inches tall. He was friendly and had a friendly face. He looked a lot like my dad, except he had heavier cheekbones, was much shorter and a little stooped. Olive, a little younger, was a pretty lady with hairs growing out of a large mole on her cheek. She was not skinny, fat, or tall. Dorothy was a little fat but not tall. She had large breasts.

Lawrence and I checked out their barn, swung on the haymow track rope and dropped in the hay, took walks with my BB gun and plinked away at blackbirds. We more or less stayed out of the way. But we did hear Dad telling the Thompsons that his marriage was not going well, and he was thinking of getting a divorce. They encouraged him to move to Spring Valley. They said there was plenty of work in the area, and Albert could get him a job with the local pea and bean vineries that Monarch Foods owned. Albert said he was a foreman for one of the vineries. They talked of old times. Lawrence and I were pretty much bored and wanted to go home to Kewanee. Soon we were on our way.

We left Spring Valley early in the morning and arrived in Kewanee early enough for Lawrence and me to catch the late afternoon movie. We were back in familiar territory. We spent the rest of the summer working at the bowling alley, tearing our bikes apart and fixing them, going swimming, eating at Dairy Queen, playing with friends, and preparing our own meals. Mom was gone. She was not home when we returned from Minnesota. She did come home for a while in August. She and Dad got into some terrible arguments. She accused Dad of having a girlfriend in Minnesota. He accused her of having boyfriends and having been with them most of the time lately. She always denied everything. She said that when she didn't come home for days at a time that she was staying with girlfriends. Dad would just go "Harrumph!" which meant, "yeah, sure!" Lawrence and I believed she was with other men.

One day a letter came from Dorothy Thompson. My mom got to it before Dad. She read it, and she was mad as hell. She waived it menacingly at him and said, "Here is the evidence that you have a girlfriend, you SOB!" Blah, blah, blah. I don't know if it was or not. Dad denied it was evidence. I never read the letter.

I was soon out on the front porch with my mom, and she was quizzing me. "Who do you like the most, me or your Dad?"

"I like you both the same," I said. She wanted me to stretch my arms to show how much I loved her. I stretched them wide.

She said, "Now show me how much you love your Dad." I stretched them wide. She became furious with me and said, "How could you like that son of a bitch?"

I said I loved both of them. But there was no satisfying her. I refused to show her I loved her more. In a few days she was gone. We got a letter telling Lawrence and me to be at the pay phone near the corner store at a certain time on a specific day, and she would call us to talk. We never had a telephone at any of our houses.

Lawrence and I went to the pay phone at the appointed time. She called, as she said she would. We wanted to know when she was coming home. She said she wasn't sure. She wouldn't tell us where she was. We wanted her to come home before school started. She said she did not know if she could or not.

She never came home again.

CHAPTER 11

SEVENTH GRADE, AUTUMN 1946

We carried on our lives without Mom. I cried a lot. I missed my mother, and I wanted her back. I just kept on praying that she would come home. Dad said we needed to start school, which we wanted to do.

I started the seventh grade at Kewanee Central. Lawrence started the ninth grade at the same school complex, only the high school. I made the football team and was a good player. I loved football. One of my classmates was Mickey Bates, who went on to play for the University of Illinois.

I made new friends easily at Kewanee's big public school. I liked it much better than St. Mary's. My teacher was Mrs. Curly. She had blue gray hair and was very pleasant. I was particularly good at art. We had a competition among the seventh and eighth graders to see who could come up with the best Halloween window designs for some of the stores downtown. We had to think up a design, draw it, paint it, and submit it knowing that we'd later have to enlarge it significantly on a big store window. I won a store window. I had chosen to make a hobo walking, carrying a little bag of his clothes fastened to the end of a long stick carried over his shoulder. A large black cat with yellow eyes trotted along side of him as they walked through a patch of pumpkins. I drew it all out on the big window and then painted it. I did much better than I thought I could, and I was very proud of my work, as was my teacher.

As I look back now, I find it curious that I may have unconsciously projected my own situation into the picture I painted, complete with an ominous bad-luck black cat.

Lawrence and I went trick-or-treating on Halloween and gathered up loads of candy. By chance we happened to stop at our old school teacher's house from near Shanty Town. We were surprised that she lived near us. She was pleased to see us and asked how we were doing. We told her we were fine and where we were going to school. She asked about our folks. We said our mother was missing, and we didn't know where she was. She was shocked and wanted to know what had happened. We said we really didn't know, but we thought maybe she had been kidnapped or something.

She comforted us by replying, "I'm sure your mother will return home soon. I am sure she has not been kidnapped."

We kind of mumbled a reply and my brother said, "Yeah, maybe."

She gave us each a big kiss, a big hug and some candy. We walked home chomping on the good things in our bag of treats.

In early November my dad said we were going to move to Spring Valley, Minnesota. We would stay with the Thompsons for awhile and then see what was best. He said he was getting a divorce, and the papers would be signed in the next few days. The day before we left Illinois, in the hall toilet of our Vine Street apartment, I crossed "Mom" off the wall with a pencil. My mom was gone. There was just "Dad, Lawrence, and me" remaining.

The next day we met Aunt Rachel in the parking lot at the bowling alley, and she and Dad went somewhere. When they returned, my dad had the divorce papers. He said they were all signed. Rachel came over to where Lawrence and I were waiting in the car. She was crying. We got out of the car to greet her. She hugged and kissed us both and told us to take care of ourselves and she would see us soon. Lawrence and I were both crying. We soon pulled out of the parking lot and Dad deliberately pointed the car towards the roads that led to Spring Valley. We had only a few clothes and no household belongings. No family pictures. The pictures had been destroyed in the house fire. No furniture. Dad had sold or disposed of what furniture we had in last few days. I did have my BB gun.

I never returned to the Illinois school system. I never again saw any of the families we had befriended or any of the friends I had made in Illinois.

68

CHAPTER 12

AUSTIN, MINNESOTA, WATERLOO, IOWA, WINTER 1946 AND SPRING 1947

I did not want to go to Spring Valley. I cried and whimpered all the way. I wanted my dad to take me back to Kewanee so I could stay with my mom. He said that was impossible. He didn't know where she was, and if she had wanted me, she would have taken me with her long ago.

I was very upset. I kept arguing and whining. I told Dad that I knew I would never see my mom or Aunt Rachel again. He said that was ridiculous. He insisted that I just get over it. Dad said we were going to Spring Valley to stay, and that was that. I complained that they didn't like Lawrence and me. He said that was ridiculous too. He said the Thompsons liked all of us. It was a long and emotional trip.

We arrived at the Thompson farm late that night. The next day we spent getting reacquainted. I wasn't sure what was going to happen next, but within a few days, Dad said he and Dorothy were going to be married. I remember it. Dad took Lawrence and me for a walk down to the creek in the Thompson's pasture. On the way back to the house, Dad told us of his marriage plans. I became very upset and began screaming at him and crying. He told me that I would not believe how good a life we were going to have. I told him he was lying. Lawrence took it better than I did. I whimpered around for several more days. I was heartbroken.

I didn't realize what had happened between Lawrence and Dad. Dad had made a deal with Lawrence that he could quit high school and go back to Minneota and live with Grandma Blomme once Dad and Dorothy were married. I would have to stay because I was not old enough to quit school, and I had not completed the eighth grade.

Within a couple of weeks Dad and Dorothy were married in a nearby "Little Brown Church in the Vale." They went off by themselves for a few days and then returned. Lawrence and I stayed with Albert and Olive. When Dad and Dorothy got back, Lawrence willingly went to Minneota. I don't remember how he got there. He was a very big fifteen-year-old, probably five feet nine inches tall and 160 pounds. He may have gone by Greyhound bus.

I was so upset that in my mind, I crossed Lawrence's name off the toilet-room wall of the Vine Street apartment. Dad and I were the only ones left.

Very early in December Dad, Dorothy, and I moved to an apartment in Austin, Minnesota, where Dad had found a job with a plumbing and heating company.

Dorothy took me to Austin Central Junior High School to enroll in the seventh grade. I didn't want her to, but she and Dad insisted. I was angry that she was acting like my mom. I was embarrassed that I had a stepmother and didn't want anyone to know. I did not want her around at all. She wanted me to call her "Mom," but I absolutely refused. I would only call her "Dorothy."

I was angry and sad, but school was a place to make friends and get attention from teachers. It was easy to get attention because I was good at my school work. We studied the countries of South America that spring. I became an ardent student of the economics, geography, and history of South America.

I liked English too. I sat next to a big sixteen-year-old who had large greasy chapped hands and smelled like gasoline. He said he had a car and worked on it a lot, and that was why he smelled like gas. He was not too good in English, so I befriended him by helping him with his work. It was good to have a big friend. Miraculously, I did not get in any fist fights at the new school. No one teased me about my thick glasses.

I walked home from school most days. It was several blocks. The weather was cold, and I had gotten a new pair of corduroy pants. They would go "whip,

whip, whip" as I walked and the inside of my pant legs rubbed each other. I amused myself by imagining I was a little professor, bespectacled and carrying my books going "whip, whip, whip" down the sidewalk.

A couple of times a week I would go from school to a gymnasium over by the large downtown grocery store. They taught boxing there. I started to take boxing lessons and in general just messed around there with some other kids. We would spar with each other in the ring, jump rope, and hit the punching bags. There were pictures of Willie Pep all over the gym. Someone said he had trained there. Dad or Dorothy would pick me up from the gym and take me home. I began to eat regular meals. And my Dad made me stop smoking cigarettes, which I needed to do if I was going to be a boxer.

The house we moved into was owned by an elderly Jewish couple. They had converted their second floor into a small apartment. This was my new home, which I shared with Dad and unwillingly with my new stepmother. The friendly old couple who lived downstairs owned a produce market. Over the next few months they often brought us fruit and vegetables that were on the edge of spoiling

The couple must have noticed I was unhappy because they soon befriended me and often asked me into their apartment to have a piece of cake or some cookies and milk. They taught me how to play a card game called Big Casino, and I spent many hours with them playing cards.

At the end of February, Dad said we were going to move to Waterloo, Iowa. He had taken a job with the John Deere Company working in a factory. I really didn't care. My life was so interrupted, and I had learned that what I wanted made no difference to anyone. On the first of March we moved to Waterloo.

At twelve years old, I had by now been enrolled in the seventh grade in three different schools in three different states.

I was only going where my dad was taking me. The September before, I had started out rebellious and full of grief over losing my mother. During that winter I was angry and sad that my dad had married Dorothy. And now I was beginning to accept that my fate was not in my hands. It was in my dad's hands, and maybe God's. God was not answering my prayers. Neither my mother nor any other relative had as much as written to me, not even my brother. I had been praying for one or all of them to rescue me. None did.

At Waterloo, we moved into a two-car garage. The people that owned it lived across the highway from the garage. It was a busy highway between Waterloo and Cedar Falls. The garage consisted of one room divided into a kitchen, dining area, and a place for two double beds. There were no partitions. There was an indoor flush toiled enclosed with a curtain. I slept in a double bed next to Dad and Dorothy's double bed. There was absolutely no privacy.

Dorothy helped me get enrolled at my new school. I think it was called Washington Irving Junior High School. It was early March 1947, and I was one unhappy kid. The boys at school were soon picking on me. Because of my thick glasses, taunts of "four eyes" and "sissy" began the first day. Those were fighting words, and I liked to fight. There were soon a lot of kids who wanted to fight me, and I was constantly in fist fights, always getting the best of anyone who challenged me. But I did get some lumps on my cheekbones and some black eyes too. Bare-handed knuckled fists hurt.

One day after gym class several of them wanted to fight me. I agreed to fight each of them, but one at time with boxing gloves after school. They agreed, so that day we got some gloves after school and went to the gym. I easily beat them up. Fortunately they did not all jump on me at one time. This was a gentlemen's sport. I immediately gained a reputation for being a tough kid. The challengers decreased in number, and I earned a prominent place in the school's seventh grade pecking order. I also made friends.

I found a new girlfriend who taught me to roller skate. I played marbles on the playground. I learned about math formulas for finding areas of rectangles, triangles, and circles, and those for volumes of cylinders and cubes, and so forth. I did well at school. I got a job delivering newspapers after school and was settling in to a difficult situation.

Shortly after I started school, Lawrence miraculously showed up on our doorstep. He had apparently become lonesome and unhappy living with Grandma and Grandpa Blomme and wanted to live with us. I don't know how he knew where we lived. I was so happy to see him. I had been afraid he was gone forever. We were soon teasing and arguing with each other again, just like the old days.

He and I had no choice but to sleep in the same bed together. When Dad and Dorothy were in their bed and Lawrence and I were in ours, our noses were only a few feet apart.

Lawrence had made it through puberty and now acted in a strange manner in bed. I had not made it to puberty yet. At night, if he couldn't sleep—and it was hot in our little garage at night that summer—he would play with his penis and then rub his fingers under my nose. He would say, "Here Donnie, have some cheese." This would make me furious and I would slug him. Then he would try to pin me my arms down on the bed, and I would kick and bite him. Needless to say, the ruckus was soon very loud. Dad and Dorothy were only fingertips away and of course we woke them up. Dad would threaten to beat us because he needed to sleep in order to work the next day. We tried to live together in harmony, but there were too many people and not enough two-car garage.

Dorothy became very unhappy with our living situation and made her feelings known to us. We had a telephone, and she talked to her mother on the phone a lot. I overheard her many times telling her mom how unhappy she was. She often cried. We taunted her. Lawrence and I didn't like her, and we began to "sass" and talk back. I soon heard heated conversations between Dad and Dorothy. Dorothy wanted to go back to the farm at Spring Valley. She couldn't stand this living situation anymore.

Lawrence and I said cruelly, "Great! Go on back. We didn't want you anyway."

Lawrence got a full time job at a laundry and bought himself a Cushman motor scooter to go back and forth to work. He soon had a pretty girlfriend and was spending a lot of time at her parent's house. He was getting a paycheck every week and becoming more and independent.

I made friends with the neighbor kid who was a little older and bigger than me. We had a few fist fights, and then we became friends. Boys seem to work relationships out that way sometimes. One day, my new friend and I went camping over the weekend down on banks of the Black Hawk River. That evening, two young couples came down to the river near where we had made our beds on the ground. They didn't see us. The couples stripped naked and went for a swim in the river. Then each couple dried themselves off, found a place on the river bank and began making love. We watched undetected.

We spent a lot a time at the public swimming pool having fun and hoping not to catch polio. We built a tree fort in my friend's back yard. We entertained ourselves playing cards, counting and naming the makes of cars going by on the highway, and visiting the nearby animal shelter. We were barefooted kids doing kid things in the summer of 1947.

Dad began to talk to Lawrence and me about leaving Dorothy. He said the three of us would have to stick together. I was beginning to like my dad better. He was finally making sense. He even took me shopping for some clothes and shoes. I needed them badly because I was growing and my feet were getting huge. But then suddenly in late summer, Dad announced that he, Dorothy and I would be moving to the Thompson farm at Spring Valley. They were going to rent more land and begin farming the place with Dorothy's folks.

I didn't know that he had already talked to Lawrence about the move and had made a deal with him to stay in Waterloo by himself. I was angry at him for making those plans. I didn't want to move to Spring Valley. I wanted to stay with my brother. Dad said I couldn't because it was against the law. I would have to come with him. I had made new friends. I had a paper route, and I didn't want to leave. I loved my brother, and I still wanted my dad to go back to my mom.

My birthday came in the first part of August, and I turned thirteen. I had already been to about twelve different schools, and we were moving again. I had not received any letters from Mom or any other relative. I didn't know if anyone knew where I lived. No one came to rescue me from my situation, not even God.

Lawrence found himself a place to stay in Waterloo with his girlfriend's parents. Dad, Dorothy, and I moved to the Thompson farm at Spring Valley in late August.

In my mind, I crossed Lawrence's name off the Vine Street toilet wall once more.

CHAPTER 13

PRELUDE TO SPRING VALLEY

Our family had lived in and around Spring Valley for nearly one hundred years. Albert Thompson was my dad's first cousin. Albert and his wife Olive had been successful at farming. They had owned and operated a large farm near Racine, Minnesota, until only a couple of years before we came to visit them after Grandpa's funeral.

Their Spring Valley farm was their retirement place. In the days before Social Security and retirement plans, it was common and desirable for a successful farm couple to provide for their own needs as they grew older. Albert and Olive kept only a few cows and about hundred chickens because that is all they needed to provide them with an income. In the summer and fall, Albert supplemented his income by working at a vinery, running machinery that processes vines of peas and beans by separating the vines from the legumes and shelling them.

They grew in their garden most everything they ate. They preserved from their garden and nearby orchards nearly everything they would need over the winter months. They owned their car and an old 10/20 McCormick Deering tractor. They had only electric and telephone bills to pay each month. The farm was paid for. They had money in the bank from the sale of their big farm, and they had interest income from their money.

Their recently divorced daughter, Dorothy, had been living with them only a short time when we came to visit. Now Dorothy was married to my dad, who had these two undesirable boys. They knew that Dorothy hated me

75

and Lawrence, and they didn't want us around. We were going to disrupt their peaceful lives. Dorothy had been talking to her mother all along. They apparently had agreed that Lawrence was not going to be part of the package. He would have to go, and Dad took care of it. I am sure they were planning to get rid of me, but they hadn't found a way yet.

CHAPTER 14

SPRING VALLEY, EIGHTH GRADE, SEPTEMBER 1947

We moved to the picturesque little farm with the pretty stucco-covered house. The white picket fence still surrounded it along with the pine and arborvitae groves. I had once thought maybe they made gingerbread men for kids to eat at this place, but that had only been my imagination.

The chickens were still out scratching and looking for food, making their comforting clucking little utterances as they searched contentedly. The two large draft horses, Fanny and Ned, were still living in the east lean-to when they were not in the pasture grazing. The four contented cows could still be found chewing the cud quietly in the west lean-to at milking time.

The farm was mostly pasture land. A stream flowed toward the northeast dividing the pasture in two on its way to town. There it meandered though Spring Valley, cutting it almost diagonally into two equal parts. The town was nestled in the valley with hills rising up on the north and the south of the bisecting stream. The hills were covered with hundreds of hardwood trees. Many Protestant church steeples poked through the trees toward the sky. The steeples were dwarfed by a water tower sitting on the hill overlooking the stream and next to my new school. The houses were small, constructed mostly of wood and painted white. Within them lived about two thousand five hundred residents. The Catholic church was small, wooden and white.

It's steeple far less prominent on the landscape than the Protestant ones. It was a picturesque little town, but it was not Catholic country.

This was not Kansas. This was Minnesota. Dorothy did not wear red shoes. Or did she? She had gotten back home. There was not a yellow brick road, only a crushed limestone road that led east to Spring Valley and west toward Grand Meadow. Although pretty, Spring Valley was not the Emerald City. The wizard was never heard from. Or were we listening to a wizard? There was a dog but her name was not Toto, it was Lady.

Lady was a house dog, an old graying black female rat terrier. She was thirteen and crabby, and she didn't like kids. All my attempts to befriend her were met with snaps and growls. Lady was fed store-bought food and taken to her toilet on a leash. She was treated like a lovable child.

Albert was sixty-four years old, still kindly and a little stooped from his years of hard farm work. He remained soft-spoken and friendly to me, although, like my dad, he never spoke unless it was for a purpose. He liked to smoke his pipe. Every evening he sat in his chair with a spit bucket next to him. He would sit and smoke and spit in his bucket while gently rocking back and forth. I was fascinated by his manly manner, and I was warned by the ladies to never sit in his chair.

Olive was still the same sixty-year-old woman, neither fat nor thin and about five feet four inches tall. She talked and moved very quickly. She was obviously the most intelligent and the boss of the family. She had a large mole on the left side of her cheek, a few short thick, clipped hairs grew out of it. Her hair had been black but it was now turning gray. She had an ever-so-slight mustache and was a bundle of nervous energy. Her lips frequently twitched when excited or upset. It was easy for me to imagine her with a pointed witch's hat nervously flying around on a broom. I thought she might be some kind of evil witch. She definitely engineered the plans with Dorothy to get her back home on the family farm. She was proud of her English heritage and her Protestant beliefs, and she despised Roman Catholics.

Dorothy, as I mentioned earlier, was about five feet three inches tall, heavy breasted and heavy boned, not pretty but not ugly, and about thirty-four years old. She was not as mentally quick as her mom. She moved more slowly with less nervous energy. Her legs seemed too skinny for her upper body. I thought she was built like a smaller feminine version of Babe Ruth.

Dad was forty-six years old, about six feet tall and about 175 pounds. He was still a handsome slender man. He had taken on a mental quality that was tentative with the Thompsons. He never seemed sure of what he was going to say. He would start a conversation in one direction with them, and if he sensed disapproval, he would change directions. He never did like conflict; now he seemed determined to avoid it. It seemed to me he was trying to please the Thompsons with whatever he said.

I was kind of skinny at five feet two inches and about ninety pounds. My hair was turning light brown and would never stay anywhere I tried to put it. I still wore those thick wire-rimmed glasses. People would often say to me that I looked like a little professor. In truth, I was a kid who learned easily, and I probably projected a little-professor image in my glasses. I liked to read and had a large vocabulary. I had been taught by my teachers over the last several grades to enunciate my words clearly, and I projected my voice loudly and with confidence. I was opinionated and verbal like my mom. I thought I was smart. But underneath the scholarly facade, I was a frightened, lonesome, and unhappy kid.

The Thompson family didn't know me very well or how I had been raised. They knew my dad. I don't think they cared enough about me to find out what I thought or felt or what I had been through. I know Dorothy thought I was just something unpleasant that she may have to put up with to be with Dad. I am surprised that Dad did not try to get rid of me in some way, perhaps by giving me to Aunt Rachel. Maybe he tried and didn't succeed.

By the time we left Waterloo, Dorothy and I were openly hateful towards each other. I heard her telling Olive how difficult and mean Lawrence and me were. Dorothy, Dad, and me had driven from Waterloo to Spring Valley to spend several weekends over the summer at the farm. It was obvious during those visits that Olive began to see me as an unnecessary nuisance. She was no longer thoughtful or kind toward me. She was just tolerating my existence in her house. I felt more unwanted than ever. I began to feel like a huge crying sob was caught deep in my chest, and it wouldn't come out. My chest ached.

Every friend I had ever made anywhere was gone. All the kids who had become my friends in every school I had attended were gone. Every family that we had befriended along the way was gone. I never saw any of them after I left a place. We never went back to visit anyone. Every one of my relatives on my mother's side was gone. Aunt Rachel was gone. My mother was gone. I had not a heard a thing from her. My brother was gone.

I had not one picture of any of them. I had not a single letter from anyone. I found it difficult to remember what my friends and relatives looked like.

My Catholic church was gone. I hadn't been to church since we left Kewanee. My dad was back among his Lutheran people, and although the Thompson family did not go to church, they were Lutherans, and I had learned over the past year that the Thompsons did not like Catholics. I knew that is why my dad was not taking me to my church.

Right after Labor Day, I enrolled in the eighth grade at Spring Valley's public school on the hill near the water tower. As I recall, I did it myself. Someone may have driven me to the school, but they didn't go in. I had been through this procedure many times and knew how to do it. The next day I started riding the bus to and from school.

The seventh- and eighth-grade classes were combined in one large room on the second floor of the elementary school building. There were about sixty of us in total. The seventh grade was on the right side of the room, the eighth on the left. Miss Markson, a teacher who was also the principal, had her desk on an elevated platform in front of the room. From her vantage point she could survey all her students. She ruled the school and our large room with apparent ease. Controlling the sixty of us was not an issue for her; she was in complete control. She was an able teacher and principal, pleasant in demeanor and appearance. She was thin and tall. Her hair was turning gray and she wore glasses without rims. She was kind and very proper. I liked her immediately.

I sat in the second row of the eighth-grade section. I was toward the back among the other children with "H" names. Nancy Gynild sat in front of me, Bob Healy in back and to my right, a fourteen-year-old, six-foot-three-inch, 180-pound Donald Byers. I liked to talk. I wanted to talk with the kids sitting near me during class. When we were supposed to be quiet, I would lean way over or twist around to get the attention of my neighbor. My behavior did not escape Miss Markson's ever-present gaze. She gave me some leeway for a few days then called me to her elevated platform. She stepped down from behind her desk and stood in front of me. I looked up at her as she spoke.

"Donnie, where did you go to school last year?" she asked.

For some reason I said, "Illi-noise.

"Don't you mean Illinois?"

"Yes, Miss Markson."

"I believe you went to an Iowa school last year."

"Well, I went to three schools last year in three different states. I guess I forgot where I went last."

"The proper pronunciation of Illinois is not Illi-noise, but Illinois."

"Yes, Miss Markson."

Then she kindly but firmly told me that she knew I could be a very good student. She expected me to be a good student and that I needed to stop disrupting the classroom by talking to my friends. She would expect better self-control and better behavior from me. She said something like, "Donnie, I expect you to live up to my expectations as long as you are in my school. And in my school you will obey my rules."

I said, "Yes, Miss Markson." I was impressed. She knew who I was, where I had come from, and she was in charge.

Autumn was warm and long. My classmates accepted me, and I had not been in any fights. I made friends with some of the seventh-grade boys who rode the bus. I spent most recess periods and noon hours playing tackle football with them and some kids from town. We soon knew who was good at football and who wasn't, and who could play what position. The way we started a game was for all the kids who were going to play to choose two captains, and then each captain would select their team by choosing alternately from those playing. I usually was named one of the captains and would choose my team. The other captain would choose his team, and we'd go at it for the day. The days turned into weeks for me as a captain. I usually played quarterback, halfback, or a receiver. I was good at football. I could run a lot better than I could pass, so I usually carried the ball. It was easy for me to run and elude tacklers. My friends began to call me "Slippery," or "Slip" for short, because I could easily slip out of a tackler's grasp. I was happy with my newfound friends and popularity on our playground football field.

I did make friends with some eighth-grade boys. Our friendships started in English class. The boys I chose as friends and sat next to were rowdy. I tended to migrate toward that type, the pre-delinquent kids. They were slow learners, and I needed to act dumber than I actually was to fit in with them. So I did.

We gave our young, first-year teacher Miss Shaw a terrible time. We constantly talked, laughed, giggled and teased each other in the back of the room, frequently disrupting the entire class. It was so much fun. I was disciplined many times by the teacher. She would give me extra work. That did not slow me down because English was easy for me. I aced my tests and got an A in English. But my deportment grade was D. The unfortunate young teacher was overwhelmed by her first year with us and quit teaching at Christmas time. Rumor had it that she had a nervous breakdown. I felt a little guilty for my part in making her life miserable.

English was the only class in which I behaved badly. I loved art class and was often embarrassed by my enthusiasm for projects.

All of the Thompson family and my dad worked at the nearby Monarch Foods vinery that fall. It was located just up the road a couple miles west of our farm. Albert was the foreman. Sometimes Dorothy would pick me up after school and take me to where they were working. I would spend the rest of the afternoon there messing around or doing my school work.

The vinery was fascinating to me. It could do amazing things. Monarch Foods had thousands of acres of land near our farm planted into peas, lima beans, and sweet corn. This time of the year they were harvesting lima beans. They collected the shelled beans and sorted them according to their degree of dryness, then sent them down a multitude of chutes into large collection boxes. The boxes were then stacked by hand on to a truck and hauled off to Monarch's food-processing factory in Rochester. The vines were piled up automatically by an elevating device into large stacks. They would cure for a while and then be used to feed the company's beef cattle in winter.

A machine pulled by mules cut the bean vines in the field and loaded them onto large wagons pulled by other teams of mules. A mule driver sat on the vines stacked high and drove the load to the vinery. The mules also pulled the sweet-corn pickers and hauled the corn to large trucks that took it to Rochester. There were thousands of mules in southern Minnesota busy harvesting the nation's vegetables.

Dorothy and Olive began to talk in front of me about my dad and his behavior at the vinery. They were angry at him for talking to the other workers. They said he was telling lies about them to their friends. They said he had told other workers he was going to leave Dorothy. Dad had said before we had left Waterloo that he was going to leave Dorothy. Maybe he was saying this now to other people. I hoped so.

Dad seldom talked to me directly. I began to sense the Thompsons did not want us communicating because they feared we might make plans to leave together. They never said, "Do not talk to your Dad." But the message was implied by the fact that I was never alone with him. Olive or Dorothy was always around; Dad and I were seldom alone together.

One day late in November, I got hurt playing football. I was trying to tackle a ball carrier, another good player, who elbowed me in the Adam's apple. I had tackled him too high on his body and paid dearly for it. I fell immediately to the ground clutching my throat. I was having trouble breathing. I thought I was going to suffocate. All the other kids playing gathered around to see what the problem was. Soon I was on my feet and hustled into the school. They told Miss Markson what had happened. I was speechless. Miss Markson said she would observe me for awhile. In about an hour my voice came back. I spoke in a squeaky hoarse whisper. Miss Markson said she was sure I would be fine but that perhaps my parents should take me to a doctor to have me checked out.

I could not speak above a whisper when I went home that afternoon. I thought I should go to the doctor, as Miss Markson had suggested. Olive, Dorothy and Dad all agreed that I would be fine. Their opinion was that a doctor would just cost money and was unnecessary. I would be fine.

I was very concerned about myself. My throat hurt. I couldn't speak above a hoarse whisper for about two weeks. When I could speak aloud again, it was in a raspy, squeaky hoarse voice.

About this time, our music teacher was holding voice evaluations for the school chorus and wanted to listen to each of us to determine who should be recruited to join the chorus. I told him I couldn't sing because I had hurt my voice box playing football. He asked if I had gone to a doctor, and I told him I had not. He just shook his head in disgust with me, and said "that was really dumb" and that he did not understand farm people. I didn't either. I had never been taken to a doctor for any reason that I can recall, except to the optometrist, and the time I was bitten by a dog years before. My dad did not believe in spending money on doctors. The Thompson family had the same philosophy.

My concern for my throat continued. I had a small lump on the side of my Adam's apple where the injury occurred, and it was getting bigger. The thought of cancer crossed my mind and then stayed there. Maybe I was getting cancer of the larynx from the injury. I imagined the left side of my face getting dark and rotting away from the cancerous growth in my throat. So I checked it frequently in the mirror, and one day I was stunned to see the left side of my face had turned dark. My heart began race.

The cancerous growth on my larynx was destroying my ability to speak and rapidly turning the left side of my face into a blood-starved dark color. I tried turning the kitchen light on to see if it was just my imagination driving me nuts. The light made no difference. Nor did it make any difference when I examined the spot in the daylight. Over the next several days I worried about how much time I had left. I wondered why no one in the family said anything to me about my rapidly deteriorating condition. I thought they didn't care and would all be glad when I was dead. But I also wondered why no one at school had said anything to me about my face.

After several days of torturous thoughts over my impending death, I took the mirror from the wall and went and stood in the sunlight streaming through the kitchen windows and examined my face. The full brightness of sunlight revealed that both sides of my face were exactly the same color. The lump on my Adam's apple was smaller. I couldn't see it in the mirror, and I could barely feel it with my fingers. I did not have cancer.

I was enormously relieved by my self-discovery in some good bright sunlight. My mind was eased and my "cancer" was "cured." I probably would have had a more rapid cure if I had trusted my family enough to ask them if the left side of my face was turning black or if they thought I had cancer of the Adam's apple. But I didn't trust them to tell me the truth about anything, to say nothing of trusting them with my health or my life.

The chill of autumn was rapidly turning into the freezing cold of winter. The work at the vinery ended. Dad, the women and Albert now spent their days at home in the house. We only had four cows and a few chickens. There wasn't much for them to do.

We started going to dances on Friday or Saturday nights. We went to Rollie Pollie Little Ole's plays and dances. It was a troupe that presented a short comedic play, and then there was dancing. I liked the plays but the dances were boring. I didn't have any of my mom's relatives to dance with, and I didn't know the people at these dances.

Occasionally, we went to the home of Albert's sister, Lena, on Sundays for dinner. Her daughter Evelyn, her husband, Elmer, and daughter Betty always dined with us. It was large group all eating together. We were all related through my great grandparents, but I had no idea at that time where these people fit into my life.

The dinners were very pleasant. Lena was motherly and kindly. Norwegians were big people, and both Lena and Henry were well into their seventies. Betty, a pretty and friendly girl, was only two years older than me. She went to high school in Stewartville. All of them were very thoughtful and attentive toward me.

The food was good but different from what I was used to with my mother's relatives. These people ate Norwegian food like lutefisk (fish soaked in lye), klube, fatima and lefse. All of these were strange to me, except lefse. They talked about people I had never heard of, like my father's Norwegian relatives from Grand Meadow, Racine, Stewartville, and nearby Bear Creek. Bear Creek is where my great grandparents had settled in the 1850s. All of these folks had stayed in this same Bear Creek area for a hundred years. Unfortunately I knew nothing of their history or who they were, for the most part. I couldn't keep track of who was related to whom, and I really didn't care. Everyone, except for Betty, was old, and they were all Lutherans. I was getting acquainted with them for the first time, but I really didn't want to. I wanted my brother, my mom, and her people.

Occasionally we went to Olive's brother's farm too. He was a friendly unmarried man who lived with his folks. He was considerably younger than Olive. They had a nice farm and a new Kaiser automobile, which fascinated me.

We played cards in the evening after chores before we went to bed. The women, Dad, and I would gather around the kitchen table. Albert would sit in his chair a few feet away from us in the dining room and smoke his pipe. We played whist, a popular game in Minnesota. Olive and I would play against Dorothy and Dad. We usually beat them. These were very animated games for me because I loved to play and win. I couldn't help but jump around with joy after taking an unexpected winning trick. I took joy in beating Dad and Dorothy. Olive was impressed with my card playing ability too, and that pleased me.

We listened to the radio, but we only had one radio: the Thompson's. They and my dad liked to listen to the news and "old-time" music. I liked to listen to programs like "The Lone Ranger." I would frequently turn the radio on when we came in for the evening and begin listening to what I liked. Dorothy or Olive would soon come by and change the station to what they liked, while advising me on what they preferred to listen to. My usual reply was that I like what I was listening to, and I would like to be able to continue listening to it. Their reply was that the adults were in charge of what we listened to. I was often upset by their domination.

In this household, I was expected to respect the wishes of adults without argument. They often reminded me that children were to be seen and not heard. My opinions were to be kept to myself. I had grown up as an active and vocal participant in my family. Lawrence and I were permitted to listen to what we wanted on the radio. We had never had an argument over what we listened to, probably because no one was usually around except the two of us. And we liked stories like "Jack Armstrong." "Sky King," "The Lone Ranger," and "The Shadow." I didn't like the news and I hated old-time music.

Dad and the Thompsons talked about expanding the farm operation. They made plans to rent more land, buy more cows and chickens, and get some pigs. They decided this would be better than for any or all of them to work for someone else. I was hoping Dad would get a job somewhere.

I wanted Dad to get a job because I needed things, like shoes, pants, and shirts. I was outgrowing the clothes I had. No one was buying me clothes even though I was asking for them. Before we moved to the Thompsons' farm, I did have clothes that fit, for the most part, even if buttons were sometimes missing. My mom had seen to it that Lawrence and I had the clothes we needed for school. I think she had bought most of our clothes out of her own money.

I asked Dad for an allowance. He said he could not afford it. I asked Olive and Dorothy for an allowance, and they said I didn't need one. I told them I was the only kid at school that did not have any money. I needed money to get a haircut. The other kids were going to the store at noon and buying candy bars and soda pop, and I did not have any money to buy anything. My arguments were quietly stated. I also screamed them at the ears of my dad and the women, but they were deaf to my pleas for money. They said they had never gotten an allowance, and I didn't need one either.

I needed a haircut before Christmas. The other kids at school were beginning to tease me about my long hair. I had to beg and beg, and it soon became obvious that my dad wouldn't stick up for me. I tried asking him for things in front of Dorothy or Olive. He would still deny me. I wondered why he didn't say, "Yes Donnie, you need a haircut. I will take you this Saturday morning." Or, "Yes Donnie, you need some new clothes, I will take you on Saturday and buy you some new clothes." I wondered why the Dorothy or Olive could not see what I needed and just get it for me. I knew they didn't like me, and I was beginning to realize how stingy they were.

I thought a lot about my mom and brother. I prayed every night for Mom to come and get me. I pleaded with God. I begged him. I moved my prayers from my back in the bed to my knees on the floor, thinking God would be more pleased and grant me my desires. I asked for my mom and dad and brother and even Albert, Olive, and Dorothy to be blessed. I thought it might please God if I was not selfish. I never missed a night.

Christmas came, and I did get a haircut. I got a paperback book, a pair of pants and a shirt. Winter turned to spring, and I got another haircut. These haircuts had become real important to me, and I would start lobbying Olive and Dorothy for one long before I really needed it. I had given up on Dad as a source for anything I needed or wanted. He was hopeless. Olive and Dorothy were the bosses; they controlled him *and* the money. Albert was a silent benign partner with his wife and daughter.

During the summer, I began to hear Olive and Dorothy talking with each other and to my dad about the uselessness of high school. According to them, high school just ruined kids. It had no practical value. You should have learned everything you needed to know by the time you completed the eighth grade. They all agree on that. All of them had only completed the eighth grade, and that was all anyone needed. More education was a waste of time and only led to a life of devilry.

Soon the women were telling me that I didn't need to go to high school. They wanted me to stay home and work on the farm. I argued with them. Today it's different, I said. Everybody needed to go to high school and college, and I wanted to do both. I reduced myself to begging them to let me go to high school. I told them I would run away if I couldn't.

On summer evenings, we would all get into Dad's old 1942 Plymouth and drive to Spring Valley. We always bought ice cream at the Dairy Store. I would generally go in and buy the ice cream cones and bring them out to the car. I would buy five maple nut ice cream cones, and we ate them on the way back to our farm. I was always glad if I didn't see any of the kids from school at the dairy store so they wouldn't see my strange family.

I didn't see any of my school friends during the summer. I spent most of my time helping with the five hundred Leghorn pullets we were nurturing for laying hens to be housed in a newly built chicken house. We had a sign out in front of the farm advertising spring fryers and at times fresh strawberries.

I helped kill and clean the spring fryers (young three-to-four-pound roosters), which we sold to people who came to our farm because of our sign. I had graduated to killing chickens myself. I had seen my mother chopping off the heads of chickens years earlier. Now I could easily stretch their necks across the chopping block too, and, with one quick blow of the axe, imagine cutting Dorothy or Olive's head right off, fling them to the ground, and watch them jump around headless. Sometimes my imagination would send a shiver through my body as I watched the life slowly drain out of them and into the dirt.

I spent a lot of time picking strawberries and weeding and cultivating the one acre garden with a hand hoe. I hated picking strawberries. It was a back-breaking job. I was not to step on the strawberry plants or their fruit, and I was not supposed to eat the big fat juicy ripe ones. I ate them anyway. Some days I think I ate more than I put in the boxes.

I had taken a fancy to track and field while in seventh grade in Kewanee, and I became interested in it again. I made a high-jump apparatus, complete with a movable bar, and I made a pole vault stick out a long bamboo pole. I would use it to jump over fences. I created a long jump area and a place to run the hundred-yard dash. I tried to jump higher and higher, farther and farther, and run faster and faster. This was how I entertained myself when I wasn't working.

We seldom went to Spring Valley to shop. The women liked to go to Chatfield, about fifteen miles away. I don't know why, because we did also shop in Spring Valley for groceries in the market across the street from the ice cream store. Dorothy and Olive would sell eggs and buy groceries with the money. The egg money was theirs to spend as they pleased. Groceries in this case meant staples—flour, salt, sugar, baking powder, baking soda, and yeast. We grew most everything else we needed, or the women had preserved it from the previous summer and autumn. The flour was always in fifty pound sacks made of printed cloth. They treasured flour sack cloth and used it to make dresses and aprons for themselves.

Summer was soon over, and I had gotten my way. I was going to Spring Valley High School. I had forgotten about one of my art projects during the eighth grade. I was always fond of pocket knives, and I used one to make a wood carving of one of our barn cats. When I finished the carving I painted it black and white just like our cat. Although I believed I could have done a better job with a better knife, I thought it looked real nice. My teacher submitted it for a competition at the Fillmore County Fair. I was to learn of its fate after school started.

CHAPTER 15

NINTH GRADE, SPRING VALLEY HIGH SCHOOL, 1948 AND 1949

I got a new pair of blue jeans, a new shirt, and a new pair of shoes for school. Best of all, I had a fresh haircut. My old jeans, shirt, and shoes became my "after school" clothes. I had a total of two shirts, two pair of blue jeans, and a pair of shoes for school. I don't recall if I had any underwear. I don't think I did or I would remember it. Pajamas were never a part of my clothes inventory. I had always slept naked. I knew that some people slept in pajamas.

I was delighted to be back at school. I learned almost immediately that I had won first place at the county fair for my carving of a cat. I was surprised and happy. I never knew what my competition was; we didn't go to the county fair. It made no difference, because what I had done was judged to be very good, and I was grateful that my teacher had submitted my work.

Most of the kids from the eighth grade were back to start ninth grade, and there were several kids from various country schools. There were about seventy freshmen all together.

The high school was located just a couple of hundred feet east of the elementary school I had attended the year before. Between the two buildings was a basketball court of hard packed sand and gravel. A huge playground was directly to the south of the two brick three-story buildings. We used the east side of the playground to play softball, and the west side to play football.

The entire south side of the high school was covered with windows. The windows of the lower two floors were protected by metal grids to prevent breakage by errant balls and whatever. The third-floor windows were unprotected. It was a long distance from home plate to those third floor windows. It was considered a magnificent athletic feat if you could hit a softball and far enough to break a third-floor window. No freshman ever did it, that I know of, but we tried.

The third floor of the high school contained the large assembly room that had an elevated stage on the west end and a small library on the east. The students assembled between the stage and the library in the morning when school started. When I was not attending a class, I belonged in the assembly room. I was assigned a seat in the second row from the coveted south side windows near the front. Tenth, eleventh, and twelfth graders sat to my right in that order. The principal sat at a desk up on the stage at the beginning of each school day. From this vantage point, he could easily survey the room. Nothing escaped his gaze or the prompt dispatch of a cure for a problem. After morning assembly, he would return to his office and other teachers would be in charge of our home room/assembly hall. His office was on the right, next to the stage. This system worked well and helped maintain complete order among the two-hundred-plus students.

I had some problems at the beginning of the school year with fights. The first one occurred in mechanical drawing class, an all-boy class. We learned to make scale drawings of projects using drawing boards, T squares, triangles, French curves, compasses, and so forth. For some reason the boy immediately in back of me said something about my thick glasses, and before I knew it, I had turned around, jumped up, and punched him several times in the face. He began to bleed and cry immediately. The teacher was out of the room when I did this. By the time he came back, the fight was over. But he could see what had happened, and I owned up to what I had done. I had to go to the office of the superintendent, who scolded me for my behavior. He threatened to call my parents if I continued to behave like this and made me sit in his office for a couple of hours. I got in a couple of more fights on the playground, but I was not turned in for them. The kids were learning not to say anything to me about my thick glasses.

I had several friends at school. One of my closest friends, who was somewhat delinquent and two years older than me, wanted to join the Navy, which he said he was going to do as soon as he turned seventeen. The Navy recruiters had given him some pamphlets. The one that interested me the most was the one that illustrated the Navy's clothing allotment. The Navy gave you three complete sets of clothes, including pants, shirts, underwear, socks, a wool jacket, and a cap. I was so envious and couldn't wait until I was seventeen to join the Navy and get those clothes. But it would be three years before I could join, an eternity to my mind.

I was fourteen years old now, about five feet four inches tall, and a little over 110 pounds. I wanted to grow tall, but growing was a slow process for me. That hoarse and sometimes squeaky voice I acquired after my football injury mellowed some and became my permanent voice. I had squeaked and squawked my way through puberty, which no one explained to me I was going through. I was growing body hair instead of fuzz now.

Albert, Olive, Dad and Dorothy all returned to the vinery to work. It was the same arrangement as the previous year. Dorothy picked me up most of the time after school and took me to the vinery. I would stay there until quitting time, and then we would all go home do chores. I would help the women with the egg gathering and then help prepare supper.

During the late summer and fall, we went to farm auction sales to buy cows. We soon had eight cows in the west lean-to of the barn. Each of them had a name.

I wanted to try out for the high school football team. I asked Dad and Dorothy, but they said they needed me to help them. I argued that I didn't help much at the vinery, and I could walk home after football practice. I could help with the chores when I got home. I pointed out that other farm kids played football. I was good at arguing and presenting my case. But my arguments fell on deaf ears. Their answer was that those kids had richer parents and could afford to hire help. They needed me to help. I didn't believe them.

It was becoming apparent from conversations that I overheard that the Thompsons had thought my dad had a lot of money when he married Dorothy. They said he had lied to them. According to them, he had nothing but an old 1942 Plymouth car and a couple thousand dollars. That was all. As a consequence we would have to be frugal and work hard to earn enough money to live on. One thing they did not want to do is draw from their bank savings to pay anything. That was their money they had saved for their old age.

Despite my difficulty in getting clothes and our alleged poverty, my life had taken on a strange stability. I was not going to two and three schools a year. We were staying in one place. We ate breakfast, dinner, and supper everyday. We ate meat, vegetables, and fruit. There was no soda pop or candy. I had enough to eat, and I never had to fix it for myself. I never saw another can of Campbell's soup or pork and beans. I was no longer skipping school and wandering with kids carrying guns and knives. I didn't work in a bowling alley, strange men didn't come looking for my mother, and I didn't smoke cigarettes anymore.

But I was disconnected and lonely. My dad seldom spoke to me. He hardly said a word to me and treated me as if I didn't exist. He never touched me, not even with one finger to see if I was there. I desperately wanted to be touched, to be hugged. My chest ached once more from swallowing the tears that never ran down my face.

I was able to ride the school bus. I was the last one picked up in the morning and the last one dropped off after school. In the afternoon this meant that I rode with many of the kids for almost the entire route. I had a lot of fun on the bus. I liked to flirt with the girls, and some liked to flirt with me. I never spent much time with the girls at school. I ate lunch and played sports with other boys at noon hour, but on the bus it was very different. I could tease and be teased, laugh and giggle with them for about an hour five days a week. I liked hanging out with kids my own age, like on the school bus, because it was so much fun. I liked girls—just being with them made me feel great. Thank you, Beverly Larson and Delores Johnson; you tremendously improved the quality of my fourteenth year of life.

As I sat next to her on the bus one day, Delores Johnson asked me, "Would you like to have intercourse with me?" I had no idea what she was talking about. I knew what fucking was, but I knew nothing of intercourse.

So I answered her by saying something like, "I don't know."

"Do you know what intercourse is?" She asked me.

"Yeah, sure I do." And then I just kind of felt embarrassed and mumbled something.

"No, you don't," she said. "You don't even know what I am talking about." She laughed. I didn't, but I was beginning to get an idea of what intercourse was, and it sounded good to me.

I had no one at home to talk with. So the kids at school and on the bus were God-sent. There were no neighbors with kids near my age. I didn't want to invite kids from school to my house. I was ashamed of my stepmother and her parents and my dad. No one encouraged me to invite friends home, either. The farm had become as an island unto itself, as if surrounded by an ocean. It was unreachable by any of my friends or relatives.

I helped the women with their work, instead of being outside with Dad and Albert. It worked out that way, I suspect, for two reasons. One is the men could easily handle the work on this small farm without my help; and two, because the women didn't want me talking to my dad and stirring up trouble. I think they thought I might encourage him to leave Dorothy and the farm. But the women did have a lot of "women's work" to do, and I was their chosen helper.

I brought in wood for the cook stove and fuel oil for the parlor furnace. I dusted furniture, wiped dishes, and scrubbed the kitchen floor. I scrubbed that kitchen floor on my hands and knees every Saturday. At first, I thought it demeaning for me to scrub the floor. But then I began to take pride in how well I scrubbed it. The women would say how wonderful I was at scrubbing the floor. I soon became a willing floor scrubber hungry for every scrap of praise they would give me.

I helped with the eggs from five hundred chickens, cleaning and putting them in thirty dozen cases. We would gather over four hundred eggs per day. It was a lot of work to wash them, candle them, and put them in the cartons of each case. The other job I had was splitting wood for the cook stove.

The kitchen cook stove was a wonderful piece of gleaming yellow, polished chrome and cast iron. It was a wood-burning masterpiece of good looks that required vast amounts of wood to be split just right for an entire year. It had a water reservoir on its right side, which kept water constantly hot for washing dishes. It had a huge oven below the cook top and to the left, an ash and cinder drawer that needed to be emptied daily. Above the flat shiny cook top were two large warming ovens with drop down doors. The left side of the cook top had a large opening for the wood. A simple hinged cast-iron door covered this opening when the fire was not being fed. There were four other removable lids over holes in the cook top. These could be removed to feed the fire directly below a lid, if one wanted to. Next to the cook stove stood a large woodbin that held eight or ten armloads of split wood fifteen inches long.

I had managed to get haircuts when I needed them by begging and pleading. Somehow my hair length had become a focal point of concern. None of the other boys had long hair, and I didn't want it either. I wasn't so successful begging for clothes.

The women had established a pattern of behavior towards me regarding clothes and gifts. It appeared that I would get one new pair of jeans, one shirt, and a pair of shoes a year. I needed a new coat for school, and I was beginning to worry that the one I had would be too small soon and I would freeze. Gloves and mittens were hard to come by too. Birthday and Christmas presents had become a thing of the past. The women apparently decreed it to be so. Santa Claus was one dead SOB according to them.

I knew the Thompsons weren't poor. They had owned a large farm and sold it. They had money in the bank, and they owned all their personal property. Their monthly expenses were low. I didn't know what they were doing with the money from the sale of eggs and milk. I was certain my poverty was a direct result of their stinginess. I think Dorothy and Olive hated me and were just plain neglectful and mean because that's how they wanted to treat me.

Spring came and, unfortunately, the end of my freshman year in May. It was back to the farm for the summer.

I spent most of the summer of 1949 working in our large gardens. We planted an acre of potatoes in one garden and carrots, onions cabbage, beets, beans, peas, tomatoes, parsnips, turnips, asparagus and more strawberries in the other.

Albert plowed both gardens with a walking plow and the draft horses in the spring. In the fall, he plowed up the potatoes the same way. I had never seen anyone do that before, and I was utterly fascinated with the way the horses could turn over the soil with that simple looking plow. He used a different plow to turn the potatoes from their home in the soil. Picking up an acre of potatoes in a bucket, carrying it to a trailer and dumping it was hard work. Once the trailer was full, the horses pulled it near the archway of the picket fence. There we again loaded the potatoes into a bucket and carried them to the back of the house and down into the dirt-floor basement. We couldn't pull the potato-laden trailer inside of the picket fence and across the lawn; there was no gate large enough to accommodate it. It was a labor-intensive job. I thought it would be easier to put a big gate in the picket fence and pull the trailer around to the basement door. But no, that would ruin the look of the fence and put wheel ruts in the yard. Besides, I was the one who unloaded the wagon and carried the potatoes, bucket by bucket into the basement for the most part.

The strawberry patch was a nemesis of mine. It was a haven for mosquitoes that loved to bite my body. And the strawberries were not planted in rows and kept in rows by thinning and pruning. They were in one huge patch. And the women still did not want me to be wasteful by stepping on strawberries and killing them. We had frequent heated exchanges over how to pick strawberries.

The potato patch was a lot of work too, not only hoeing the weeds between the rows but also catching the potato bugs. I would catch them and put them in a large can then poor fuel oil on them and set them on fire. This was the accepted way of killing them. There was row upon row of other vegetables to hoe as well.

We stored our potatoes in the dirt basement of the house. We grew enough to last all year. We stored carrots in sand in the same basement. We canned beans, peas, and corn from the garden to last a year. We boiled sweet corn from the fields, and cut the corn off the cob and dried the kernels in the oven. Then we put the dried kernels in sacks and stored them in a dry place for use during the winter. We dried apples by slicing them and drying them in the oven. We stored the dried apple slices in bags too. Peaches, apricots, and raspberries were bought in season and canned and made into preserves for the winter. We also gathered sacks of dried lima beans. I helped in all this food processing and storage. I learned a lot about canning and preserving food.

We increased our flock of young pullets to one thousand. They would replace the five hundred hens when autumn came. We had three chicken houses now.

We were expanding our herd of cows. The west lean-to that housed Ned and Fanny became home for four more cows, complete with drinking cups. We didn't have running water in the house, but we had running water in the barn and a drinking cup for each cow. The rationale was if they were to give a lot of milk, they needed to drink water whenever they wanted it. Our cows were bred every year so that they would continue giving milk. Their calves were kept if they were heifers, if they were bulls we sold them as veal calves. We had Jersey and Guernsey cows; they gave milk that was high in butterfat. We had decided to get a Holstein bull to breed these cows. Then we would get calves that grew into cows that gave a lot of milk, rich in butterfat.

Our Holstein bull was absolutely huge. He weighed a little under one ton. He scared me nearly to death. He had a ring in his nose and a long chain attached to it. The chain was long enough so hopefully he would step on it when he began to charge at you if you were in the pasture with him. This bull wanted to kill anyone who came near his cows. He did not distinguish between man and beast. Dad and Albert both treated him with fear and respect.

Dorothy enjoyed my fear of the bull. Often the cows would need to be brought into the barns for milking. Dorothy's face would light up with a smile as she'd say, "Donnie, go put the cows in the barn."

"But the bull is in there," I would say.

"You are not afraid of a bull are you?"

"Yes, he scares me to death."

"Elling or Dad will get them in if you are afraid."

I saw this as hateful, but a challenge nonetheless. It meant that I had to get in the yard with the bull to prove I had courage. The yard was surrounded by a woven wire fence with two strands of barb wire on top. My only hope if the bull charged me was to scale the fence before he got to me.

I didn't like Dorothy, and I hated and feared that bull, but I was not ever going to back down from her nasty challenge. As soon as I would get in the cow yard, that bull could smell my fear and begin scratching the earth with his front hooves. I would be shaking inside with fear, but I tried not to show it. I tried to be cool and watch him out of the corner of my eye, if he began to charge, I would run for my life and try to scale the fence on the north side of the yard, where a large hardwood tree served as a post. He charged me nearly every time I went into the yard. I always made it to the fence, flew up the woven wire in a couple of steps and started climbing up the tree. The bull would come smashing headlong into the tree while I hung on several feet above him. There were many near misses, but he never got me. It became a dangerous game between Dorothy and I. A test of my courage and will against her ridiculously dangerous suggestions. A hundred-and-ten-pound green kid is no match for a charging two-thousand-pound bull.

I was now allowed to do some manly type of work in addition to helping with the women's work. I began milking cows. From this point in time, I would milk four cows in the morning before school and at night before supper each day. I milked Daisy, Rowdy, Gretchen, and Lady. They became my gentle and motherly good friends. I would lay my head against their big bellies as I sat beside them on my milk stool and pulled the milk from their teats. I listened to their bellies rumble as I daydreamed about any number of things. Occasionally I would squirt a stream of milk towards a barn cat and watch him open his mouth and catch nearly every drop. I learned to do that from watching Albert. The cats were expert milk catchers.

The cats came and went. Mostly they went by dying from distemper, because we had not been giving them shots. I would get so upset when they would die. All of us were upset when a cat got sick, but there was no way of saving its life. Vaccination was the only way, and it cost quite a lot to vaccinate six or seven cats. We began taking them to the veterinarian to get them shots that kept them free of distemper.

We called the veterinarian to treat sick animals, and the cows had frequent illness. Cows can get "milk fever" after giving birth to their calves, and some did. Some had difficulty while birthing their calves. Breeding a large Holstein bull to Jersey cows probably was not a good idea. They often got mastitis, a serious inflammation in the udder rendering their milk unfit to sell. The disease threatened the cow's life. Our chickens would suffer from outbreaks of coccidiosis and Newcastle disease, both serious, contagious, and fatal. The hogs could get erysipelas, a crippling fatal disease. Our vet was a frequent visitor and very good at his profession. He impressed me with his skill and friendliness, and I wanted to be like him. I decided during the summer that when I grew up I would be a veterinarian. I found out what courses were recommended for high school students to take and what I needed to get in to a veterinarian college.

CHAPTER 16

THE TENTH GRADE, SPRING VALLEY HIGH SCHOOL

I turned fifteen in August. I had grown a lot over the summer. I was now about five feet seven inches and about 125 pounds. In school I was an average size kid but one of the toughest. In morning assembly I used count all the boys I could beat up, which was most of them. There were some juniors and seniors who were much bigger, and I didn't think I could beat them with my fists. I would need something else to take them on. I think this is one of the dumb macho things that fifteen year olds do. At least I did.

The women would not let me go out for football, which would have been a great outlet for the anger and hostility I felt. I had given up on ever having a chance to play.

Because I had decided to be a veterinarian, I took required subjects like biology and geometry for, plus typing, English, and history. I would take chemistry and physics over the next two years.

My clothing allotment this year was a new pair of jeans; I didn't get a new shirt. I had only two or three shirts to wear, all from years gone by. One was a yellow square-bottomed pullover shirt with a knit cuffs and a badly stretched out neck. I strung a piece of elastic through the neck band so it fit better around my scrawny neck. But it made the collar bunchy. Some of the kids were beginning to make fun of my clothes.

I wanted to earn some money to buy clothes, so I decided to trap mink and muskrats that fall and winter. I found some muskrat traps in Albert's workshop and cleaned them up for trapping season. Starting about the middle of November, I began setting the traps for muskrats, mink, and whatever I could catch. I was not very experienced at trapping, but I had learned from my Uncle Henry, a trapper, how and where to set the traps.

I caught only a few muskrats, several skunks, and a badger. I learned that most animals will chew their leg off to escape the trap. I found several partial legs in my sprung traps. I learned to drown the muskrats by holding them under water with a big stick. I had a difficult time killing the badger. I caught him in the middle of our stubble field. He was tough, vicious, and tried to bite me. He died hard. I beat him to death with a piece of fence post. The skunks were even more difficult.

My dad and Albert told me I could kill a skunk before he sprayed me by sneaking up on him and hitting him over the back with a piece of two by four. If I hit him hard enough, I would sever his spinal cord and he would be paralyzed and unable to spray. I tried this method on my first skunk. It didn't work. The skunk just whirled around when I was close, lifted his behind up over his back and sprayed me at the range of a few feet with a nauseating yellow mist. I immediately felt like vomiting. I beat him to death with my two by four, but I paid a big price.

The women wouldn't let me in the house, I smelled so bad. I had to take my clothes off in the grove and come back to the house naked. I was very cold and still very stinky. There was maybe a foot of snow on the ground. My clothes were useless. They hung in the trees for months and never did lose their skunk odor. I smelled like a skunk for days both at home and at school. The kids would pinch their noses shut when I sat next to them in classes or ask if they could set somewhere else. It was hard to get the nauseating odor off of me. Soap and water did little. I tried bathing in a jar of canned tomatoes, but it didn't help much. I sold my catch of muskrats and the badger for about twenty dollars, which I used to replace my stinky clothes. From then on if I caught a skunk, I never messed with him; I just let him die in the trap and decay.

I was still praying at night. I prayed to catch a mink; I prayed for my mother to come and get me; I prayed for my brother to come and live with us; I prayed for clothes and haircuts and money.

On weekends in late autumn, we drove to the Forestville area with our car pulling an open trailer for hauling logs. There we got permission to cut down dead hardwood trees, cut them into lengths to place on the trailer, and haul them home. We cut the trees down with a two man saw. Then trimmed them with axes and cut them into lengths with a bucksaw. Once we got the logs home we stacked them up to be cut into stove sized lengths with a buzz saw. The buzz saw was powered by our old 10/20 McCormick Deering tractor with a twenty-foot long belt attached to a pulley. This gave the saw enormous power to cut through thick logs, or your fingers, arms, head or anything else that got in the way of the whirling thirty-six-inch diameter saw blade. We created a small mountain of fifteen-inch chunks of wood, enough to feed the cook stove for a year. With an axe, we split these chunks into pieces that would fit easily into the stove. The more difficult knotty ones required a sledge hammer and splitting maul.

I became the primary wood chopper, and I liked the job. I wanted to build muscle, so I pretended I was in training to be a boxer. Dorothy would stand and watch me split wood with the axe. It was often cold outside, but she would bundle up and come and watch. I didn't need her supervision, so I don't know why she did that.

I often felt like hitting her in the head with the axe. I had learned to hate her. These murderous thoughts were beginning to frighten me. They were no longer imaginative thoughts; they were real and becoming obsessive, and they were no longer pleasant thoughts for my amusement. I actually wanted to kill her.

We butchered a hog in late autumn. We had to wait until cold weather because we didn't have a freezer to keep the meat. Hog butchering was a gruesome task for me. I knew the pig; he was one of our own. I believe I had named him Henry. Dad and Albert brought the pig over to a place near the barn where they had rigged up an apparatus that allowed them to lift the two-hundred-pound hog high enough so that his nose was off the ground.

The lifting was accomplished with a block and tackle. One end of the block and tackle was fastened to the top of the apparatus, the other to a singletree.

Dad struck the pig in the head with a sledge hammer. The pig was knocked unconscious and fell to the ground. Albert immediately pounced on his hind legs and with knife slit the pig's skin between his Achilles tendon and the bone, then inserted the hooks of the single tree into each leg between the bone and the tendon. Dad immediately hoisted the pig into the air until his nose was off the ground, while Albert went to the pig's throat with his knife and slit it. Warm blood gushed out of the nearly decapitating wound. Dorothy and Olive were there to catch ever drop in a large dish pan. The whole killing process was over in less than a minute.

The pig went from a friendly fellow just "oinking" around to very dead, almost in an instant. Dad and Albert took the skin of the pig off with knives and cut open the belly and chest. As they did this, his guts came tumbling out along with his liver, kidneys, lungs, and heart. They were careful to remove all these edible parts from the intestines. The intestines were handled separately. They were thoroughly washed and used as casings for some of the sausage. The head was cut off. Soon the pig was headless, split into halves and then quarters.

I was amazed, sickened, and awed by how fast a living thing could be killed and cut into small pieces. I thought they could kill me in the same way they killed the pig. Who would know if they killed me? Who would wonder what had happened to me?

Soon sections of the pig were brought into the house and cut into more sections, and the process of preserving the meat began. The bacon was put into a large crock of salt brine for curing. Roasters were brought out to begin roasting most of the meat on the cook stove. Other pieces unsuitable for roasting were put in a pile that we ground into sausage and fried. The roasts and sausages were then put in fruit jars and preserved in a pressure cooker.

We feasted on blood sausage, liver, heart, fresh pork chops, and ribs for several days. The process of cooking the meat and preserving by canning and salt brine took about a week. The women and I did most of the work after the hog had been cut up. We lived off the canned meat in the winter, and then in the spring we butchered another hog.

Canned pork roast and sausages are delicious. My sandwiches that I took to school in my lunch bag were made from Henry Hog, whom we had killed and canned. Other hogs took his place when we needed more meat. I often placed pieces of them on homemade bread along with some homemade mustard to carry off to school for my lunch each school year. They were crude sandwiches next to those my friends brought to school. They ate store-bought bread with cold cuts and lettuce, or they ate from the cafeteria. I was ashamed of my sand-wiches, but they tasted good. I wanted to eat cafeteria food, but it cost money, and I had none.

I frequently helped the women make bread, cake, frosting, and cookies. This was at least a twice-weekly undertaking. I became the official frosting pan licker. My tongue could whip around an egg beater with the agile dexterity of a kid after a sugar fix. There were times when the women and I would get along splendidly. These times were often centered on cooking and baking in our very cozy kitchen. Over time, I became familiar with women's work, and I was pretty good at it.

The woodbin in the kitchen next to the cook stove was a favorite place to climb up into and sit. It was always warm there. I could hunker down on to the wood and prop myself up to read comfortably in good light and in the warmth from the stove. Another place of comfort was the dining room oil furnace. I would scrunch into a small space between the oil burner and the wall and put my feet against the metal pad that protected the floor from the heat of the stove. I could set there for hours and read in absolute comfort. On the other side of the burner was Albert's smoking chair, strategically placed so he could get heat from the oil burner and survey the kitchen, parlor, and the rest of the dining room.

I began to notice that Dorothy sometimes did what to my mind was a most peculiar thing. Directly across from where I sat and read by the oil burner, about ten feet away was the front door with a large window. Southern light came streaming through it. Dorothy would go to the door with a mirror and a tweezers in her hands. She would stand in the light of the door window, lift up her dress, place the mirror so she could see her crotch, and begin picking things from her vaginal area with the tweezers. Her back was to me and generally no one else was around except her mother. I have no idea what she was doing, but I saw her do this many times. It did not seem to bother her that I saw this. I never asked her what she was doing. I thought she was a little crazy.

One day that winter, Lawrence came to the farm. It was a Saturday morning, and I was scrubbing the kitchen floor. He just walked right into the house. He was mad. He had probably encountered Albert or my dad in the barnyard, and perhaps it had not gone well. He was taller and heavier than when I last saw him. I felt small, skinny, and vulnerable standing in front of him.

I was dressed in ragged jeans and a shirt, clothes from previous years, now too worn out to wear to school. The women had taught me to sew, and I patched my own jeans whenever they needed it. I probably had a bunch of patches on my clothes this day. Lawrence said I looked like a rag muffin and wondered why in hell I was scrubbing the floor. The women were in the kitchen too and angry at his intrusion and belligerent manner. They said he was causing trouble and told him to leave. I told Lawrence it was just my job to scrub the floor and I didn't mind. I was actually scared of him. He was big and talked mean. During those few minutes I felt alone, defenseless, and, in some kind of way, ashamed.

Lawrence came to school the next day. I was called out of class and told to go to the superintendent's office, where my brother was waiting. I was wearing one of his old short-sleeved shirts. He wanted to know why I was wearing such a dumb-looking thing. I didn't tell him that I was not getting new clothes when I needed them. I just told him that I liked his old shirt. He didn't like me calling him Lawrence. He said he had changed his name, and I should call him Larry, which I did. He wanted me to go with him on the back of his Cushman motor scooter to Waterloo. I told him I didn't want to go. I wanted to stay at the farm and go to school. He said I was a dumb shit. I asked him where Mom was, and he said he didn't know. I asked him about Aunt Rachel, and he said he didn't know anything about he either. He told me he was living in Waterloo, and he didn't know anything about the people from Illinois or Minneota. Larry gave me some money and told me to take care of myself. He rode off on his scooter, and I didn't see him again until June 1952.

Larry's gift was the first money I can remember having since the beginning of the eighth grade. I didn't tell the women that my brother had been to school and given me money. I hid it along a fence line in a field next to a fence post I could recognize again and used it as I wanted to. One day I forgot and left some change in my pocket and Olive heard it jingle. She insisted on knowing where the money had come from. They said they knew Lawrence had been at school and had given me the money. I denied everything.

They hated my brother and told me he was no good. He was nothing but trouble and that I should stay away from him. I did, but not by my own choice. Larry went back to Waterloo and enlisted in the Air Force almost immediately.

In truth, it bothered me that Lawrence had changed his name. Lawrence was my brother, not Larry. I wasn't sure I wanted Larry for my brother. He acted so mean. He was like a stranger. I liked Lawrence much better. I had not seen him since the summer at the end of the seventh grade. He had changed and so had I. I crossed Lawrence's name off the toilet-room wall again.

My sophomore year was tough on me emotionally. I was ragged, and had no money. I had to work hard. The school district had decided that if I were to ride the school bus I would have to pay for it because we only lived 1.8 miles from the school. The family decided I could walk back and forth to school. I missed the kids on the bus. My dad and Albert were of absolutely of no help to me.

I acquired another job on the farm—to run the electric water pump in the pump house, which was right outside our back porch door and filled the large galvanized tanks on the second floor of the barn and the horse tank in the horse barn. The pump forced the water down to the barn tanks, and gravity allowed each cow's drinking cup to fill with water when they put their nose against the release device in the bottom of the cup. It was a simple and efficient system. I had to watch the overflow spout coming out of the second floor of the barn and shut the pump off when the water began to run out of it. I could do this easily by just moving in and out of the pump house to observe the spout and still keep an eye on the pump. If I did not shut the pump off in time and overflowed the inside tanks, I'd create a big watery mess in the barns. When the weather was cold, it was warmer to stay in the pump house and just run out and peak at the spout when I thought the tank was about full.

One cold evening while pumping water, I saw a package of arsenic behind a picture sitting against the pump house wall. Albert used it to poison rats. Suddenly an overwhelming fear swept through my body. I was in a panic. I felt a rush of heat go up through me and into my face. I could hear my heart beating, and my head began to spin. I had an inexplicable urge to take that poison and kill myself. I had no idea why this urge came over me, but it was terrifying. I didn't take the poison, but that strange compulsion petrified me with fear. I had never experienced anything like that before.

I couldn't understand why these terrible thoughts and feelings were coming to me. They were not welcome. I was becoming afraid of what I could think or imagine. Indeed, horrible ideas would just pop in to my mind, and it seemed I could not control what came to my mind or imagination.

Everyday I had to go to the pump house and pump water for the barns. Every day the arsenic was there. I feared I would take it. So I would begin to count to keep my mind occupied while I was in the pump house. I knew that was crazy. So I soon gave that up. Instead I prayed to God for help. I was terrified. I prayed for him to keep me from killing myself. I asked him to make me strong so I could be with my mother and brother again. I thought if I could last until I was able to be with my mom, I would be alright.

My preoccupation with suicide and praying kept me busy. I couldn't concentrate on doing my chores. I would forget things. I put things in the wrong places. Spoons in with the dishes, wood in the porch instead of the wood bin, I sat down to milk the wrong cows, and on and on. The women became furious with me about the mistakes I was making and scolded me. They told me to pay attention. I should think, and not daydream about devilry. They reminded me of how much trouble my brother had been. I would be like him if I did not shape up. I didn't tell them that I was thinking of committing suicide and praying for help.

At this time, Spring Valley High School started a program of religious instruction. Once a week I could be excused from school to attend religious instructions at the church of my choice. It was not a requirement but a choice my parents and I could make.

I wanted to practice my faith. I brought the permission slip home for my parents to sign. I gave it to Dorothy, but she refused to sign it. She didn't want me to go to the Catholic church. I didn't even show it to my dad. I knew she would convince him not to sign it. I knew that if I wanted to go to the Lutheran church, she would have signed the permission slip. But I wouldn't give up my Catholic faith. It was my faith and my link to my mom, her family, and my past.

The Thompson family disliked Catholics with a zeal I had never witnessed before. They had a ton of stories about priests and nuns to support their claims against my church. Most of them were the same old things. The convent nuns were a sexual harem for priests. The Pope told all Catholics what to do. Catholics would sin like hell during the week, go to confession and communion, and then go right back to sinning again after Mass on Sunday. They worshiped the Virgin Mary instead of Jesus, and on an on. Albert had been a member of the Woodsmen and the Masons. Olive's brother was a Mason. I did not know anything about those groups at the time, but both sounded anti-Catholic to me. The Thompsons hatred of Catholics was irrational and, I think, pathological.

I signed the permission slip myself and went to religious instructions at Spring Valley's little white wooden Catholic church. The priest asked about my parents and why they didn't come to church. I told him my parents were not Catholic. My mother had been, but my dad had divorced her, and she lived somewhere else. That surprised him. He looked at me with a quizzical look, but he never asked anymore questions about my parents. That was odd how-ever, because I usually looked like a refugee. I was the only one whose parents didn't go to the church. The Thompsons never did find out I signed my own self into religious instructions. The priest was of little help to me. He either didn't take notice of my shabby clothes or decided not to get involved in to whatever problems I may have had.

I was in desperate emotional trouble. I needed someone's intervention. I couldn't seem to handle my anger and fear. I was doing a lot of obsessing about what was happening to me. My sudden urge to take the rat poison haunted me. I wanted God to give me some peace of mind, some rest from my fears. I considered asking my Catholic friend, Nathan Collins, if I could come to his house and tell his parents that I needed a place to live. I wanted to live with him and his family because I knew his dad, who had an egg-buying store, and I knew his brother. They seemed to be such a nice family. Maybe after they heard of my plight they would take me in. But I did not pursue it.

God must have become very ill that winter because he was not answering my prayers and there was no evidence that he was listening at all.

One day while at the dining room table doing my school work and worrying about my mental health, I just blurted out, "I need a doctor, I need a doctor." I was thinking that to myself, but I didn't intend to say it out loud. It just came popping out of my mouth. I was so surprised. Ordinarily, when the women were around I never said anything without considering what I was going to say first. This was like involuntary speech.

The women were in the parlor. They wondered what was wrong with me. I told them I had just said, "I needed a doctor."

They asked me why and I said, "I didn't know, but I don't feel very good."

"That is what you get for reading so much," Olive said. They said if I kept reading so much, I would go crazy. Now I had another worry: the fear of going nuts from reading too much.

I didn't really understand what was happening to me. I knew that I was unhappy, and I was being treated badly by the family. Albert was another story. He actually seemed a lot like God to me. He was an impartial silent observer. He never intervened for any reason regarding anything. He just did his chores and smoked his pipe. When he did speak, it was only about farm work or the past. He was like God: benign, but of absolutely of no help to me whatsoever.

I realized the thoughts that were coming to my mind in regard to killing Dorothy with the axe and committing suicide were probably due to the situation I was in. I realized too, that there probably was no one who would be rescuing me from the Thompson farm. I considered running away, but I didn't know where to run to. God was not giving me any peace of mind or helping me. And Mom was not showing up and probably never would.

I was maturing sexually. My penis would get hard for no reason. It just did. This seemed to happen if I had to leave my desk at school and go to the blackboard in geometry class. Mr. Reps taught geometry, and he frequently asked me go to the board and work out a geometry problem for the class.

I would walk to the board, and wham, a hard penis would push my pants out. I was sure everybody could see it. At those times, I would try not to turn around, but instead keep the front of my body turned toward the blackboard and only turn my head towards Mr. Reps. Mr. Reps was a big fat assistant football coach and our only math teacher. He seemed to me to be a complete ass. I hated him for always calling on me. It embarrassed me to get up in front of the class with my ragged clothes and long, shaggy hair. And now I had acquired this penis problem. He frequently made comments to the class about my shyness, which embarrassed me even more. Perhaps he knew of my adolescent problem and was enjoying making me miserable. I thought of killing him too.

If I were at home and in my bed at night, I discovered if I would play with my penis it would ejaculate, and I would have the most peculiar and wonderful feeling. I wasn't sure if this was going to hurt me. I had heard from the priest and other kids that if you masturbated you could drive yourself crazy. I had another thing to worry me.

What I really needed was God and my dad, or most any rational sane adult to set down and talk to me about adolescence, puberty, and the changes going on in my body. I needed to learn how to harness anxiety and fear. I knew this at the time. The problem was, there just wasn't anyone to talk with. If there had been someone, it would have improved the quality of my life immensely.

Spring Valley had become a nightmare. The farm with the white picket fence was a place of evil. Dad had said at the very beginning that I would not believe how good we were going to have it on this farm. He was so wrong. The women and my dad had placed me in hell. Olive was the boss in hell. Her suspicious nature, stinginess, superior intelligence, and outright lack of compassion made her a perfect Devil. Her slow-minded daughter was the human "apple of her eye." The Devil protected Dorothy with every fiber of her mind and body. The Devil controlled the money. Her hoarded money was never used to relieve suffering. Her control over Dad, Dorothy, and Albert was remarkable and unshakable. Every once in a while I would find myself cozying up to the Devil in attempt to have her like me.

Why was this small, nice looking, nervous old woman so powerful? I knew she was only a human being, and I could kill her, but then I would go to jail. I could not escape her power, neither could Dad or Albert. And Dorothy basked in the control of all the resources her mother had at her disposal. I wouldn't understand the basis for her power for many years later.

CHAPTER 17

SPRING VALLEY, 1950–51

I had grown to five feet eight inches tall and weighed about 125 pounds. There was no fat on me. I was strong from splitting wood and pitching tons of cow, horse, pig and chicken manure. One thing you get from livestock is a lot of shit. During the winter, we had to haul it out on a sled and pile it west of the grove for spreading in the spring. We built small mountains of shit over the winter.

We now had about twenty-five head of cattle, about fifty hogs, and a thousand laying hens. We were renting an additional forty acres of land about two miles from our farm. We needed even more land to feed the increasing number of livestock. We were milking about eighteen cows without a milking machine. We didn't have a tractor; all the farm work was done with the two draft horses, Fanny and Ned. The old McCormick Deering tractor had iron lugged wheels that were not permitted on the public roads.

The family decided we needed a rubber-tired tractor. They bought a 1950 Ford tractor with a three-point hydraulic hitch. This was a nice little machine. It made field work a lot easier for Albert and Dad. I didn't get to drive it. I was relegated to the horses, and my primary machines were a manure fork and the manure spreader.

The draft horses were huge, weighing about one thousand eight hundred pounds each. Ned was an easy-going laid back Percheron gelding, but Fanny was a nervous, high-strung Belgian mare. They reminded me of Albert and Olive in personality.

I first became acquainted with Fannie's high-strung ways while watching Albert feed the horses. Fanny would try to bite him if he did not get the hay in her manger fast enough. If she succeeded in biting him, he would hit her in the head with the back of his pitchfork. She would jump back in shock and anger and kick backwards with both hind legs. Her hoofs over the years had beat huge dents in the water tank several feet behind her. If you should be standing behind her at these times, she would surely maim or kill you. While striking Fannie in the head, Albert would let loose with a string of profanity that impressed me.

I soon learned that Fannie would try to bite me when I was slow to get hay in her manger. And often times she succeeded. She would usually get me in the top of the shoulder with her huge teeth and pick me right up off the floor. I would howl with pain, smack her in the head with the pitchfork, and scream profanity at her. She at the same time would pull back on her halter rope and kick the crap out of the water tank. She was a piece of work and a dangerous horse to be around.

But overall I loved the sense of power I felt by being able to control these two huge beasts and direct their energy to purposeful work.

I had to walk back and forth to school again. The district still insisted that if I were to ride the school bus, Dad would have to pay for it. Of course, he and the women agreed that I should walk. I was used to walking to and from school. I had learned to manage the bitter cold winters somehow. My old wool mackinaw coat was getting pretty shabby, but it was warm. My wool stocking cap was barely adequate. In mid-winter, temperatures could be thirty below zero in the morning. An average day started got up to fifteen or twenty degrees during the day.

I froze my ears several times, once so badly that they swelled up turned black, and all the skin fell off. The snow was sometimes so deep I walked along side the telephone wires strung between the poles along the road. The snow plow would come through and push the snow to the side, and it would pile up to ever increasing altitudes. New snow would fall again and the northwest wind would blow drifts in to the plowed out road, filling it in completely, until it would be ten or twenty feet deep in places. At these times, no vehicle could get through on the roads, not even the big truck of the milkman, who picked up our large cans of milk each day.

Our milk could not keep; it could sour, and we did not have cans enough to store it. So we would hook up Fanny and Ned to the sled complete with sleigh bells and haul the milk to the creamery in town. That was fun, and I would usually go along. We'd bundle up under wool blankets covered with horse hide to stay warm.

I believe it was during that winter that the snow was so deep we actually made a tunnel between the barn and the house. We did this by shoveling out a path and piling snow on the sides, then placing boards on top. When new snow fell, it made a tunnel. Under the boards we had a very nice covered pathway from the house to the barn.

The work was hard on the farm that winter. I was bigger and stronger now, and I did more outside work. I still milked my four cows before and after school. We got up every morning around 5:30. During trapping season I got up even earlier. I was tired at school a lot of the time.

There was hay to cut from stacks to feed the livestock. We hauled that in by horse-drawn sled. There was straw to haul in for bedding and manure to haul out to the mountains of shit. There were hogs and chickens to feed. There were eggs to gather, clean, and pack in cases.

I was concentrating hard on keeping my sanity. I filled my mind with school and farm work. I wasn't entirely successful, but I was better.

I tried reading the Thompson's Bible for comfort, but I found none. The stories seemed so outrageous. I just could not find comfort in reading their Protestant Bible. I thought maybe I would do better with a Catholic Bible, but I doubted it. I only found comfort in daydreaming and work.

By now I was truly the poorest dressed kid in the entire Spring Valley school system. I was entirely shabby. But no one dared tease me at close range. They knew I would fight, and they had come to accept the fact that I probably could not help the clothes that I wore. I often smelled like skunk or the farm yard, and they accepted that too. They accepted this goggle-eyed kid who dressed like a bum but was as smart hell in class. Indeed, I was some kind of weird nerd. My friends were some of the school's smartest students. I fit in with them because

I was their equal academically, if on no other basis. Their lives of sports were different from mine. They dated, and some had cars now. I didn't.

I daydreamed about what I was going to do when I got out of high school. I would get a job in Rochester at a department store and buy myself a lot of clothes and a car. I would save money to go to the University of Minnesota and become a veterinarian. I took chemistry that year; next year I would take physics. It was just a matter of time.

School soon ended, and I was headed for a summer without my school friends. We rented more land and had even more work. I was kept busy, and I buried myself in work.

Albert had decided the previous year that we should get a threshing machine to thresh our oat crop. I thought we should hire someone to harvest our grain with a combine. He thought that wasted too much grain, so he bought the threshing machine. We cut our grain with a binder and placed the bundles of grain into shocks. We placed the grain side up, six or eight bundles to a shock, and two or three bundles to cap the shock. This is typical.

Our next step was atypical and a page from Albert's past. He wanted us to haul the shocks of grain into an area just west of the grove and pile them into beautiful conical stacks. The stacks were really nice looking but a lot of unnecessary work. After a couple of weeks, we pulled the threshing machine up to the stacks. We brought out the old 10/20 tractor and connected the large drive belt to the pullies on the tractor and the threshing machine. We were ready to thresh the grain the old-fashioned way, pitching bundles into the machine hopper from the stacks. The tractor's engine strained and the machine rumbled and shook into operation. The grain came out of an auger into a wagon and the straw got blown into a large pile. It worked great, but it was an awful lot of work. Albert said it was just like he used to thresh in the old days, only then they used a steam engine. He was very happy.

The next year we did it an easier way. Albert and Dad joined a threshing crew with a group of other farmers. The crew went from farm to farm with the threshing machine and harvested directly from the shocks in the field. The shocks were loaded a bundle at a time on to a hayrack and then hauled to the threshing machine. There the bundles were loaded into the hopper and threshed. There were no conical stacks.

I expected there would be some kind of trouble because Dorothy or Olive were usually with Dad wherever he went. But there was no trouble when the crew came to our farm. We put on big dinners and lunches for them, and everything worked out fine. In fact, it was fun. We had large meals and there was lots of talk and laughter.

We seldom visited Henry and Lena Simonson's or Olive's brother's. We had stopped going to dances long ago. Our lives had become one of work, work, and more work. My life was one of work and school. Fun and games were not part of what we did.

Dad set right next to me at our dinner table everyday. But he had become a stranger to me. The man who sat next to me seldom spoke to me directly. He hardly acknowledged my presence. He did nothing to me or nothing directly against me. He never touched me. I did not love him. I felt sorry for him. Dad talked to the Thompsons, but it was obvious to me that he only said what they wanted to hear. There were no arguments. He always agreed with them.

Dorothy touched me one time. I made some smart remark to her while cleaning string beans at the kitchen table.

"Are we going to eat before or after supper?" I said. She didn't think that was funny. I thought it was funny because we had all noticed that my dad was getting thinner and thought maybe he needed to eat more. It was not wise of me, and my timing was wrong. She was using a butcher knife to clip ends off the string beans. She walked behind me grabbed me with one arm across my chest and with the other put the butcher knife to my throat.

"I will kill you if you say one more word," she said. I kept my mouth shut, and she let go of me. I realized again who the enemy was. But the truth is that she didn't hurt me. I could have killed her easily anytime. I was much taller, stronger, and quicker than she was. But I never hurt her.

Indeed, there was no physical punishment dealt out to anyone in our strange family. There were no firearms, except for Albert's old single shot shotgun hanging in his bedroom. I never saw him use it. There were knives, axes, pitchforks, sledgehammers, hammers, and hatchets. But no threats were issued by anyone until the string-bean remark. I never saw anyone else threatened with a weapon, and I thought occasionally of using one of these potential weapons to kill.

We were just a family that did not touch to comfort, give pleasure, show passion, or hostility. The Devil ruled by spoken and unspoken word. All her subjects willingly submitted. I probably was the only one who tried to resist the Devil. Our relationships were filled with stubborn silence and quiet, unshed tears. We led lives of obedience to a small, nervous, paranoid old woman whom any of us could have easily killed.

CHAPTER 18

GOD WAS SURELY DEAD, 1951 AND 1952

In September I started my senior year. The women tried to persuade me to stay home and help with the farm work. I said no; I was going to school. I was still ragged, but I had a fresh haircut. It was far better to be at school than at home with the women. I knew school was necessary for my future plans and for my mental health. I was looking forward to the spring of 1952 when I would graduate. I would leave the farm then and go to work in Rochester. I daydreamed all the time about what I was going to do once I finished high school and moved away from the farm.

My hair was cut very short a couple of weeks before school started. I wanted to lose the untanned ring around my ears and the back of my neck before school started. I didn't want to look like a dumb farm kid with a white ring around my head where my long hair had been during the summer.

I also knew our senior class pictures would be taken right after school started, and I wanted to look nice for the picture. I had been lobbying for a suit or a sport jacket to wear for the photo. It was the custom for the senior boys to have their pictures taken in suits. Pictures of previous graduating classes hung in one of the long hallways at school. All the boys wore suits and ties, since the beginning of time.

But I didn't get a suit, or a sport coat, or a tie. My picture was taken in a short-sleeve light-blue open collared shirt. I was the only boy in the school's history that I know of who appeared in a senior class picture without a suit.

I was different, and I was embarrassed by my differences. But I had grown accustomed to it and carried on anyway.

At this same time, I began lobbying for money to order a senior class ring. I was unsuccessful in that too. All efforts fell on non-compassionate ears. The fact that all the other seniors had ordered rings did not move the family one emotional bit. They didn't care what the other kids did. There would be no money for a class ring. Over the past several years, the Thompsons had demonstrated a lack of compassion for me. They expressed no interest in my wants, hopes, or needs. They were consistently and pathologically cruel in their frugality.

Dad was getting thinner and thinner. He had always been thin, but this was different. He was becoming frighteningly thin. He ate much more than the rest of us, but still he got thinner. The only one of us who was overweight was Dorothy, and she was only a little fat. I had grown to five feet nine inches and weighed about 130 pounds. I was very conscious of my height and weight because I wanted to grow to be at least six feet tall and weigh 180 pounds.

Christmas 1951 was like other Christmases at Spring Valley: no presents. Santa Claus died long ago. Lena Simonson had died the year before, so we did not go there for Christmas. We did not go to her daughter Evelyn's house either. I don't know why. I think Evelyn's husband Elmer may have died too.

I think it was a little before Christmas that I had to each give a speech in one of my classes. I dreaded the thought of getting up in front of my classmates. I was embarrassed by my appearance. My hair was long and shaggy, my clothes were old and patched, and I often smelled bad.

I stunk from hog slop spilling on the pant legs of my jeans. I carried two five gallon buckets of ground oats mixed with water to slop the hogs every morning. Each bucket weighed about forty pounds and often a little slop would spill on me and turn sour after a day or two. The odor was often accompanied by the smell of cow manure, which would cling to me like bovine cow pie cologne. In addition I often encountered a skunk in my traps, even though I did not take them from the traps anymore, proximity was sufficient to add more cologne. We did not have hot and cold running water or a bathtub, and we didn't take baths in the winter. I had kind of a sour, manure smell about me, mixed in with a little skunk and body odor. I was stinky enough so that I could smell myself if I stood or sat near a source of warm air, like a heat register.

I prepared my speech on trapping, I couldn't think of anything else to talk about. I spoke on how to catch, kill, and skin muskrats and mink. As I gave the speech, I knew no one in the class gave a damn about what I was saying. I knew I looked like a ragged beggar and that I smelled bad. I saw the snickers in the back of the room as the kids whispered to each other. Some made suggestive gestures by pinching their noses. But I gave the damn speech anyway, although I was embarrassed and angry. I held in my emotions and never wavered in my delivery.

I often presented myself in my classes in pretty much this same costume and barnyard cologne. They could see the way I was dressed. Why didn't one or more of the teachers ever ask the school to check on my home life? I was a freaking mess! They never said a word to me or, apparently, to the principal. No one ever investigated my home life.

On the last day before Christmas break, the kids in my English class, apparently inspired by a very popular classmate, presented me with a Christmas gift. Actually everyone in the class received some kind of a gag gift. This classmate stood up near his seat and read out loud the card in the envelope and then presented it to me.

"In consideration of the fact that several kids in the class have recognized that Donnie needs a haircut, they have all chipped in money so Donnie can get one, therefore we present you with this gift Donnie."

He walked over to me and handed me a card containing money. There was uneasy laughter in the room, one of those uneasily smiling was me. I was stunned by this unkind gesture of Christmas spirit. My face must have turned pale, I thought my heart would stop; it was beating furiously in my chest. The teacher did not say. "Hey wait a minute, this is out of line and cruel." No! She just went along with it.

I was furious and humiliated. I wanted to run, cry, and kill. If I would have had a gun, I would have killed everyone in that classroom. I have hated that classmate ever since that day.

The kids at school had been my salvation. Home was a nightmare. I was unable to handle this kind of embarrassment. Most of the kids in this class had been in my classes since the eighth grade, and they more or less accepted my poverty. I was severely wounded by the fact that they were making fun of me with this supposedly humorous Christmas gift.

God was surely dead. Where was this compassionate God? What was he good for? He was useless; he was dead! What had I ever done to deserve what was happening to me?

Over the next several weeks, I became very depressed and began to feel as if my mind and body were two separate things. I felt alone in my head, and my body meant nothing. I could feel the essence of my being, my soul. I kept thinking what a weird feeling it is. I thought I was on my way to complete madness, hanging on to my sanity by a thread.

Then one day, by some miracle, some inner, wiser, older being within me began to release into my thoughts. These were kind, understanding, and positive thoughts about me. I felt it would be all right, that I shouldn't worry. I should take care of myself. I was good, and I had a right to be here on earth. I had a purpose for being. It was powerful. I felt better immediately, even though I did not know where this inner support was coming from. But that support made a difference.

Sometime in late spring, while Dad and the Thompsons were in Spring Valley shopping, Dad bolted from them. He apparently jumped out of the parked car when a police officer walked by and told the officer that the Thompsons were holding him captive. The Thompsons apparently told the officer that Dad was a little "off" and said they were taking good care of him. The Thompsons knew the police chief, so apparently he believed them.

Dad came home with the Thompsons. The women told me what had happened when I came home from school. I was so embarrassed for him and myself. I knew that the kids at school would probably hear about it. But none of the kids said anything, so maybe they didn't hear about it.

Dad looked awful. He was so skinny, his eyes were sunken, and he showed no emotion. I was afraid he was going to die. I felt sorry for him, and I wished he had gotten away when he tried. Maybe someone could have done something for him.

I began taking over most of the work Dad had been doing. He just was not strong enough to do his share.

The women said he was shelling corn from the corn crib and filling his pockets with corn. He was reaching into his pockets and taking handfuls of corn and putting them in his mouth. I watched him with the women from the kitchen window. He was eating field corn. I began worrying about him all the time. I needed to do something, but I didn't know what. I didn't know what was wrong with him.

The chores for me now were horrendous with Dad sick. We had so many cows, pigs and chickens. I missed a lot of school because I had to stay home and help get the farm work done. At times I tried to deny that anything was wrong with my dad, but it became obvious something was.

I was physically strong now, and I received praise from the women and from Albert. I was a man, they said. The women said I could keep up with any man when it came to work. I harnessed the horses, hooked them to the sled or the wagons, hauled manure into the fields, cut hay from the stacks and brought it to the barn to feed the horses and cattle. I milked my cows and most of my dad's. I helped with the gathering of the eggs, cleaning and putting them in thirty dozen cases.

The women were helping with the milking now too. I began lobbying for a milking machine and thought we should buy a new Surge milking system. It would save us so much time and effort. I almost had Albert convinced. His years of hard physical farm work were catching up with him. He was nearly sixty-nine years old, arthritic, and he suffered from a painful prostate problem. He told me he had to "empty his water" often. I don't think he got much sleep at night because he was up peeing. Olive was sixty-five years old and slowing down herself. She and Dorothy wouldn't agree to buy a milking machine. They vetoed the idea. They said the machine did not milk the cows dry and as consequence the cow would stop giving milk earlier than if milked by hand. I claimed we could "strip milk" after the machine, which avoided that problem. The answer was no. So because of their stubbornness, there were five of us milking cows every morning and night when two people could have done it easily with the Surge system.

Dad and Dorothy had the upstairs bedroom. The stairs went directly into their bedroom. There was no door at the top of the steps. My bedroom was to the left at the top of the steps. It was really the Thompsons' storage room. Most of it was filled with a lifetime of their accumulated artifacts. A curtain was stung across the heirlooms to hide them from view. This gave me about half of the room for my hide-a-bed. There were no doors to the bedrooms, so I could hear them making love at night. I could also hear Dorothy complaining to my Dad about his lack of interest in sex and his inability to please her. I felt sorry for the poor man.

The senior prom took place at Spring Valley High School on May 4, 1952. I wanted to go and asked the women if I could go. They said I could. I was the only boy there without a suit. I had no date. Dorothy took me to the school and dropped me off.

After the prom, I went with some of the kids to nearby mystery cave. There we drank some beer and smoked cigarettes. We stayed out all night. I did not get home until about six on the morning. The women were angry at me for not getting home in time to help with the morning chores. Even though I had been up all night, I worked all day and was very tired by late afternoon.

That evening while milking a cow, I went to sleep. The milk pail slipped from the grasp of my knees, fell and spilled onto the floor. Dorothy was standing across the gutter from me and saw what happened. She was furious. She began yelling, insulting me, telling me that an education hadn't done me any good; I couldn't even milk a cow.

Before I could think, I leaped to my feet with the milk stool in hand. I shouted at her, "I will kill you if you don't shut up." She screamed for her father. Albert came running as best he could and told me to put the milk stool down. I told him I would kill him too if he didn't leave me alone. I would have too. I was in a rage. I threw the milk stool at Dorothy's feet; she jumped out of the way. I walked out of the barn and out to the road and started walking east toward town.

I had gone about a half a mile when Dorothy came down the rode in the car. She wanted me to come back. She apologized for yelling at me. I told her I was tired, and I couldn't help what had happened. I got into the car and returned to the farm with her.

Dad was gone. While Dorothy, Albert, and I were having our confrontation, he had slipped away. A police car came to a neighbor's house a little later in the evening. Our neighbors were just a few hundred yards west and on the south side of the road. My dad was in the police car when it went by our house toward town.

The next day and in the days that followed the radio and newspapers reported the story my dad had told the authorities: that he had been held prisoner by the Thompsons for the past five years.

At first I was relieved that Dad was gone. I had been very worried about him for months. But I was embarrassed—by him and his story. I was devastated by what my friends at school would think.

My name was mentioned in the newspapers and on the radio. Elling Haugen had a seventeen-year-old son who attended Spring Valley High School and remained at the Thompson farm. Dad's picture was in the Spring Valley newspaper and the Rochester *Post Bulletin*, and perhaps many other papers. Dad looked emaciated and terrible in that picture. I was ashamed of myself for not having done anything to help him earlier.

I stopped going to school. I was too upset and embarrassed. People from the sheriff's office came to the farm to talk to me and the Thompsons. Several times they took me to the county jail in Preston where Dad was being held. They apparently kept him in the jail because they didn't know what else to do with him. Each time they picked me up, they took me to the jail and put me in a room with Dad so we could talk. He was generally sitting in a chair and keeping warm with blankets he had wrapped around himself over his clothes. He said he was cold all the time. He was such a pitiful site to behold. He said he wanted me to help him and support his story. I knew he was upset and disappointed in me. He knew I was not supporting the story like he wanted me to. I was ashamed of him and myself. I was very sad about the whole situation and frightened of what might come next.

After visiting with my dad, the deputies would take me into another room and question me. They sat me in a chair with a bright light shining on me, like I was a criminal. They asked me over and over about how the Thompsons had treated my dad during the years we had live on the farm. They asked about my treatment over and over in many different ways.

They wanted to know if I thought Dad had been held a prisoner by the Thompsons and if I had been held a prisoner. They asked if my dad had ever been beaten or threatened with a beating. I said I had never seen him beaten, and I never had heard any threats or been beaten myself. They wanted to know if I ever saw any of the Thompsons with a pitchfork, and if anyone had threatened to use it as a weapon against my dad. I said I had seen each of them with a pitch-fork or manure fork while with my dad, but I had never seen them threaten or try to stab or hit him with it. I told them I had been threatened once, and I told them about the incident at the kitchen table with the butcher knife.

They wanted to know why my dad was so skinny, and I told them I didn't know. Did he and I got enough to eat? We did. Had I ever seen him take field corn from the corncrib and fill his pockets with the kernels and then eat them? I had. Why did he do that? I thought it was because he was hungry. We all worked really hard on the farm, and we had to eat a lot. I'd had trouble gaining weight too, because of the amount of work I do.

They asked me why his clothes were so ragged. I told them my clothes were ragged too and full of patches, as were Albert's. The only ones who did not have really ragged clothes were the women, but some of their jackets and sweaters were ragged. Did I think we were poor? I didn't know for sure. I didn't think the Thompson's were poor because they owned the farm. I thought they were just stingy with their money. We were raggedy because the Thompsons didn't like to spend money on anything they didn't think was necessary.

I was interrogated several times, and it bothered me to be in the room with my dad. I had to look at him. Somehow I felt that I was responsible for his terribly emaciated condition. At the same time, I really felt that Dad had gotten himself into this situation by his own doing. If he had only stood up to them, none of this would have happened, and the last five years would have been very different. Why didn't he just drive off with the car one day and pick me up at school? If someone tried to stop him, he could have just beaten them up and drove away. We could have gone anywhere he wanted to. I talked to my dad like this when they put me in the room with him. I told him I thought he could have left at anytime he wanted to, except for maybe the last couple of months. He was convinced he couldn't have left because Dorothy or Olive would have killed him with a pitchfork.

I tried to be honest. I couldn't say that my dad had been held a prisoner for the past five years against his will, but I couldn't say for certain that he had been held against his will in the last few months. I knew that his condition had deteriorated terribly over the past few months and that he had approached a police officer in Spring Valley during that time and asked for help. I believed then, and believe now, that the only way he could have gotten away from the farm was by force. But in those last few months I don't think he was strong enough to use force.

I conveyed my thoughts to the police as best I could. I think they saw that I was trying to be honest and that I was conflicted and frightened. I believe they thought I was telling the truth as I saw it.

I had not been kept on the farm against my will. I had stayed there because these people, as stingy, strange, and mean as they were, were my family. In retrospect, I remember trying many times over the years to figure out where I would run away to. I could have run on most any day I had left the farm and was at school.

Over time, I had pretty well forgotten about my Aunt Rachel, my mother, my brother, and all my mother's relatives. I had forgotten what they looked like. I didn't have pictures of them or letters to refresh my memory. I had no pictures of myself from any time in my life, including the past six years. Not one relative ever called or wrote to me. If they had, the Thompsons or my dad must have intercepted every communication. But I don't think anyone ever tried during those six years, except my brother.

I learned from the police that my brother was in the Air Force. They must have found out where he was stationed. He came to see me on the farm and wanted me to go with him to Minneota. Reluctantly, I agreed and we left together in his car. We stopped in Austin overnight. I couldn't sleep and wasn't sure I wanted to go to Minneota. I didn't know "those Minneota people" anymore. I decided during the night I wanted to go back to the farm. I got up and wrote a note to Larry telling him I was going back to the farm. I slipped out of the motel room while he slept. I went to the highway and hitched a ride back to Spring Valley and the farm. The Thompsons were glad I had returned. But I was not sure what I was doing or where I belonged.

Dad had left the Preston jail and returned to Minneota. I heard later his brother Harland (Holly) had picked him up in Preston.

I crossed my father's name off the bathroom wall that I imagined still existed in Kewanee. I was the only survivor. I had ended up alone on the farm, where I had not wanted to go, with people I had never wanted to be with. The family I had been born into had completely disintegrated.

I quit going to school and hadn't been there for more than a week. Then one day the principal came to see me at the farm. He talked to me and the Thompsons. He wanted me to return to school. I said I was too upset and ashamed. He said it would be all right; he had talked to my classmates, and they wanted me to come back. I don't know what had been said on my behalf, but I went back and the kids treated me well. No one mentioned my dad.

I felt great at school now. It was as if a gigantic burden had been lifted from my shoulders. I was absolutely giddy at times. I laughed so easily at things. Everything had become less desperate and serious. I had fun. I felt relaxed. The kids must have thought I was a new person. I was happier now than I could remember being in years.

Within a matter of days I graduated. The Thompsons didn't attend the ceremony, nor did any other relative. All the other boys wore suits to our graduation ceremony except me, but my gown covered that up well. And I did get a ride to the school that evening. Dorothy took me and dropped me off.

Someone called out the names of the graduates; as they did, each went on stage to receive their diploma from the school superintendent. I was very anxious. I didn't want to walk up on stage in front of everybody. I knew they all knew about my dad. It had been the talk of the town for the past month.

Finally my name was called to receive my diploma and, to my surprise, everyone in the auditorium stood and applauded as I walked toward the stage. They kept on applauding while I received my diploma. I had been very uneasy, but the applause made me feel wonderful. I was so grateful for their support and acceptance. Many of the people in the auditorium came to me after the ceremony and wished me success and good luck. Not a single one of them mentioned my dad. Tears of gratefulness welled up in my eyes and trickled down my face. I couldn't believe that everyone was so thoughtful of me. They were proud of me.

I stayed on the farm after graduation. There were crops to attend to. All those cows still needed to be milked twice a day, there were hogs to feed and eggs and chickens to care for. The animals and the crops didn't disappear with my dad. They were ignorant of our family problems.

Within a short time there were trips to Preston to meet with attorneys. I attended some of them, but I was not always included, and I still don't know how everything was settled. I think there must have been an out of court settlement.

My dad received a sum of money for the time he had spent on the Thompson farm. I think it may have been as much as five thousand dollars. Dorothy and Dad were granted a divorce. I was emancipated from my dad, Dorothy, and the Thompsons. I could legally make all decisions regarding myself as if I were twenty-one years old. The Thompsons were ordered to pay me sixty dollars a month while I continued to work on the farm. I was also awarded a small sum of money for my work on the farm for the past few months, something like two hundred dollars.

And that was it. It was all over. As far as I know, Dad returned to Minneota. I returned to the Thompson farm.

It is hard to believe, but after the court procedure, Dorothy told me that she wanted my dad to come back. I don't think she was able to grasp the fact that she and her parents had almost killed him. She did not comprehend how serious the accusations had been against her and her parents, or how physically damaged and emotionally distraught my dad was. She was about as wise as a rock. I told her that if he loved her, he'd come back. But I knew he never would.

CHAPTER 19

ESCAPE, SUMMER 1952

It was strange being with Thompsons without my dad. Dorothy was not my mother; Olive and Albert were not my grandparents. Many years before Dad had said I would "learn to love them." I never did. At times I liked them, but most of the time I did not.

My dad had put me in the care of the Thompsons when we moved from Waterloo to the farm at Spring Valley. He should have been responsible for me and ensured my proper care and supervision. I was barely thirteen years old. I was at Dad's mercy, and he put me in their hands.

I decided to stay with Thompsons because they were the only family that I knew of for certain. I did not know what was going on with my dad; my brother was in the Air Force; I had no idea where Mom, Rachel or any of my relatives were, even after all the publicity and court appearances. No relative showed up at the farm to see how I was doing. No one wrote or called.

When the Thompsons paid me that first sum of money I bought a typewriter and some clothes. I had my hair cut from then on whenever I wanted it cut. I was no longer dressed in ragged clothing as I worked around the farm. I looked good while working, and I looked real nice when we went to town, which was usually Rochester now.

In a peculiar way, I had become the most powerful person in this strange family, or what was left of it. Dorothy and Olive would ask me for advice on things. I told them that if any questions that were asked about my dad just tell the truth. What was the truth? I guess each one of us had our own interpretation. But they were no longer in charge of me. I was in charge of me.

I had been terribly pained by my dad's illness and emaciated condition, but I was pleased by the court's resolution of our family problems. I felt joy at my graduation ceremony. I was happy with my consequent freedom from poverty and my rise to independence. But this satisfaction and ecstasy rapidly deteriorated.

The burden of farm work was near overwhelming. I was not following my dream of leaving after graduation and working in Rochester and saving money to go to college. It was going to take me forever to get enough money to buy a car. I wanted to go to see some of my high school friends, go to parties and dances. I wanted to date girls. None of this was happening. The women would neither loan me their car nor loan me money to buy a car. I was stuck with nothing but work, livestock, manure, Dorothy and Olive.

We began to visit again with some of the Thompson relatives, something we had stopped doing a couple of years earlier. We began visiting with neighbors too. This bothered me. It didn't seem fair or right. Why hadn't we been doing this before?

I bought myself a cocker spaniel puppy and named her Peggy. I wanted something to love. I was feeling lonely and that old lump came back to my chest, like a giant crying sob that was stuck and trying to get out. I needed to belong to someone. I wanted to be hugged, but I didn't get hugged. I wanted to cry. I felt like I could cry forever, but I didn't shed a single tear. But the puppy was very good at joyfully playing and licking my face.

I started to think the most peculiar thoughts. I began to see the Thompsons as talking heads. I wanted them to just shut their mouths. Their bodies were used to propel only those damn talking heads. I saw myself as just a talking head too. I just needed my body to propel the head around and so I could eat and keep my head alive.

I was trying to figure out life, and I concluded that life was just in one's head. The body was to keep the head alive. I wanted us all to turn into stone. I wanted no more thoughts or feelings. I had had enough. I wanted to curl into a ball and never speak again. I felt only contempt for the Thompsons and myself.

I couldn't turn anything into stone, and I couldn't immobilize myself into an unanimated blob. My choices seemed to be to continue living like this or death. I wanted someone to wrap their arms around me and hug me.

I began to think of the earth in a different way. It was not a beautiful planet created by God, where plants grew in the rich soil. Soil was nothing but shit, dead plants, and animals that had accumulated and deteriorated over eons of time.

The earth was a large sphere. At its core was a mass of molten rock, then a shell of hard rock. This latter shell was covered with the remains of dead plants and animals and their excrement. These things just decayed over time so that no one recognized what dirt really was.

The rich soil on which we lived was just a thick layer of shit and dead stuff. I was devastated. I could not see God or good in this "dust unto dust" realization. Only the dust was made up of the shit and the dead. I was very disappointed. Living things had created the earth by living, shitting and dying on it, not by God in a miraculous supernatural seven-day creativity binge. What did God do? Everything went on without him. He did not intervene in anything. There was no God.

I was spending entirely too much time alone with no one to talk things out with. I decided in desperation to reach out to the Thompsons.

I told them that I had decided that Olive, Dorothy, and Albert should be called "Grandma, Mom and Grandpa." They were somewhat surprised by this decision. I had refused to call them anything but their first names for six years, so I think they were really kind of shocked. So was I.

It was not a good idea, and it worsened rather than improved my mental health. Within days, I felt like a traitor to my own feelings. I had sold out in an effort to get some affection.

A few nights later we were visiting some friends. These were new friends we had made since Dad had left. We were all eating dinner. I was the life of the party, however small it was, telling jokes and laughing. I was the center of attention.

I was in the middle of a funny story. Suddenly I forgot what I was talking about, and all the secret, suicidal and homicidal thoughts I ever had came rushing into my head in an instant. I wanted to blurt them out.

I put my hand to my forehead and muttered that I couldn't remember the rest of the story. They gave me a funny look and laughed and said that happens sometimes.

I was stunned by what had happened to me. The incident frightened me, and for days I thought about it. My feelings and thoughts were nearly out of control. I was having trouble with guilt, shame, and hostility. They all wanted to jump out of me at once. I knew I was in deep trouble emotionally. I couldn't sleep at night, and I now weighed less than 130 pounds, despite eating as much as I could.

It was September, and I had had enough. I had to leave the Thompsons. I decided to leave at night while they were sleeping so there would be no attempt to try and stop me. I did not want to hurt any of them.

Olive always locked the doors at night. She kept the key in her bedroom on the dresser in a porcelain dish. I had seen it there many times over the years. I made plans to leave on a night when I knew for sure that the key was in the dish. A few nights later, I heard the tinkle of the key against the porcelain as she dropped it in the dish.

I kept my puppy in a wire and wood crate at the top of the stairs at night. Dorothy slept in her bedroom, and I was still sleeping in mine. Of course there were no doors upstairs, and sounds from one room could easily be heard in the other.

I knew the exact spot in Olive's bedroom where the key was. I planned to take the puppy with me. That meant I had to take the pup out of the cage without waking Dorothy. Then I would have to creep down the creaking wooden steps and go into Albert and Olive's bedroom without waking them, get the key, unlock the house back door, and be on my way before anyone was awake enough to stop me.

About two o'clock in the morning, I got up. I quietly put on my clothes, opened the crate, took the puppy, and slowly and quietly crept down the stairs. I don't think I breathed, I was so quiet. It took me about twenty minutes to go down twenty steps. I slipped into Olive's bedroom and took the key. I walked backwards through the short hallway out of their bedroom, past the stairwell, and to the back door in the kitchen. I unlocked it in an instant and was in the porch, unlocked the porch door, and I was outside.

I knew I may have made some noise, so I decided not to go down the road, but instead I cut through the grove on the north side of the farm yard. I crossed the fence on to the neighbors land and headed northeast along the railroad tracks. This area could not be approached by car. I carried my puppy in my arms.

About ten minutes after I left the house I saw our yard light come on and I saw a car leave the yard. I had made a wise decision on the route to take. I walked several miles through other farmers' fields until I came to the main highway toward Austin and Rochester. It was a foggy morning. A slight mist was falling. I waited for the good light of dawn before I got up on the shoulder of the road to hitch a ride. It was very difficult to see what was coming up or down the road. I was worried that the Thompsons may think to look along the highway I had chosen. I stuck my thumb in the air at the first vehicle that came by, a semi truck. It stopped.

The driver must have thought it was a little odd that I was hitching a ride on such a miserable morning with a puppy in my arms. He asked me if I was running away from home. I said, no, I needed a ride to Racine, I was going to my grandma's house. He told me to get in, and I was on my way.

The driver dropped me along side the highway when we got to Racine. He wished me luck. I thanked him for the ride and began walking toward Evelyn Miscke's house on the north side of town.

Evelyn Miscke was very happy to see me. She was Albert Thompson's niece. I had always gotten along well with her. She knew all about the problem with my dad and the Thompsons from the radio and newspapers—and the gossip. She was not judgmental about the case or me. I asked her for help. I wanted to go to Minneota, where I thought my dad was. I thought I could take the Greyhound bus from Racine. I think she knew how to contact my Dad through his sister Bertha, or maybe it was his brother Harland. At any rate, it was not long before my dad called Evelyn, and he and I agreed that I should take the bus to Minneota. The following day I boarded the bus for the nine hour trip to Minneota, via Minneapolis. Evelyn kept my puppy and shipped her to me a few days later.

The Thompsons and their farm were now history. The nightmare of the past six years was over. It had started just after my twelfth birthday and ended shortly after my eighteenth.

I never saw Albert again. He died five years later of a heart attack in his cow barn, probably while hand milking one of his favorite cows. I only saw the Thompson women once, about twelve years later for about twenty minutes. Then I never saw or heard from them again. They were just a reoccurring bad dream that diminished in frequency over time.

That twenty minutes I spent with them was in the spring of 1964. My wife and I and our two children were visiting with some friends we had met while I had been attending the University of Minnesota. They lived in Rochester. My wife knew I had gone to school in Spring Valley and wanted to see the infamous Thompson farm. I really didn't want to go there, but I was curious too, so I said okay. We drove by the farm. It was beginning to look very run down. The buildings were no longer brightly painted. The white picket fence had faded. A few of the mixed breed cows were still in the pasture.

"Let's stop," my wife said, "I want to see if anyone is home."

"And then what?" I asked.

"Well, we'll talk to them."

"Oh great, that is just what I wanted to do!" I said sarcastically. My hands were already sweating and shaking. I felt very nervous.

I went up and knocked on the door. Both women came to the door. They knew who I was right away. They looked much older, and Dorothy had gotten fat. They invited me in, but I said my wife and kids were in the car, and we had just stopped by to say hello. They walked out to the car with me, and I introduced everybody. I was very nervous while making small talk, and I wanted to leave. My wife seemed to enjoy chatting with them; she could talk to anybody. But she hadn't spent six years in hell with these women when she was a kid.

Finally my own children saved me by beginning to squeal, "When are we going, Daddy?" I said real soon, and we were out of there shortly. As we left, my wife remarked that they did not seem that bad. I was nervous and my hands trembled for several minutes after leaving the driveway.

Many years later, long after 1964, I learned that Olive had had a nervous breakdown prior to our moving to the farm in 1946. She had been hospitalized for a mental disorder long before Dad and I had set foot on the farm. One of her symptoms had been paranoia. She had been a suspicious and distrustful person before Dad and I had ever laid eyes on her. The very intelligent, cruel maternal leader of our strange little family group had suffered from mental illness. She lived past ninety years old. I hope God had mercy on whoever else came under her influence during the following decades.

Dorothy married again, but I don't know to whom. She lived into her eighties. Both she and her mother lived out their lives on that once pretty but soon deteriorating little gingerbread farm. I watched it decay over the years from a distance. I never approached any closer than to drive by it and check it every other year or so. It began to look darker and more evil with each passing year. Every time I went by I would stop on the road down by the creek near our old potato patch. By 2005 most everything from the original farm had collapsed or was gone except for a little stub of a silo. I had hoped that by viewing it on those visits, I would become less emotionally affected by being there. That never happened. Even in 2005, even though it looked drastically different from 1952, it still made me tremble.

CHAPTER 20

MINNEOTA, LATE AUTUMN 1952

It was nearly dark when the Greyhound bus stopped at the Atlantic Hotel on the corner of Main Street in Marshall, Minnesota. I looked out the bus window to see if anyone was waiting for me. No one was.

I got off the bus. I had no luggage. I waited on the side of the hotel for a few minutes then started walking toward the corner to Main Street. Before I got to the corner my Aunt Rachel, Dad, and another woman appeared.

Rachel extended her arms to embrace me. She was crying with joy. She hugged, kissed, and cried on me. It felt good to be in her arms. I hadn't been hugged by anyone for six years.

I had not seen her since November 1946. She looked and smelled just like she had before. Dad stood nearby, still very thin. He stepped forward and hugged me. He said he was glad to see me too. Mary, the woman with them, said she was glad to see me as well. Mary was quite fat and had a large beak-like nose. She thought I should remember her from when I was little, but I didn't. She seemed disappointed.

We walked around the corner to where Rachel had parked her car. She drove us to Minneota. On the way, she said she wanted me to come home with her. I wanted to go home with Rachel because I had no idea where I would be sleeping otherwise. We stopped in Minneota and let Dad and Mary off at Mary's tiny house. I wondered why Dad was staying with her. But I wondered only for a moment. I knew he had found another woman to take care of him. I was disappointed, but I said nothing.

It was a long way over gravel roads to Rachel's farm, about twenty miles. This part of Minnesota had not caught on to the blacktop road yet. On the way, she told me I had gotten so big she could not believe it. I told her that I was a lot older now and that is what happens to kids; they grow up. I was kind of nervous. I hadn't seen her for so long. I knew she was wondering why I had stayed with the Thompsons after my dad left. That question would be coming up very soon.

I asked her when she and Henry had moved back to Minnesota from Illinois. She told me it was shortly after Dad, Lawrence, and I had left. Donnie Pete was a senior in high school and Patty was in junior high. She said that Dad was working for her brother Rene, my uncle, doing farm work. And gossip had it Dad was sleeping over at Mary's house. She told me Mary had seven kids. Larry was out of the Air Force and working in Waterloo. She didn't know where my mother was. The last they had heard, which had been some years before, she was living in Kentucky and was married, but they did not know the man's name.

Uncle Henry, Donnie Pete, and Patty were waiting for us. They were happy to see me. They thought I had grown a lot too, but I looked skinny to them. I had lost weight. I only weighed about 135 pounds. Henry wanted to know why I was so skinny. They asked me if those people had given me enough to eat. They did, I told them. I was just skinny.

"They sure as hell starved your Dad," Henry said.

I acknowledged that Dad certainly had been very skinny. Henry said I had changed a lot since Kewanee. I wasn't as cute now as I was then. I was probably eleven years old years old the last time he saw me. Henry was determined to find out what had happened at Spring Valley. He was antagonistic and had some notion in his head that I knew more than what I was telling.

Donnie and Patty were grown. I would not have recognized them if I had seen them on the street. I had imagined over the years that Donnie had grown tall and probably was playing basketball. He was not as tall as me but he was much heavier. Patty was as cute as when I had last seen her. She was thirteen now and hardly remembered me.

Rachel had Dad, Mary, Rene and his wife, and some friends over to see me during the next several days. I guess everyone wanted to see Elling's kid who had stayed at the Thompson farm. Everyone told me they were glad I had come back to Minneota, where I belonged. They said I did not belong with those people at Spring Valley. I belonged with them.

They were curious as to why I had come to Minneota now. Why hadn't I come out earlier with my dad? I told them I didn't know for sure, but the Thompsons and the farm had been my family and my home since I was twelve. I told them I had gotten lonesome, and I wanted to be with my dad again.

The next few days were filled with uncomfortable encounters, with Henry in particular. He was unable to understand what had happened at Spring Valley. He thought I was lying and became dogged in his pursuit of the truth. Often we'd sit at the kitchen table. The light over the table flooded me and the table with illumination. But I didn't want to be illuminated. It felt like I was back at the sheriff's office in Preston. I didn't want the spotlight; I wanted to hide in a little darkness. I wanted to be with Henry and Rachel, but Henry was making me uncomfortable.

At that time, and in my mind I was not sure what happened at Spring Valley to Dad and me. I couldn't explain the reasons for Dad's emaciated appearance and pathetic condition at the time he had returned to Minneota. I couldn't explain why I hadn't run away from the Thompsons years ago. I couldn't explain my unbearable sadness in the last months at Spring Valley.

I was not going to shame myself by accepting responsibility for Dad's treatment or condition. I wasn't responsible for what happened to him; Dad was. I was innocent of any wrongdoing. I needed to believe Dad was responsible for what had happened to him and what had happened to me. He was the person responsible for the nightmare at Spring Valley, no one else.

Rationally, I would argue with myself and Henry that Dad had brought it all on himself because he was looking for a cozy place, for people with money on a nice little farm. He found the farm and an eligible woman in Dorothy and married her. It was their decision. When things turned sour for him and Olive's paranoia began to set in, he should have stood up for himself. If he had, nothing bad would have happened to him or me at Spring Valley. He should have stood up for himself because he was an adult man and a father. He should have stood up for me because I was his child.

Rachel spoke up often during my confrontations with Henry. She'd say, "Leave that boy alone, Henry. You know how Elling was; he never ever stood up for himself. And lie—I never saw a man who could lie like him."

I repeated in a hundred ways to Henry and the other skeptics on my Mom's side of the family that Dad should have just assumed responsibility for himself and me. I was the kid, and he was the adult. Fathers are supposed to look out for their kids. Most were sold on this argument, but Henry remained skeptical. Henry implied that I had somehow been disloyal to my dad.

I pushed back. I asked the skeptics why they hadn't visited, written, or telephoned. They could have contacted us at anytime in the past six years. Why didn't they? Their answers were feeble. They did not know where I was and didn't want to interfere.

"You could have found me if you wanted," I told them. It was true. They knew where we were. My brother had told them years before, when he was fifteen and had come to Minneota to stay with Grandma Blomme.

I wanted the whole nightmare to go away, but it was not going to die easily. The monsters lurked in the shadows. I was a survivor, but I was one of the walking wounded. I was having difficulty reconciling my feelings about who was in the right and who was in the wrong about Spring Valley. Had I been disloyal, or just honest to a fault, or was it no one's fault and inexplicable?

I soon made the rounds visiting Dad's relatives too—Grandma Haugen, and Dad's sisters and brothers. It became apparent that most of them blamed me for not getting my dad away from the terrible Thompsons before they nearly killed him. They were worse than Henry. They seemed to forget that the Albert Thompson was their first cousin, and I don't think they ever asked themselves where they had been during the past six years. They knew Dad had married Dorothy and we lived on the farm near Spring Valley. But none of them ever contacted us.

The seeds of my alleged disloyalty had been obviously planted in the minds of my Dad's family by someone, probably Dad's brother Holly, and maybe by

Dad himself. His sister Bertha and her husband Henry and their children, I soon learned, were convinced that I was in some way responsible for what happened to Dad at Spring Valley. Soon they began to shun me completely. The same was true for Dad's sister Marie and her children. His brother Sanford, however, befriended me and spoke to me. He said he had always gotten along well with the Thompson family; he just could not understand what had gone wrong at Spring Valley. Where had *he* been for the past six years? Why hadn't he come to visit us?

I was getting emotionally beat up by these people. The Haugen family had sided with my fifty-two-year-old dad, and I was the bad guy. It hurt. Couldn't they understand I was still a kid? So one day when no one else was around, I asked Dad if he felt I was responsible for what had happened. He just expelled some air from his chest in a Norwegian expression of something unintelligible to me, kind of like a guffaw. Then he said something like, "Of course not. It was the Thompsons fault."

"Are you sure Dad?" I said. "Because Bertha, Holly, Marie, and Norman all think I am responsible."

He said something like, "They just don't know what happened. That's all."

I told him they were really making me feel like shit. He said I should just forget about it. That was what he was trying to do.

Forgetting about it was hard to do. I wanted these people to care about me, but I felt like they hated me. The Thompsons had treated me better than Dad's relatives.

Believe it or not, I began to miss the Spring Valley farm. I had become a part of the strange Thompson family during my adolescent years. They were my family, and I was used to them and a daily routine. I got up in the morning, milked cows, ate breakfast, and I either went to school or went about doing other farm work. I became familiar with our farm life over the years. We ate dinner and supper together. We milked cows and did our other chores in the evening. I missed the horses, which I liked working with. I was used to a purpose-driven farm life. I often wondered what the Thompson's were doing and how they were getting along. How were they managing all that work by themselves? But I knew I could not return to the farm. They had mistreated me for years. It is strange that I became so attached to the very people who were almost indescribably mean and neglectful of me.

I couldn't go back. At the same time, I felt there was little hope for me to have a good relationship or a home with the Haugen side of my family in Minneota. I was unacceptable to my dad's family. I was a painted bird among the Haugen flock. Maybe it was those thick glasses that made me so easily identifiable as different.

As I thought about it, I remembered that the Haugen relatives had shunned Mom, Dad, Lawrence, and me when I was a child because we were Roman Catholic. I had never known any of them very well. They were strangers and never liked me. The shunning was only a continuation of where we had left off twelve years before. I never had been acceptable to them.

Larry came up from Waterloo. Of course, he needed to learn what had happened in Spring Valley too. But like the others, I was unable to convince him completely of my innocence. We didn't dwell on the subject, though. It seemed nothing could be explained to anyone's satisfaction.

Larry was a good-looking hard-living man. He had a lot of drinking to do, and then there was fighting, dancing, and woman chasing. He was good at all four.

I was not.

Larry got a job as a bartender at a nightclub in Taunton. He bought a beautiful dark blue 1948 Dodge four-door sedan in which to do his thing, and now my thing. I soon learned to drive it, and when he felt generous, I could use it.

Larry was a little taller and much heavier than me. He talked and acted mean. He carried a .25 caliber pistol in the glove compartment of the Dodge. He liked to whip it out and shoot through the passenger side window at fence posts, while I sat in the passenger seat. He scared the hell out of me.

This was the Wild West, and Larry seemed to fit in. He had quit school in the ninth grade and spent four years in the Air Force. He seemed to lack any inhibitions. I completed high school, wanted to go to college, and was afraid of my own feelings. I was a nerd; he wasn't. We did not fit well together.

Frankly, I had gained a self-righteous sense of moral conduct from somewhere. Somehow I identified with a different class of people, not the class my brother was in. My moral code did not include carrying a gun, drinking to get drunk, and trying to fuck every girl I liked the looks of. I talked differently than Larry. I enunciated my words clearly and used a different vocabulary. There was a gap between us. What was the right way for me to behave?

Rachel said I could leave Peggy, my cocker spaniel puppy, with her and Henry until whenever. They still had Puppy, but he was an old dog now. Peggy lived out her long life with them. I saw her frequently over the years, and I often played with her. I used her as my hunting companion over the next many years. She was a natural for flushing out pheasants.

I made my temporary home with Rachel and her family, so did Larry. Rachel treated us like her own kids. She was very kind, accepting, and loving to me. I became her favorite child. However, Donnie and Patty were not jealous. They treated me like a brother. Rachel told me she needed to show me a lot of love because she had missed me so much over the years and wanted to make up for lost time. She felt she should have gotten in contact with me at Spring Valley, and maybe she could have done something for me while I was there. She was right. She could have taken me home with her. I am sure everybody on the farm would have been glad to get rid of me, including my dad. That is, until I became an able-bodied farm hand at about fifteen years of age.

Soon after I arrived in Minneota and had made my home with Rachel, I placed a series of ads in the personals section of the Cincinnati and Covington newspapers. The ad asked for anyone knowing the whereabouts of Martha Blomme (Haugen) to contact me at Rachel's address. In the ad I indicated I was her son and needed to get in touch with her. There was not a single response. I was very disappointed. I wanted my mother. Over the years I had turned her into a saintly mother who could solve all my ills with her love and affection, if only I could find her and be with her. I had worked on this canonization of my mother in my troubled little mind since I was eleven. I had made her bigger and better with each passing year of her absence. And when the Dorothy and Olive would criticize her for being a slut and no good, she became even more saintly in my compensating protective mind.

Larry and I began going to dances at Glady's Ballroom in Montevideo. I was under aged to drink alcohol, so Larry would order 7-Up and make drinks from a bottle of alcohol we brought with us and kept in a box under the table.

I was soon getting up enough nerve to ask the girls to dance. My early training as a child dancing on my mother's feet paid off. I soon felt comfortable dancing and had no trouble finding partners. I was beginning to live like my peers—to drink, dance and flirt with the girls. I liked it.

As soon as the weather began to look like spring, probably mid-March, Larry and I rented a room in Marshall on Main Street near the Coca-Cola plant. It was a nice room in a nice house. We found work with the Miller Construction Company as laborers. Our hourly wage was one dollar per hour straight time, no extra pay for overtime. We worked sixty hours a week and made sixty dollars, less deductions. I had been used to hard farm work, so I had no trouble adjusting to the labor. Larry was used to bartending, so it took him a little while.

We spent our leisure time at the bars, dance halls, and restaurants where people our age hung out. I wanted to try out for one of Marshall's city baseball teams, but I was unable to convince Larry to try out. He had no interest in play-ing baseball. Larry's main interest was girls, and he was good at picking them up. He had a car, so he had a big advantage over me. But I dated some of the girls I met through coworkers. We went to movies and dances.

Larry was drinking a lot and was often drunk at night. He could consume vast quantities of whiskey, and you could hardly tell he had been drinking. I, on the other hand, after four or five drinks, would get sick and throw up. I couldn't keep up with my brother. One night Larry was on his second fifth up in our room and fell asleep with the open bottle next to the bed. He must have knocked it over during the night. The whiskey soaked the floor and ran through into the ceiling below in the landlord's living room. This made them very mad, and we were evicted the next afternoon. We rented an apartment in a building about a block up Main Street and moved our things the same day. We now had a lot of room and could make more noise as we sat and drank or when friends came over. It was a good place to bring dates and try and make out.

I formed a good relationship with Mr. Miller's son, and another boy named Don. I began to hang around with them. They did less drinking and lot more of what I would call typical dating—like movies, and drive-ins for burgers. I had a brief relationship with Don's sister, Karen, who was a very pretty blonde.

Spring passed quickly and we were into summer. The construction work was hard. Larry tired of Miller Construction Company and went to work for a road contractor. The work I did was laborious. I did things like unload boxcars full of eighty-pound bags of cement onto trucks. For days on end, I and others would shovel rock and sand into cement mixers for pouring concrete foundations and floors. I mixed mud and tended bricklayers. I did house framing and roofing. It was hard work and the pay was poor. Soon Larry was going out of town a lot. It was late summer and, since he was gone so much, we decided to give up our apartment. This put me in a bind because I didn't have a car.

During the summer I had become acquainted with my dad's girlfriend's kids. I became good friends with Mary's oldest boy Ronnie, who worked at a gas station in Minneota. He was a senior at Minneota High School and a football player. I also became friends with his friend Jimmy. Ronnie told me the gas station in Minneota needed to hire someone, so I applied and was hired by the MGT Co-op. I moved into Mary's house along with Dad, Mary, Mary Ellen, Angie, Norma, Adrienne, Duane, and Ronnie. It was a tiny house of four small rooms and an attic. I slept with the two boys in the smallest of rooms in one double bed. The girls all slept in the attic. I never was up there, but I know you could not stand up because the ceiling was so low. God have mercy if the house ever caught on fire at night. There were too many people in too small of a house. There were many moments of friction between myself and some of the girls who felt I didn't belong there. I felt I didn't belong there too. It was a temporary thing for me, and of course everybody involved wanted me to be there only on that basis.

Ronnie was a good kid. He had a girlfriend named Midge. She was a very buxom girl with a fun personality. So we all got along very well. I soon met some of Midge's friends and began dating one named Pauline. I also met Midge's younger sister, who was thirteen. She was a gangly but a strikingly tall blonde who looked much older than thirteen. She was bold. One day while I was over to her house, she asked me why I never asked her out. I told her because she was too young. Midge had warned me not to date her sister, and I respected that request. But I liked her younger sister's looks and personality.

Pauline was Catholic and very pretty. I dated her many times. We went to movies and drive-ins and did some petting. I could occasionally borrow my dad's car. That was a good thing. Pauline was determined that she was going to the convent after high school to become a nun. How far can you go with a girl that wants to be a nun? Not far! Kissing and hugging is about it. However, she was a fun, intelligent girl to be with. And I had a girlfriend to do things with. She had one habit that really bugged me, however. She made the sign of the cross every time we went by the Catholic church. She lived near a Catholic church, so she seemed to be making the sign of the cross all the time. I was greatly disappointed in God anyway, and the constant sign of the cross stuff got to me. I would have rather been going out with thirteen-year-old Lorna.

During the course of the summer, Jimmy, Ronnie, and I decided to enlist in the Navy. We would do this next summer after they graduated. Although they were the same age as me, they were still in school. We went to Montevideo and took the Navy's written tests. We all did well, but I did exceptionally well. The Navy considered me eligible for officer candidate school. I didn't even know what that was, but for some reason there would not be an opening for me for several months for this particular naval school. I would have to wait until after Ronnie and Jimmy went in the next summer.

One day during the summer, Grandma Blomme heard from my mother. She was coming to Minneota visit Grandma and Grandpa. Larry and I went over to Grandma's house the day she arrived.

I had not seen my mom since I was eleven. I didn't know what to expect. I was apprehensive, and my feelings were confused. I had canonized her into sainthood while I was at Spring Valley. But I was in for a surprise.

Mom hurried into the front yard when Larry and I drove up. She did not look like my mom. She was old and fat. She spoke with a southern accent. I really didn't know this woman.

Mom started talking as she approached us. She said her husband was with her and that he didn't know she had been married before or that she had two children who were now grown. She said we could come in, but we must not tell him we were her kids. She didn't want any trouble.

We asked what we should call her.

"You call me, Martha!"

We were both immediately angry, but thought, what the hell. It really didn't make any difference to us! We had just come over to see Grandpa and Grandma anyway. We went in. Her husband was sleeping on the couch. We had a look at him. He didn't look like much to me, just an average looking kind of skinny man, kind of redneck-like. We talked with Grandma and Grandpa for a few minutes. It was a very awkward situation for them and us. They knew Larry and I were upset. They did not know why my mom had not told him about her two boys. They thought it was shameful of her.

I went out to Rachel's later that day and told her that Mom was in town. I told her what happened when we met her at Grandma's. She said she didn't know why Martha behaved like she did; she must be crazy. She was ashamed of her sister. I was the very upset. Rachel gave me a big hug and told me that I should not worry about it. She said to me, "I love you, you know that."

I did not see my mom again. She returned to Kentucky the next day.

I couldn't believe my mother was so calloused. She didn't love me! At Spring Valley, I had desperately hung on to her memory with every bit of strength and energy I had. I prayed for her to rescue me. I begged God a thousand times to let me live with her, to reunite us.

I was devastated by the realization that she was never going to be a mother to me. She was not going to be anything to me but a source of anguish and disappointment.

She denied our existence to her husband, and she had the nerve to ask my brother and me to support her lies. She had rejected us again. I wanted to tell her, "You mean nothing to me, absolutely nothing." But she was gone. I could not tell her how worthless she was.

She did mean something to me: I despised her very existence, her damned selfish existence. I felt contaminated by her. I wanted to divorce myself from any memory of her. I hated the fact that I had born from her womb. I cursed God for allowing this woman to be my mother. The fact that she gave birth to me made me cringe with contempt for myself. I hated the very blood I carried from her in my veins.

I hated her.

CHAPTER 21

LATE SUMMER AND AUTUMN, 1953

I fit in well with my new friends in Minneota. I hung around with Ronnie and Jimmy and their girlfriends and sometimes Pauline. They were all still in high school; I had already graduated from a school they had never heard of. The dreaded Spring Valley loomed in the background, that strange place where my Dad had been starved. The stigma lived on. The kids neither understood that aspect of my life nor did we talk about it. We ignored it.

Autumn soon arrived, with it the high school football season. I went to all the games with my friends to watch Ronnie play. I loved the excitement of football—the crisp air, the pretty cheerleaders, the bands, and the cheering crowds. I had always been a good sandlot player, and I think I would have been a good high school player if I would have had the chance.

I was becoming more and more disenchanted. My brother said I should go into the military. It would be good for me. I could take advantage of the GI Bill and go to college afterward like I wanted to. He had a steady girlfriend now and was thinking about getting married.

I felt lonesome a lot of the time. I couldn't describe what I was lonesome for. I wanted something I wasn't getting, and I didn't know what it was or how to get it.

Mary's tiny rundown house was filled with kids and Dad and Mary. I often would clash with some of the girls, and I felt a desperate anger toward them at times. It seemed I had no place to go. They had my dad, and he was as useless to me now as he had been at Spring Valley. I had known for years that he would never be a father to me, and it was far too late now. I could expect nothing from him, not love, not advice, not a relationship, or any interest in me.

I decided not to wait to join the military. On November 3, 1953, I joined the Army for three years. I was sent to Fort Riley, Kansas, for eight weeks of basic training. After two days, I realized that three years was an incredibly long time.

CHAPTER 22

THE ARMY

I was assigned to H Company of the Eighty-Fifth Infantry Regiment, Tenth Mountain Division. There were about two hundred men to a company. Our company was made up of four platoons of about fifty men each.

I was in much better shape than most of the other recruits. There was no aspect of training that was difficult for me. I found it easy, and I actually I enjoyed basic infantry training.

I was surprised by the physical condition of my fellow soldiers. I never knew there were men who would pee their pants or faint if they stood in formation for a couple of hours. I did not realize that a lot of men my age could not walk ten miles with twenty-five pounds of equipment on their back and an M-1 rifle in their hands. Frequently we would go on the long forced marches and a dozen or more men would "fall out" along side the road unable to make the distance.

There was no softness or leniency on the part of the Army in terms of training. If someone fainted in ranks, they would lie on the ground where they fell. The rest of us were not to move to help them. If a man urinated in his pants, he stood there with urine soaked trousers until the entire company was dismissed from formation, no matter how long that was. If you fell out on a march, we yelled insults at you as we passed by. Later a truck would come by and pick up the guys who couldn't make it.

Men who could not stand up to the rigors of training were unmercifully taunted by the rest of us. Shirking responsibility was not tolerated. Thievery was not tolerated. We were encouraged to taunt and threaten those who couldn't live up to what the company demanded of its soldiers.

One day upon returning from a difficult five-day exercise in the freezing cold of the Kansas winter, a young recruit who had begged off the exercise by complaining of illness was caught with another soldier's personal items, which he had apparently stolen while the rest of us were on maneuvers.

Justice was swift and partial. We determined the guy guilty. Two of our strongest men took the accused thief into the barracks' large community shower. The rest of us in turn, beat him with our fists until he lay unconscious and bleeding on the shower room floor. He was then picked up bodily by several of us and thrown naked outside the barracks front door.

When the company commander made an inquiry about what happened to the young man, no one admitted any knowledge of how he had been beaten and bruised. We were not expected to step forward and tell what happened. We were expected to keep our mouths shut.

A few days later, this young man returned to our barracks, but he was taunted so badly, he drank a bottle of Lysol or something from the latrine. An ambulance came and took him away while we were standing at morning formation. We broke formation long enough to cheer wildly as the ambulance drove away. He never returned to the company, and I never saw him again. I have often wondered what ever happened to him.

The eight weeks were soon over and I went to Fort Leonard Wood, Missouri, for eight more weeks of training as a combat engineer. It was like infantry training, but now we had to build bridges too. Here I had an opportunity to make some choices. I could have applied to go to officer candidate school. I could have also applied for airborne training or helicopter pilot school. However, anyone of these choices would have required me to extend my enlistment by as much as a year. Another problem was my poor eyesight.

I passed all these choices up. By this time, I didn't want to spend any more time in the Army than necessary. Nonetheless, I had noticed that being an officer was much better than being a grunt. You got better food, nicer uniforms, more pay, and more respect. I didn't know that when I enlisted, or I would have perhaps thought of some way to go directly to officer candidate school on a three year enlistment.

From Leonard Wood, I was sent to Fort Belvoir, Virginia, for training in water purification. After completion of this school, one of my school friends and I received orders for the worst possible place at that time: Korea, for a long tour of sixteen months.

CHAPTER 23

KOREA, JUNE 1954 TO OCTOBER 1955

We arrived by ship in Pusan, South Korea, one morning in early June 1954. The harbor was crowded with ships and small boats. The tiny civilian boats that came to greet us were filled with people, many of them children. Our ship towered over them, the little boats and people looked like play things in the water below. I could hear children begging. Their arms were stretched upward and hands open waiting to catch the candy, gum, and cigarettes we threw down. They maneuvered their boats and caught their booty with uncanny expertise. They had done this before.

The late morning sunlight, diffused by the high humidity, illuminated the ancient treeless hills surrounding the city and harbor. The unusual light brushed the hills in an eerie pale yellow green. The worn down hills were planted all the way up on every side, neither an inch of earth shown through the pale green, and no ground wasted. There was not a tree in sight. I had never seen anything that looked like Pusan.

We were unloaded from the ship into eighteen wheelers with open trailer boxes, the sides of which were near shoulder height. Perhaps there were a couple hundred or more of us crowded into each trailer. We each had all our possessions in our duffle bags, and we were packed so tightly that one could hardly fall over as the truck bumped along the streets. I felt like an animal being hauled off somewhere. It reminded me of trucks taking cattle to the slaughterhouse in South St. Paul.

The trucks carried us through the streets of Pusan to the Army processing center for all new arrivals. There were no tall building anywhere that I could see; all the buildings seemed to be shacks. The streets were muddy with puddles of water here and there. There was a mixture of odors. Some were sweet, others were of burning charcoal, and there was the unmistakable smell of human waste.

I saw pretty young Korean women in American-style clothing on the streets mingling with other Korean women, men and children in typical Korean dress. Some of the guys riding in the back of semi-trailer with me said the pretty ones in American clothes were prostitutes. They said you could get a "blow job" through the fence at the processing center for a pack of cigarettes. I was skeptical; I wondered if the Army would allow that.

After processing, we were allowed to roam around in the large chain-link fenced enclosure surrounding the compound. The fence was very high and topped with barb wire. Sure enough, gathered along the outside in various places, were American-dressed Korean women and up against the fence. On the inside were GI's. They appeared to be engaging in oral and vaginal sex. I could figure out how the oral sex was accomplished, but not the vaginal. I could not believe what was going on here. No military authorities seemed to pay attention to what the men and women were doing. This compound was the indeed the most unusual place I had ever seen. It was in the middle of a pale yellow-green covered landscape with dripping hot humidity, and men were having sex with women through a chain-link fence. Everything about it was new to my eyes and mind, and it seemed unreal.

Soon I and many other soldiers were on an antique train heading north to Seoul. The train was of a vintage I had never seen in the States. It was tall and narrow with wooden benches for seats. It was old, rickety, and full of rattles as we bumped and rolled slowly northward. Its ancient steam engine pulled us past rice paddies and small treeless hills clad in pale yellow green.

In Seoul, my friend from Fort Belvoir and I were separated. I never saw him again. I was picked up by a jeep and taken to a railroad battalion headquartered in Yong Dong Po, which is south of Seoul just across the Han River.

My new assignment was with a group that provided water for the steam engines on the Korean rail system, among other things pertaining to water. Our battalion was housed in a set of brick buildings that had been a boarding school for Koreans prior to the war. This was my new home. We had a mess hall that doubled as a nightclub. We ate our meals of dehydrated reconstituted food there during the day, and at night we bought beer for a dime and mixed drinks for a quarter.

Across the street from us was graves registration, were they brought the body bags containing dead soldiers for whatever processing the Army does to the deceased. The guys on the trains said there were still a lot of body bags coming down from the north. I couldn't tell you if there were or not. I never went over there, and I didn't pay much attention to any danger I might be facing. I just never spent time worrying about it. It would be a waste of time.

A mile or so north of my battalion, there was a PX on the main road toward Seoul, past the dilapidated open-fronted shacks where Korean merchants sold their wares. I could buy cigarettes for one dollar per carton, shaving equipment, cologne, perfume, cameras, film, and so forth. I soon learned that these were valuable items that could be traded on the black market.

The Korean merchants sold Korean items and a lot of black-market stuff. They all changed American GI script money for Korean money illegally. I could get about four hundred wan for a dollar. You could buy or sell anything with these merchants, ranging from cigarettes to jeeps.

The merchant shacks lined the street on both sides of the road nearly as far north as the airport and the Han River. Each store crowded tight against the next. Many sold food like dried squid, raw fish, and red meat. Many of the meat and fish items were unrecognizable to me. The meat looked like it may have come from small animals, like cats and dogs. Other stores were sex shops. Small children would come and grab your hand and say, "You come with me GI. You watch number one skivvy show." I would find out later on what that meant.

The smell in the street was completely unique. There was no refrigeration, and the odors of partially spoiled meat and fish mingled with those of charcoal smoke and feces from "honey buckets" that rumbled through the streets.

The honey bucket was usually a large wooden barrel cradled on its side by a wooden frame. This frame and bucket sat upon a heavy two-wheel cart pulled by an ox and guided by a Korean man, known as a papa san. The barrel was used to collect human waste in liquid form from cesspools. The liquid feces were used to fertilize Korean cropland.

These barrels had an opening on top in the center through which papa san filled the barrel with a long handled dipper. He was usually not entirely accurate in pouring directly into the hole. The fertilizer ran down the barrel's sides building up rivulets of feces, much like melted wax on a candle. They seldom covered the opening and waste sloshed out of the barrel on the bumpy roads and spilled onto the streets. The smell was always there, mingled with other smells, such as ever-present smoke from charcoal fired hibachi pots. After a rainstorm, when the sun came out and warmed the streets, the stench was incredible and unforgettable. But if it hadn't rained for a while and the weather was mild, the smell from the hibachi pots was really pleasant.

The walkways in front of the shops were usually crowded with Koreans and American soldiers. So full in fact, people often spilled out into the streets in an effort to walk by each other. The pretty Korean women with American dresses were among them. Small children from six to ten were seemingly everywhere and, unfortunately, were sometimes run over by our military vehicles.

My work at my battalion was easy. I seldom needed to go out on the rail lines to maintain the water pumps. The men who were about ready to ship home were called "short timers." They had earned the better jobs and were not about to give up their work and trips to the "long timers," who still had several months or more than a year to go.

It was boring back at the battalion, and time passed slowly; the short timers knew it. Long timers like myself, and there were several of us, fought the boredom by playing cards, reading, writing, working out, and drinking.

I read a lot—everything I could get my hands on. I wrote letters to Aunt Rachel, Larry, Pauline, and Midge. They always wrote back sooner or later, but I never received enough letters quickly enough to please me. They seldom sent their letters by air mail, so it took three or four weeks for them to arrive. Most letters came by boat mail. Midge was by far and away the best and most faithful letter writer.

One, two, three, and four months went by. During those first months I refused to have anything to do with the Korean prostitutes. I thought it was degrading to have sex with them, and it was morally wrong. The guys making love to the prostitutes were depraved. And what about venereal disease? What about saving yourself for the woman you would marry someday in the future?

Several of us thought we should be saving ourselves for the future. The short timers told us it was just a matter of time and we would be as depraved or worse than they were. I said, no way!

We spent a lot of time drinking and talking about what we were going to do when we returned to the States; lots of lies and bullshit for the most part.

It was a tough trip for the morally pure to walk the mile to the PX. Prostitutes and child pimps lined the way. Little kids would grab us by the hand and beg us to have sex with their sister or their mother. "You have a really good time, GI," they would say. "Cost you only one carton cigarettes. No VD. My mother a virgin."

Typically, as I walked by the shops, a well-built pretty young woman took hold of my hand. She tried to get me to stop walking by telling me how much she liked me. She told me how handsome and attractive I was to her.

Once I stopped she soon rubbed her body and hands on my crotch in a most erotic way. Generally, she said something like, "Oh, GI, you are very big. You are number one. I want to make love to you. I make you very happy. Okay? GI, you come with me to my house." Once I began to get an erection, she attempted to unbutton my fly.

The girls were very good at seduction. They were professional. It was a war between my desires and my sense of right and wrong. It was a close battle each time. I tried to say no to them, but they didn't give up easily. They were persistent entrepreneurs. Often, they would be hanging on to my penis as I walked away.

I walked away buttoning myself back up, glad I still had my male organ and wondering what sex with her would be like. I was a virgin and wanted to have sex, and I was amazed by my willpower.

This same seduction scene could occur many times on the way to and from the PX. The entire mile was an erogenous zone.

What do you do with your sexual urges? Masturbation was taboo; the church said it was a sin. I did some of that anyway, and I hoped that God would forgive me, if he was watching. I didn't think too highly of God anyway, and I was very sure he was not watching me masturbating. After all, there were three billion people on this planet. A good number of them were probably masturbating or fornicating at any one time. He couldn't watch us all. I wondered if it would be better for me to make love to those sexy women. Most of the other GI's were sleeping with some "moose" (the GI name for a Korean prostitute). Nothing bad was happening to them. In fact, they seemed to be getting along better than those of us who were abstaining. They acted like they were having fun.

The word was just don't pick up a moose on the street. Get yourself a steady girlfriend and then there was little risk of trouble, trouble being anything from VD to a Communist insurgent.

One day a friend from the battalion and I went to the PX. On this day, two beautiful young women began to seduce us. Nancy, a lovely girl about twenty-one, was giving me the rubdown. I was excited and wanted to have sex with her. Conscience be damned, I was going to do what my body wanted to do. I accepted her invitation to her house for one carton of cigarettes. My righteous morality was lost in a few puffs of smoke, so to speak.

We went down some alleys into a maze of shacks and more alleys. I was afraid I would get killed somewhere. Maybe she had some friends who were going to mug and murder me. Maybe she was a Communist and would stab or shoot me somewhere in this labyrinth of shacks. No one would ever find my body. These thoughts were no deterrent. The sex drive is strong.

No problem, her shack was humble but clean. She shared it with several other people. Her bedroom had a bamboo mat on the floor and some pillows.

She took off her clothes and stood nude in front of me as I looked at her with open mouth and eyes. She was a gorgeous woman. Her body looked perfect. She laid down on the mat.

She asked me to take off my clothes. I was self-conscious and apprehensive, but I took them off. She told me to lie down on the mat extending her hand up to mine. I took her hand. She pulled me gently down to her.

"You virgin, GI?" she asked knowingly.

I stumbled around with some words, embarrassed by my virginity.

She laughed and said, "No problem. I will help you." She did. My virginity was lost in seconds. The only telling of loss was my foreskin. I had not been circumcised, and it was ripped and bleeding. No matter. Sex was absolutely wonderful.

Nancy was a very gentle person. She spoke "GI English," enough so we could communicate quite easily. I think she and her family had suffered terribly during the war. She had been married to a Korean soldier who had been killed in the fighting.

She lived with relatives in this small shack of a house. There were at least five of them. I never learned for sure who they all were. One was her mother, and one her grandmother. I believe she provided most of the income for everyone in the house.

Her shack was like the others, essentially made of tin, strips of wood, and cardboard. Much of the tin had come from GI food containers. The entire area of Yong Dong Po had been devastated by the war. The Communists and the Allies had fought their way back and forth through the city at least three times. The people had been ravaged and their country was essentially destroyed. Prostitution, money changing, and the black market had become their way of life and their economy. They were living within this new system. They were clever determined survivors.

I don't believe there was a large building standing in Yong Dong Po that was not riddled with bullet holes or bombed into rubble. I never saw one.

I saw the poorest people I had ever seen on the streets of Seoul. They were dressed in rags. Not clothes, just rags. We called them "koogies." I had been well dressed at Spring Valley compared to these people.

One day on a street corner in Seoul I saw a small group of koogies skin some rats and boil them in a large tin can over a little fire they had built. They ate

DON HAUGEN

the rats. Dogs and cats also did not last long on the streets in this part of Korea. There were many hungry people.

I was stationed at the railroad battalion for eight months. I saw Nancy often during my remaining time. We became good friends. I'm sure she continued to ply her trade with other soldiers. But we never talked about it, and I never saw any of the others.

Many soldiers fell in love with prostitutes. Several tried to marry them and bring them back to the States. We were constantly warned by the Army of the difficulties we would encounter if we took home a Korean wife.

I had a rewarding friendship with Nancy, but I never talked with her about getting married or bringing her to the States. We just ignored that issue all together.

After about eight months in Yong Dong Po, I was reassigned to a new unit in Taegu, a city far to the south of Yong Dong Po. Nancy wanted to come to Taegu with me. I told her that after I had gotten settled in, I would send a letter telling her where I was in the city and when to come.

As soon as I was settled, I sent her a letter asking her to come to me. She never replied, and I don't know if she ever received the letter. There was no way to call her. She never came to Taegu.

My new job was on a water point, providing clean potable water for the American forces in our section of Taegu. There were four of us who lived at the point. Our half-acre compound was surrounded by a high fence, at least twelve feet high, with barbwire at the top. Armed guards from the Korean Army patrolled the perimeter every day. We were in the heart of an area heavily populated with shacks. We each had M-2 carbines and plenty of ammunition.

We spent most of our time playing poker, drinking, and chasing women. I guess this is how Larry had acquired his skill and interest in these activities—the same way I was acquiring them now.

I continued to receive letters from home. I learned that Larry had married his sweetheart, Eunice. Dad and Mary had a baby. I could not believe that. It was like the world was upside down or something. Pauline had gone to the convent to become a nun. Ronnie and Midge were married, and Ronnie and Jimmy were in the Navy.

At the water point, our closest neighbor was a "honey bucket" man. When it rained, which it did frequently, the dirt road in front of the point became a sea of mud and feces. Then the sun would come out and bake this cesspool. The odor was incredible and unmatched by anything I had witnessed in Yong Dong Po.

A young Korean man worked for us as a houseboy. He lived across the street with his family. They had a small boy of about two years old named Bong Song Giddy. Bong's mother never put diapers on him. She would at times take him by the ankles with one hand and by the neck with the other and bend him in two, bringing his head towards his feet. She would hold his little butt out away from herself and Bong would poop. I couldn't believe it. I saw several women do this with their small children. It was amazing how efficiently this worked.

Our main base was about a mile from the point. It was very large and the home of the Korean Military Advisory Group (KMAG) and the Eighth Army. The Neutral Nations Inspection Team was also in the same compound area. We had a huge nightclub, excellent dining facilities, a large movie theater, and a swimming pool. I had been eating reconstituted dehydrated food for the previous eight months. But now I was eating real food, and it was fresh. This base camp was a show place for the Eighth Army, and it had the best of everything in this part of Korea.

On weekends the Army would send trucks out to pick up "business girls" to bring to the club. They all carried VD cards, which showed they had been examined by our doctors on a frequent basis and were VD-free. The Army thinks of everything.

There were a lot of girls who came to the club. They were all pretty. We danced and talked with them just like you would in the States, and if you wanted, and the girl agreed, you could take the girl home courtesy of the US Army two-and-a-half ton truck. It was a well-run system. There had been nothing like this in Yong Dong Po.

It seemed to me everyone on the base was shacking up with a business girl, officers and enlisted men alike. Some officers paid us in whiskey or favors to be able to park their jeeps at the point inside the fence while they spent the night with their girlfriends.

Occasionally soldiers from the DMZ would come down for processing at our base. They were wild and girl hungry, and fights frequently occurred at the nightclub.

One night a First Cavalry soldier fresh from the DMZ picked a fight with me in the club. He said he didn't like the way I looked. He called me a four-eyed bastard, or something like that. Those were fighting words for me, and I said a few unpleasant things to him. He hit me and I jumped on him and started beating on him. Soon everyone was fighting with First Cavalry soldiers. The melee spread throughout the club, trashing chairs, tables and whatever else was handy.

After a couple of months, it was obvious Nancy was not coming to Taegu. I started looking at other attractive girls. I met a petite, pretty girl named Linda. We went to movies together and to dances at the club. Soon we decided to live together. I felt a little guilty about what I was doing. But after a few days of guilt, I went ahead and enjoyed myself.

It was a good decision based on fact. I always thought, who really cares about me or what I do? The answer, based on my life experience thus far, was no one.

I went to Japan on R and R—rest and recuperation—for two weeks in June of 1955. I went to a resort village at the base of Mount Fuji in the lake region. It was a beautiful setting. I met a lovely Japanese girl named Tanya. We soon agreed to spend the next two weeks together.

Tanya took me to all the things that were fun to do in the region. We took the train to Tokyo. We went to movies and ate in nice restaurants. We went shopping and to the bath houses. We went boating and skinny dipping in Lake Yamanaka. We dressed together in traditional Japanese clothes and sometimes walked on the streets around the resort together in costume. We got along so well and had so much fun I could have stayed in Japan forever.

Upon returning to Korea, Linda and I did not get along well. It all started one day while we had been playing with each other at her shack. She announced that she needed to go across the street and buy some cigarettes. She was gone maybe fifteen minutes when a woman I had never seen before burst into the room and said that Linda had been hit by a truck and killed. I looked at the woman in amazement. I could not believe it. She said I should come at once. I was skeptical. There were still insurgents around, and I was not sure the woman was telling me the truth. I waited in the room for a few minutes. Finally, I went outside to see what was going on. Just then Linda came back. She was furious with me. She said that I didn't care enough for her to come and see if she was dead. I tried to explain that I thought it was a joke. She was not amused by the fact that I thought she was playing a joke on me.

I learned from Linda that Korean business girls formed strong attachments too. They tested love, not unlike the girls in the States.

Soon it was October, and I received my orders to return to the States. I needed to report to Inchon for processing out of the country. Yong Dong Po was on the way to Inchon, so I decided to see if I could find Nancy before I left. I hitched a ride from Seoul to Yong Dong Po and Nancy's old neighborhood. She did not live in the same shack anymore. I asked neighbors where she lived.

After considerable effort, I found her. She beamed with delight when she saw me. I was overwhelmed with joy to see her again. We spent a night and a day talking about old times before I had to leave. She explained that she had not come to Taegu because her family needed her where she was. She said she had not received my letter. Maybe she didn't.

I shipped out of Inchon within a few days bound for the United States. I had been gone for seventeen months.

CHAPTER 24

RETURNING TO THE USA

At Inchon, I boarded a troop ship with thousands of other GI's headed for the States. We docked in Seattle, and I was processed at Fort Lewis to go on leave and then report to Fort Belvoir, Virginia, to finish out my enlistment.

During the next two weeks, I went into Seattle nearly every day. I made some new friends at the base, and we went in for movies, girl hunting, and shopping. Mostly I was in awe of the people, particularly the children and women. I was simply amazed at how smart the children were. They all spoke English so well. And the women were so colorful. It was unbelievable to my eyes. I hadn't seen any American children or women for nearly a year and a half, and I had forgotten how they looked. That was the most remarkable thing that occurred in those fourteen days. I had been in Korea for too long!

But I learned a lot about that part of the world, and I had a gained a lot of experience with women and sex. I learned how to pass through boredom and have fun in places that were dangerous. I saw the results of war and its effect on people and their property. I saw how the South Korean people coped with the terrible destruction of the war and economic deprivation. In my mind, it seemed that the black market and prostitution were the underpinnings of the entire South Korean economy. I learned that drinking a lot of beer was a good way to keep my ugly childhood from interfering with my life.

Soon I was able to take a plane to Minneapolis. From there, the cheapest way to get home was to go out to the highway and put my thumb in the air. So I hitchhiked to Boyd, Minnesota, where my brother lived with his new wife and baby. I bought an old car and got a job with a power line construction crew for a couple of weeks to earn some extra money. All my old friends were gone. Ronnie and Midge were in the military, as were most of the other guys I had known. I visited Aunt Rachel. She and Uncle Henry treated me with welcoming warmth. I ate a lot great food over the next few weeks at their table. Aunt Rachel was one person I could count on for love and affection. I saw Dad, but spent most of my time with my brother and his family and at Rachel's farm. Dad and his new wife Mary had a small child. Their tiny rundown shanty of house was overrun with people.

When my furlough was nearly up, I drove across country in my newly purchased old car to Fort Belvoir, Virginia, a long and lonely trip on mostly two-lane roads. I took a stupid side trip to Cincinnati, to see if I could find my mother. But it was a waste of time, as I did not know her address or phone number. She was not listed in the phone book under "lost mothers," and her new husband wasn't listed either.

Fort Belvoir was good duty. I was stationed on a water point on the Chesapeake Bay, testing rapid sand water filtration equipment. This was interesting and fun to me. My mind was kept occupied, a very good thing, because it was rather boring here compared to Korea and the girls. When I wasn't working, I would go into Washington, D.C., with some guys and drink beer and try and pick up women.

I applied to the University of Minnesota for admission as a freshman and was accepted. Time went fast and the early discharge I had applied for to attend college came through. I left for Minneota on August 10, 1956, for another long trip mostly on "two-laners."

There was really no room at Dad and Mary's. The two of them had made another baby girl. The rumors were rampant that they were not even married. I don't know if they were or not. But the fact was they had two small children, and I didn't know how many of the big girls were left in the house. I could not believe my dad was still making babies. What in God's world was this man thinking? He was dirt poor, and most of the time he was unemployed. The little girls were very cute, but I felt sorry for them. I feared they were destined for the same poverty and neglect that I had experienced. Time would determine that indeed poverty and neglect would be their childhood and adolescent destiny.

I stayed with Aunt Rachel and at Larry's during this brief period before school started. Through my dad, I made arrangements to stay with his brother Holly and his wife until I found a place near the university. Holly lived in Minneapolis. He was one of those who had been shunning me for all these years, so I was surprised they allowed me to stay with them. But he and his wife wasted few words or time with me. It was understood that I would be out of their house as soon as possible.

It was at this time that I found out for sure that Albert Thompson was my dad's first cousin. I found out from Holly and another of Dad's brothers, Sanford. Sanford told me he had had a long-standing relationship with Dorothy Thompson over a span of many years. I concluded that this relationship probably included a love affair. Sanford told me he had always gotten along well with the Thompsons. Albert Thompson was indeed the son of my Grandpa Hans Haugen's sister. They all had known each other since my dad was a child. So why in the world didn't they try and talk to the Thompsons after my dad's accusations? And why did most all of Dad's relatives continue to treat me as if I was responsible for Dad's problems at Spring Valley? They continued to shun me even after I had returned home from the Army.

I enrolled in the University of Minnesota and began classes in September 1956 as a pre-veterinary medicine major. I was elated to be there. It had been a long and circuitous route. But I did it. I soon discovered I needed a job to cover the expenses that the GI Bill didn't cover—room and board, tuition and books, rent, food, auto maintenance, gasoline, clothes, movie dates, and beer. I was doing great until working thirty to forty hours a week caught up with me. Then I started falling behind in my school work. The car was a piece of junk by now and was eating money real fast. But I wanted to keep it so I could go the 165 miles to Minneota frequently to have some contact with family. I needed friends and family. I had no real friends in Minneapolis yet. By this time, family contact was my brother and Aunt Rachel almost exclusively, and I needed them for emotional support. By December, I decided I would take my final tests and drop out for a while to earn some more money. It would be the best way. I could do the college work, but I just did not have the financial means to stay in school. And I was unwilling to give up beer and a social life to do it. As it turned out, I didn't even study for my finals. I just took the final for inorganic chemistry and skipped the others.

I should have made getting my education a priority, forgetting Minneota and making a new life for myself at the university. But I didn't. I was too poor and lonely, and I couldn't handle it by myself. So I returned to Minneota.

CHAPTER 25

MINNEOTA, 1957

I stayed with Aunt Rachel on the farm a few miles north of St. Leo until I found a job. Jobs were hard to come by. But I found one working for Doc Merritt, the veterinarian in Minneota. I worked in his office and store keeping books, selling things, and kind of as a jack-of-all-trades. I helped him vaccinate pigs and unloaded cattle and hog feed from trucks owned by Sam Severson, Midge and Lorna's father.

I still had a junker of a car and little money. So I slept in the store at night on a cot. It was a miserable existence. I often thought that I was on a difficult road, and I worried about what was ahead of me. How could I earn enough money and get back to college? I would have been better off staying in the Army. I think too that I was suffering from some kind of post-Army syndrome. What I really liked to do was drink beer and have fun. After two beers I would begin to feel human, confident, and alive. My nerves would settle. So I spent a lot of time at night at Joe Dero's Pool Hall drinking beer and playing pool. Joe's was the Roman Catholic saloon. So I was for the most part, among my own kind there. There seldom was a "painted bird" attitude expressed toward me at Joe Dero's. No self-respecting Lutheran would go there. They went to Harold Friend's place.

In fact, Joe's became my dining room, living room, saloon, and pool hall. It was my home so to speak, until I ambled a few doors down to Merritt's store to go to sleep. I had learned to handle my drinking quite well. I would just get enough of a buzz to feel good about myself. This enabled me to have pretty good social life with the young women in the area.

I took a particular fancy to Lorna Severson, Midge's little sister, the one I was not supposed to date or mess with. She was about seventeen years old, but she could have passed for twenty-one. She was a very good-looking young woman now in a fine-looking body, and we liked one another.

I am not sure why she liked me, but I knew why I liked her. She was high-spirited, intelligent, attractive, liked to talk, and she was a lot of fun to be with. She liked to smoke and drink a little, and she was really good at necking.

There was only one little problem. Her mother disliked me intensely. I was Elling's kid, the one who let Elling starve at that farm near Spring Valley. Unfortunately for me, Lorna's other boyfriend was my cousin, Dick. Dick's mother was my dad's sister, Bertha, who hated me. So Lorna had been hearing venomous gossip about me for four years. I was surprised she would have anything to do with me. But I think she liked being with me because I was forbidden fruit. In fact, Lorna agreed to go out with me only if her mother wouldn't suspect me as a boyfriend. So our dates were clandestine.

I went over to her house a lot, and I don't know why her mother allowed that. Perhaps when Lorna invited me over, her mother wasn't around. The Severson's had an one-room "in-law" apartment in their house, and I would meet with Lorna there. There we sat and talked, maybe have a beer or two and act like friends, which we were. We never got down to any serious petting there because her mother was just a wall and a door away.

When we got into my car, and during the course of the evening parked, we could do some serious necking. She was a tiger—bold. I could be sitting there talking with her and she would suddenly jump on me and start French kissing. Thinking that the bold kisses were an invitation for a more aggressive move on my part, I would initiate a bolder move myself. At times this would be acceptable, and at other times, my actions would be followed by her sitting up and placing her back against the dash and passenger side door. From that position, she would slap me hard in the face. I did not like being slapped, so I would slap her right back and then she would slap me. That would continue for several minutes until we would burst out laughing at what we were doing.

Sometimes for no apparent reason she would look at me and smile and then push me really hard in the chest with both hands, I would do the same to her.

This pushing and shoving would continue until we began to laugh together at what we were doing.

She often said at these times, "I shouldn't be with you. My mother doesn't like you. We should not be doing this."

I would say, "Yes, so what?"

We had a fun time together. I adored her spirit and boldness. But I knew she saw me as a kind of a forbidden "boy toy." I was an opportunity to experiment with her own sexuality. But we never did have sex together. I always respected her wishes when she said no. She was still an adolescent, but in a woman's body, and I enjoyed being with her. But in this case I was not a boy. I was a young man with a lot of experience with women, so I didn't limit my "dating" to Lorna alone.

I went to local ballrooms and met girls. Often I would take a girl home after the dance and do some serious necking. This was a common thing to do in our part of the country. I got in a lot of fights at these dances. Usually they were not serious, and no one was badly hurt. But I was too willing to fight. As the spring turned to summer, I was dating several girls at one time and drinking more and more. I was becoming more irresponsible all the time.

I made friends with some of guys from town who were a little younger than me. I was a bad influence on them. I had become self-destructive, I think. One night I took some friends to Canby, where we had way too much to drink. Instead of driving down good old Highway 68 back to Minneota, a distance of about twenty-five miles, I drove my junker down the railroad tracks all the way to Minneota. It was completely irresponsible, but it was crazy fun. Some nights I would not even come back to Merritt's store to sleep. I would just sleep on the beach in the sand at Lake Cochran, or I would wake up in the car in front of the bar I had been in the night before.

About mid-summer, Lorna told me she would not be able to see me anymore. She did not feel our relationship was going to have a good ending. I more or less said. "Okay, if that is the way you want it. It's okay with me." She suggested we brand ourselves, and in so doing we would tie ourselves together for all time. She decided that we should burn a scar into the top of our left wrists symbolizing our unity. A good idea, I thought. So we took a lighted cigarette and held it to each other's wrist and burned a deep hole in the center top of the wrist. We even blew on the cigarette's lighted end to make it glow and become hotter. We were definitely branded for life.

I knew she had chosen Dick to be her acceptable boyfriend. Her parents liked him. Although, I pretended like I wasn't hurt by her decision, I was devastated. I loved that girl, even if she was just a teeny-bopper in a woman's body. In my mind and eyes she was wonderful. She was good looking, bold, and intelligent—just the kind of person I would want to spend the rest of my life with.

I didn't really realize how much I was in love with her until she was gone. Then I hurt. Of course, I knew I was not a prize. I was unacceptable to her parents and way too wild and irresponsible. And I couldn't seem to change my ways.

After Lorna said goodbye, I drowned my sorrows in a lot of beer over the next few weeks while I continued to pursue other girls. I got way too serious with one or two of them. But I didn't care that much for them. I was only interested in sex.

The Chevrolet dealer in Minneota approached me one day and said he would like to sell me a new car. I was tired of my old junker and wanted a new car, but I couldn't afford one. But the dealer didn't regard that as a reason not to buy. It didn't take much convincing; I was soon the proud owner of a new salmon and white 1957 Chevrolet, one of the coolest cars ever built.

It was a sure-fire car for picking up girls. Fortunately for me, one day in early fall, I met a really pretty girl from Porter while some of my friends and I were pheasant hunting. She was riding around in her parent's car with a girlfriend. One of the girls knew one of the men in my car, and that helped in picking them up. They liked my '57 Chevy. We struck up a conversation and soon the girls were riding with us. I liked one of the girls, Lorraine, right away. She seemed bright and bold, so I asked to see her again when we took the girls back to her car. She agreed to a date in a few days.

Lorraine had a slight cold and she sounded like Barbara Stanwyck when I picked her up at her parents' home in Porter for our date. She looked like a young slender eighteen-year-old version of Barbara Stanwyck too. We hit it off right away and were soon seeing each other almost everyday.

I had slowed down on drinking but hadn't stopped, and I was still doing some crazy and dangerous things. Four of us decided that we could make a little extra money by hunting jack rabbits and selling their pelts and carcasses, which were worth about three dollars a piece.

So a couple of time a week I would drive over west of Canby near the Dakota border and look for large hayfields that had been cut and now were stubble. Once in a field, we turned off our headlights and rolled down all four windows. Each of us had a loaded shotgun in the car. The front seat passenger and the rear seat passengers would put the barrels of their shoguns out the window and be ready to shoot. We would cruise the field slowly until we saw some jack rabbits, then turn on the headlights and blast away at them as they ran to escape our speeding car and the shotgun blasts. Guys were firing out of all three windows at one time. We were a jack rabbit assault vehicle. It only took minutes, and we would have several jacks.

A few fields and we would have about thirty of our prey for a short nights work. It was hilariously fun and profitable. But as I look back, it was stupid, mean, and dangerous.

Lorraine and I became more involved, and by January it was clear that she was pregnant. Her parents were unhappy, and Lorraine was very concerned. I was thinking, How did that happen? Well, it happened the way it always has happened. I proposed to Lorraine, and she accepted. Her parents insisted on a church wedding. We were married at the Porter Lutheran church on the coldest day in February 1958. It was a crystal clear twenty-five degrees below zero that sunny day.

I had one little problem come up. I had been so irresponsible in keeping up the car payments that my beautiful 1957 Chevrolet was repossessed. In addition, Doc Merritt laid me off because he did not have enough work for me. I think the real reason was that I just had been too unreliable as a worker in the past few months.

So Lorraine and I went on an extremely brief honeymoon using her dad's car. I could not believe how embarrassed I felt. I lost my job and my car just a few days before I married Lorraine. Her parents were horrified. But Lorraine was a courageous young woman. She believed in us.

CHAPTER 26

A MARRIED MAN, 1958 TO 1964

In a few days, I bought another old junker and took a job selling Culligan Soft Water door to door in the Marshall area. We rented a little house in Minneota and set up housekeeping. How strange it was to have Lorraine stay all night and be there the next morning. I saw her use the bathroom and take showers. She indeed lived permanently in the same house with me. She truly was my pretty live-in wife.

We no more than had settled in and, as luck would have it, I developed appendicitis. I needed emergency surgery and had no insurance. So we ran up a sizable medical bill. I was out selling Culligan water softeners door to door in Marshall four days after surgery. We were dollar desperate.

Fortunately, I did well selling Culligan, and soon the major employer in Minneota had heard of my sales prowess. "Doc" Kerr owned Kerr's Hatchery and Feed Store and Lord only know what else. He was probably the richest man in the entire area. He offered me a job selling baby chicks to farmers over a wide area north of Minneota and far in into South Dakota, along with a company van to use. I took the job. It was a good job, and I was very successful at it. Selling baby chicks to farmers was much easier than selling water softeners door to door in town.

Our son was born in September 1958 on a bright and sunny Labor day. He was a healthy little fellow who tried the abilities of his totally inept young parents. He soon had his nights and days mixed up. He slept all day and cried all night. Fortunately this ended after about eight months because Lorraine and

I were beginning to look pretty haggard. We were at our wit's end as how to cope with our new baby. We did not have insurance so we ran up another bill at the hospital with my son's birth too. That added to my appendectomy bill gave us a lot of unexpected debt.

Aunt Rachel had been disappointed that Lorraine and I were not married in the Catholic Church. I was disappointed too. On several occasions I expressed these feelings to Lorraine. I think to please me, she told me one day that she would like to become Catholic, which she did. She took instructions and was baptized, and a day or so later we were remarried in a Catholic ceremony at St. Edward's. Our son Donnie was baptized the same day.

Lorraine's mother was furious. Within a few days the minister of the Porter Lutheran Church started visiting Lorraine while I was at work. He told her that she could not gain the kingdom of heaven through Catholicism and was destined to burn in hell for sure. Of course, Lorraine was very upset after these unwanted visits by the preacher. So we talked to Father Hoffman, the priest at St. Edward's, about our preacher problem. He said the next time the preacher came, to send him over to talk with him about theology. He said he had not had a good argument with a Protestant for a long time. So the next time the preacher came to berate Lorraine, she sent him up to Father Hoffman. The preacher never returned, and Lorraine's mother settled down and accepted her now-Catholic daughter, son-in-law, and grandchild with love and respect.

Intolerance and prejudice among Christians had reared its ugly head again. It was still true that Lutherans and Catholics disliked each other. Fortunately, Lorraine's parents never again gave us a bad time regarding religion, or anything else for that matter.

Lorraine and I had a little baby girl in October of 1959. We named her Anastasia. She was so cute, but she began to dehydrate immediately after birth. She had to spend the first two weeks of her life at a hospital in Sioux Falls, South Dakota, to receive special care. Anastasia did well in Sioux Falls, and we brought home our healthy little girl after a couple of weeks. We did not yet have adequate health insurance, so we ran up more bills.

The car broke down, and we bought another junker. Our debt was becoming scary. Then one day, I got into an argument with Doc Kerr over some petty thing and in a fit of anger with him, I quit my job. It was stupid of me, and I realized it the next morning. I trudged over to Kerr's office and apologized to him profusely, begging for forgiveness. He was a tough character, and he sent me out of his office while he and his right hand man, Eddie, talked about the situation. I heard Kerr ask Eddie which Haugen family I belonged to.

Eddie said, "He's Elling Haugen's boy, the one that was involved in that slavery thing down at Spring Valley a few years ago."

I heard some more talk. Then Doc came out of his office and said that I could not have my job back. I was crushed. I had been his most productive salesman. The stigma attached to me because I was with my father at Spring Valley was at work again.

Lorraine and I were bitterly disappointed with the loss of my job. I was dumbfounded by my own stupidity. I knew better than to argue with Doc Kerr. There were no other jobs in Minneota. I found a low-paying job in a furniture store in Marshall. Lorraine had to find a job to keep up with our bills. She took her first job ever, as a bookkeeper at Gambles in Marshall. Our children went to childcare. We both needed to work to earn as much as I was making with Doc Kerr.

Even with both of us working, we could not catch up on the debt we had accumulated since getting married. Now we needed another car. Our clunker had died because of a cracked head, and we had no money or credit. Most of our debt had come from hospital bills. We were being harassed by a bill collection agency almost on a daily basis. I went to an attorney to see what he could do to keep the creditors from garnishing our wages and harassing us with phone calls. The attorney took a look at our debt and our income and advised bankruptcy. We were reluctant and embarrassed, but there seemed to be no other way. We were warned that our credit would be ruined if we did it. But we were desperate to escape the harassment, so we did it. To my amazement a used-car salesman came around in a few days and said he heard I needed a car. I said I do but I can't afford one. He said that would not be a problem. He could arrange a loan, and he sold us a 1958 Ford station wagon that had about 60,000 miles on it and a good case of fender rot from salt. But it ran well, and we were so pleased that we could even buy it.

One creditor came to me at my place of work with two friends and insulted me for filing bankruptcy. There was no need to try and explain. I told them I was sorry but that I had no choice. They were angry at me, and I was furious with them and wanted to kick their brains in. But I couldn't afford to lose my job. I really had had enough. Where in God's name was fairness and justice in this world? Other people seemed to have good parents and family who cared about them and helped them. In my mind, I believed I had been permanently screwed by fate. God, if he existed, which I doubted, really did not give a damn about me.

I realized now that I had a problem. My life experiences were taking their toll on my common sense and behavior. I was not doing well even though I had a loving and devoted wife. I needed some help. I learned about a psychologist in Marshall, Paul Hauck, who was well regarded. I began psychotherapy with Doctor Hauck and continued it for about one year. I went to talk with him once a week. I poured out all the miserable tales of my childhood, Spring Valley, and everything since. I talked about my mother and father, my relatives, the shunning, the drinking, the tendency to fight. I talked about everything freely and openly. I unburdened my soul to a man whose ear was totally mine. He had a kindness and understanding I had not seen before in anyone. He was the most understanding and compassionate person I had ever talked to.

During these conversations, I began to understand that I didn't belong in the Minneota area, where I would continue to be shunned and plagued with the stigma of Spring Valley. I needed a new environment in which to pursue what I had wanted to do since high school: go to college. Doctor Hauck agreed.

There were several other factors motivating me toward the decision to return to school. I needed to do well for my wife and children and create an opportunity to succeed for us. There was some revengeful anger that can be summed up as an attitude I held. It was an "I'll show you" attitude. I wanted to prove something to Lorna and all the others. I would demonstrate to her over time that I was indeed a worthwhile person. Her mother and all the others had been wrong about me. I would prove my worthiness by what I could accomplish. She could watch me from a distance. And she did.

I enrolled at the University of Minnesota in June 1961 as a freshman in the College of Science, Literature and Arts. I moved 165 miles to Minneapolis by myself and began the summer sessions. I found a room in a house within walking distance of campus. There were a few other students in the house. We each had our own bedroom and shared a kitchen. John F. Kennedy had become president and his Peace Corps program was being formed. The guys in the house listened to the radio with great enthusiasm as the names of those who had been selected from our area were announced. They were very excited about their chance to join the Peace Corps. I was excited about being in college. I had no thoughts of joining the Peace Corps. I had done my stint with the Army in Korea, but I was very happy that the Peace Corps was created and that Kennedy, a Roman Catholic and a Democrat, had been elected. I hadn't believed a Catholic could get elected president.

It had been nine years since I graduated from high school. I knew it was going to be tough for me to get up to speed with these bright young people fresh out of high school. I knew I also had a problem with public speaking. Every time I had to get up and give a talk to a group of people as a salesman, I was uncomfortable. I was able to conceal my nervousness even though I was terrified that something ugly would just pop out of my mouth. I feared something about my mother's sexual behavior or my own murderous and suicidal thoughts while at Spring Valley would come tumbling out of my conscious mind. These memories may have been in my subconscious, but they were also in my conscious self or, maybe more appropriately, they were on my conscience. Those things never did spring forth unwittingly from my mouth, but I never knew when or if they would. How strange that fear seemed to me; it was strange and yet understandable.

I decided that I must overcome this speaking problem right away, so I took a speech class on the Saint Paul campus that summer. I thought the students would be all farm kids who were less sophisticated and consequently maybe I would fit in better. I fit in fine, but they were not less sophisticated. There were about thirty young people in this class, all of them bright, and I believe they were all Republicans. At least there were many speeches praising the Republican Party. I did well on all my speeches during the term. I delivered a "bell ringer" of a speech for my last one of the class.

I spoke to these kids about the Democratic Party, President Kennedy, and the programs that we now took for granted. I informed them as to the origin of

programs such as the Civilian Conservation Corps, Social Security, unemployment compensation, worker's compensation, the Federal Deposit Insurance
Corporation, the victory in World War II, the Marshall Plan, integration of the
armed forces, the GI Bill, the Peace Corp—all started under the administra-
tions of Democratic presidents. There was much to thank the Democrats for.

That speech showed me that, when I felt strongly about an issue and my
mind and emotions were rapped up in what I believed, my fears did not haunt
me as I spoke, at least not as much. The professor who was teaching the speech
class told me I had delivered the best speech he had heard in some time. He said
he was going to give my name to the university's debate team and that I should
try out for it. The summer sessions had been successful for me.

Lorraine followed me with the children in September, and we moved into
the university's married-student housing project, University Village on Como
Avenue. University Village was a large postwar development of surplus military
metal Quonset barracks. The village was laid out in a rectangular grid, military
style. There were a great many parallel rows of Quonsets in every direction.
They were all "dressed down and covered right." There were four Quonsets,
a fence and then an alley. The four rows were repeated over and over again
towards the south. Each Quonset had a little patch of grass on either side of a
short sidewalk that led to a bigger sidewalk that joined eight Quonsets into a
common rectangular shaped block. As a result eight married couples were on
a small block, so to speak, with each couple's front door facing their neighbor
across the sidewalk.

There were two families per Quonset, one in back and one in front. Each
half was about 500 square feet. There were a lot of small children, perhaps
hundreds. Their laughter, screams and crying were a constant reminder that
this was married-student housing. There were no secrets in the Village blocks.
You soon learned when your neighbors were arguing, making love, or if the
kids were happy or sad. There was little privacy. The strife and happiness of our
neighbors flowed in, and my family's joy, anger, and sadness flowed out. Over
the years we learned to suffer the heat of summer without air conditioning in
our metal building by opening all the windows for a little cross ventilation. We
assisted the cooling by running cold water over our metal house with a garden

hose. We kept warm in winter by letting our "houses" get buried in snow except for the front door and around the small push out windows.

September 1961 was a busy one for me and Lorraine. School started and Lorraine began her office job with the Gamble Company. She had gotten a transfer from the Gamble Store in Marshall. Her daily drive was about 20 miles across Minneapolis to the western part of the city. We only had one car, our badly rusted Ford station wagon, and she needed it, so I either took a bus or hitchhiked to school everyday. Every morning we had to get Donnie and Stacy up, give them their breakfast, and get them ready to go to the baby sitter. There they stayed all day until we picked them up in the evening. Since my schedule was more flexible, I usually walked or carried the kids to the sitter and brought them home. It is an amusing moment for me to recall carrying the kids off to the sitter in the winter. They were dressed in what seemed to be very slippery snow suits. I would carry one in each arm along with my books the few "blocks" to the sitter. They seemed to slide through my arms and fall into the snow so easily. By the time I would get to the sitter I would have dropped them in the snow many times. Often I would end up carrying each around the belly with head forward and feet trailing. They seemed to enjoy this slip and drop way of traveling as they were generally giggling and screaming. Of course, the kids were little, Stacy was two and Donnie was three.

Money was tight for us and I often resented the fact that many of our neighbors did not have to work. Their parents helped them out. But Lorraine and I had to work. I worked at every quarter break and on weekends if I could find a job.

I took a full load of credits the fall semester. I found freshman English and the forty-five themes I wrote that year the most challenging. College algebra was almost beyond comprehension eleven years after high school. Like I thought, the competition was tough and most classes were graded on a curve. I needed to study to keep up.

The debate teacher did contact me, and I joined the debate team. I debated with the freshman team. Our debate topic for the year was, "Should the Non-Communist Nations of the World Form a Free Economic Union?" Sometimes I was assigned to argue the affirmative and sometime the negative. I was good at debate and enjoyed it. However, near the end of the freshman year I had had enough of it. The preparation it required while trying to keep pace with my other class work, earn some money, and help with the kids was just too much. Debate began to make me anxious, I was beginning to believe that I would never feel at ease with public speaking. I was just spending too much time worrying and working on it. My professor was disappointed when I told him I was quitting. I gave him my reasons, but he didn't believe me. He thought I could do it. But the truth was, I didn't like the pressure. If I could have learned to be more comfortable with my own fears of something unintended slipping off my tongue, I probably could have handled it. But I hadn't learned that yet.

I loved the literature part of English and humanities. I had no difficulty with Shakespeare and the Existentialists. In fact, it was like I was being fed a brain elixir. I loved literature, and the exposure to it made me feel good. Anthropology, sociology, psychology, economics, history, geography, and biology also were easy and enjoyable. I had chosen the right major.

On November 23, 1963, I was sitting in one of my favorite sociology classes when someone came to the door and called the professor into the hall. She came back into the room with tears streaming down her eyes and announced that President Kennedy had been shot in Dallas. I will never forget my reaction. I could not believe it. Tears started streaming down my face too. Class was dismissed within a few minutes, and I went home. Later that night, the news that my President, my Catholic hero, was dead moved Lorraine and me to tears as we sat and watched the TV coverage. The whole nation was in shock. Lorraine and I were sure that some group from the segregationist south was responsible, perhaps even Lyndon Johnson himself. We never have really reconciled who was responsible for President Kennedy's death to this day.

I had many jobs over those three years. I found weekend jobs on bulletin boards at school. They were often day labor jobs, the kind you would not like to have for a career, like cleaning restrooms, washing and waxing floors, unloading boxcars, taking store inventories, mowing grass, and raking leaves.

Fortunately by this time, Lorraine had taken a job in the university admissions office, so the car was available to me. As a result, during Christmas break I was able to take a job in toy store in St. Paul selling electric trains and auto racing sets. I did this for three Christmas breaks. It was a fun job because I got to demonstrate the Strombecker car racing sets as well as the electric trains. Between summer sessions, I worked for Gehl Forage Harvesting Company in the parts department in downtown Minneapolis. My job was finding, bagging and shipping machine parts. I climbed around large vertical stacks of bins of various sizes, like a monkey swinging arm over arm and foot over foot to the proper bin, collecting the parts in a bag, and then preparing them for shipment. It was good athletic job that paid well.

My last summer was spent at a junkyard in St. Paul. I worked for a man whose granddaughter worked with Lorraine and put in a good word for me with her grandfather. It was a dirty job. The junkyard was filled with wrecked cars. They were everywhere. They sat individually and in piles in the huge dirt-covered yard. The wind constantly lifted the dirt, which settled and stuck to my usually sweaty self. Often I was so filthy when I came home at night that Lorraine did not recognize me as I walked from the parking lot to our Quonset.

I started out my new job where the beginning day laborers did. I began by stripping foam rubber out of junked car seats with a box cutter. To do this, I crawled into the car and tore the seats apart and threw the foam rubber out of the car. While working on the inside of the car, I needed to leave the car doors open so the man running the forklift wouldn't come along and run the tines of his lift through the windows and take me and the car to the electromagnetic crane. There were two dangers. One was to be pierced by the tines of the fork-lift. The other was being lifted to a great height and then dropped to a tremendous impact against the hardened earth below. This was a very effective gravity method of separating the car body from the axles, drive train and engine. The dropping did accomplish this separation of parts. So imagine what the drop would do to me if I had not already been mortally wounded by the forklift tines.

Once I removed the rubber, I took the battery out and removed the wheels. Next, I shut the cars doors and smashed all the windows with a long heavy steel bar. At this point the car was ready for the forklift, crane, dismemberment, and the baler. The baler squeezed the car body into a really tiny cube; the crushed cube of a car was loaded on to a boxcar with the magnetic crane. It was a very efficient operation.

After some time I was promoted to operating the forklift, which was a cleaner, easier and safer job. One day I was busy picking up cars by running my forklift tines through cars that had their front and rear windows smashed out and their doors shut, indicating that they were ready to be taken to the big magnet. I was a happy camper and all was going well. Then I came to a car that appeared ready. The doors were shut, and the windows were broken. I lifted the tines into position and accelerated the forklift. The tines went through the passenger side and nearly to the other side when they met a firm resistance. I put the forklift in neutral and walked over to see what was wrong. I looked through the passenger side rear window and was shocked to see that I had pinned a man to the back door on the driver's side of the car. The tine was in his ribcage. I ran back to the forklift and backed up. The man fell from the tine to the floor of the car. I jumped off the fork lift and peered in the car again. He was not dead but was moaning, and I began screaming for help.

Others came running over. Someone called an ambulance and within moments we heard the sirens of the rescue vehicles. TV crews from WCCO and KSTP also arrived. The TV stations were located almost next door to the junkyard. Everything happened so quickly. I could not believe what I had done. I was concerned that I had killed mortally wounded the man . I don't believe he was conscious when they took him away. That night the story and pictures were on the local news channels, but I don't recall that it stated the condition of the man. I didn't know who he was, but I think he had just started work at the junkyard that morning. I felt terrible, and I inquired many times about the man's condition. They told me that as far as they knew, he was recovering just fine, which did not seem possible to me. I have relived with horror that moment of puncturing him with the forklift many times since then, each time with a shudder.

The next day I was moved to another job at the yard because I did not want to run a forklift again. They put me on the battery cracker. There I joined some other guys. Like them, I wore a rubber jacket, apron, gloves, boots, a cap, and goggles to keep the sulfuric acid from burning me or my clothes. One at a time, I picked up batteries that had been taken from junked cars (and there were hundreds of batteries) and held it up to a machine. I pressed a lever with my foot and the machine would crack the battery. Acid would come pouring out and drain into a trough below, usually splashing on to my essentially rubber covered body. I would then pick out the battery's lead plates from the debris and throw them into a bin. I picked out the plastic housing pieces and threw them into another bin. I don't know where the acid finally ended up. They probably collected it in barrels on a lower floor and sold it, as they did with the lead plates. I cracked battery after battery at a steady pace all day long for the rest of my summer break. It was a dirty, nasty, and dangerous job, the kind of job that will keep you in college.

Another way I earned money was to volunteer for university experiments. Some of these were easy and required only a few hours in some kind of psychological study. Others were medical experiments. I quickly learned to avoid these after participating in one to test the average capacity of the human bladder. This experiment required me to be strapped down to a bed. A catheter was inserted into my penis, and they fed me fluid intravenously. They fixed the catheter so that I could not urinate. They would not allow me to urinate until my bladder had become so full that I was begging to be able to pee. As if that were not enough torture, they injected me with something that made me feel like I was very hot. Then that feeling would pass. The purpose of this, the nurse told me, was to determine how fast my kidneys would process this substance. I began complaining about the experiment to the nurse. She was not sympathetic, and I could not just get up and leave because I was strapped down. She did tell me at the end of the experiment that I had an enormous bladder capacity: something like 1500 milliliters. I vowed that I would never volunteer for another medical experiment. I believe I was paid sixty-five dollars for my trouble.

The easiest way I found to earn money was to sell blood. When the car needed repairs, or we wanted some extra money to travel back home to Porter and Minneota, I sold blood. It was quick and easy, and my blood was always in demand because of my blood type.

In the spring of 1963 the old Ford station wagon was about ready to fall apart. The salt from the streets had nearly eaten away the fenders and the innards. I didn't know if we could get a different car. We would need a loan, but I knew our credit was probably not good because of the bankruptcy. I went to University Bank and applied for a car loan, fully expecting to be turned down.

The loan officer was very helpful and steered me to a car dealer that the bank wanted to help. He made a deal for me with the dealer that included trading in my old Ford.

I wanted to honor the deal and trade my old car in for the new one, so I made the piece of junk look as nice as possible. I knew the battery hanger was rusted nearly through, so I fixed that up with wire as best I could. But lo and behold, I was within a few blocks of the dealer on Lake Street when "kerplunk"—the battery fell onto the street, and the car died immediately. Lake Street was busy, and it was hot outside. So while cars where honking and drivers were yelling at me, I scrambled to pick up the battery, jam it in somewhere and refasten the cables. I was sweating profusely. I wanted to get rid of this piece of junk. God was with me because the car started, and I made it to the dealership with the battery hanging precariously by the cables. About an hour later, I drove out in a brand new 1962 Plymouth with push-button shift. Our junker car days were over forever.

Those three years at the university were, in retrospect, a wonderful time for us. Lorraine and I grew into adulthood together, and we did a good job of it. We were getting on our feet financially and establishing good credit. We were making it as parents. We cherished our children, and took good care of them. We were a tight-knit little family. Donnie had started kindergarten. Although we both had to work and I had to study hard, we still managed to fit some fun into our busy lives. For example, I had always loved college football. So we went to most all the Minnesota home football games. Another source of happiness and camaraderie was our neighbors in the Village and friends from school. We had many "row parties," and although we have seldom seen any of our friends from college, we kept in contact with many of them for years by mail.

Another fine thing that happened was that I got my first pair of contact lenses through the Student Health Service. I was so happy, I could not believe it. They were often uncomfortable and scratchy, but I hated my glasses and learned to accept those hard contact lenses in my eyes. Those thick spectacles were an artifact of the past.

We went home frequently during those years to see our families. Lorraine's parents grew to love me, and I loved them too. The seemingly "possible bum" their daughter had married was really a pretty good guy. He was doing well by their daughter, and she was happy. We'd visit my brother, Grandma Blomme, and Aunt Rachel, but the rest of my relatives we more or less shunned. It was pay back time. I would stop in to visit my dad occasionally. Of course he had a new family now. But their home was a tumbledown shack, and the look and smell of poverty and neglect was obvious to me. Dad's inability to relate to me on any meaningful level during my visits was always a source of lingering sadness and disappointment.

I graduated from the University of Minnesota in June 1964 with a bachelor of arts in sociology and a minor in psychology. Finally, I was a college graduate, the first one ever on either side of my family. I had made it. Lorraine and I had made it together. I finally realized the goal I had set for myself so many years before while a high school student in Spring Valley. I did not become a veterinarian. My interests changed as a result of psychotherapy. My admiration for that therapist and the helping professions inspired me to pursue a degree in social work instead of veterinary medicine.

I was accepted at the University of Michigan Graduate School of Social Work in Ann Arbor for the fall semester of 1964. The school apparently was impressed with my application and the fact that I was married with two children. I had done some volunteer work with two different social service agencies while an undergraduate. Those agencies must have given me good recommendations. Anyway, the school turned my name over to the Washtenaw County Juvenile Court in Ann Arbor, which was looking for a young couple to continue a group home in Ann Arbor for delinquent teenage girls. The home had been started a few months earlier and was in need of someone to buy the house and continue the program. It would require us to live with the girls. The group home would be our home, and the girls would be our foster children. I was enthusiastic; Lorraine was apprehensive, but she wanted to try it. The court required us to come to Ann Arbor and for interviews with various people involved in the program.

We went to Ann Arbor in early summer for the interviews. They liked us and were especially pleased to see how level headed Lorraine was. They knew she would bear a lot of responsibility on a daily basis, so she needed to be well-grounded. They wanted us to take over the operation, and they wanted the house that would serve as the group home. Its selling price was $24,000. We had zero dollars. So what were we to do?

We borrowed some money from a professor who wanted to see the group home continue, and we borrowed from the Ann Arbor Bank on the basis of a good recommendation from the judge of the juvenile court. We also borrowed from the previous owner and took over the land contract he had been paying on the balance of the house. Thus we bought ourselves a beautiful, large brick home. We had one house payment and three loans to pay each month for a few years into the future.

Lorraine was twenty-four years old, Donnie, was soon to be six, Stacy was four, and I was twenty-nine. In early August we loaded ourselves into our 1962 Plymouth, loaded a U-Haul trailer with all our earthly possessions, and moved nearly nine hundred miles from any family, friend, or relative. The group home was our very first house, and we had bought it using only our own abilities.

I began my studies in the School of Social Work in late August. The school awarded me an all-university grant and a salaried field placement. The National Institute of Mental Health awarded me a scholarship to cover the next two years of study. In addition, we were to be paid an amount of money for each girl placed in the group home by Washtenaw County. Our next two years were financially secure. We were doing work that I wanted to do. We were both proud of what we were about to undertake. The Ann Arbor community had placed a lot of faith in us.

CHAPTER 27

ANN ARBOR, MICHIGAN

By the end of August, the first girls were placed in our group home. We enrolled Donnie in the first grade and Stacy in kindergarten at Bach Elementary School, only a few blocks from the group home on West Huron Street. I started classes in the School of Social Work and worked two days a week as a paid social work intern with Wayne County General Hospital's psychiatric hospital in Eloise, Michigan. Lorraine became the mother and cook for eight kids. We were now a family of ten people. A lot had happened quickly, and it was nearly overwhelming. Fortunately the juvenile court had an excellent staff, and the group home program had been well thought out. It allowed all of us to jump into our new and hectic life.

The Washtenaw County juvenile court provided each girl in the home with a caseworker who worked with her and her family. A group worker came at least once a week for group therapy with all the girls. She also served as our liaison with the court, the caseworkers, and as our therapist, so to speak, as we interacted with the girls on a day-to-day basis. As a rule, Lorraine or I met with the group worker several times a week. We had a consulting psychiatrist and psychologist available for the girls, and often school social workers were involved too. The roles Lorraine and I played in this scenario were as parents, albeit young ones.

The girls generally ranged in age from thirteen to sixteen. They all had been adjudicated delinquent or neglected by the court and removed from their homes. The behaviors that brought them to the court varied from chronic truancy, running away, theft, assault, drug use, abuse, and parental neglect. They were deemed fit to attend public schools and live in an open setting without bars and locked doors. The girls were allowed to go up town, to date, and to participate in school activities as long as they did not get into serious trouble.

They lived in our home, which was not identified in anyway as a group home. The house looked like all the other houses in the neighborhood. The girls dressed as they chose, similar to other girls attending school. They received a clothing allowance from the court so that they could be properly dressed. They received a weekly allowance of spending money and had phone call privileges. They could move around the house as if they were our natural children and had their own recreation and family rooms. We had a system of withdrawal of privileges to correct misbehavior.

I often thought that it would have been far better for me to have been in a group home like ours than to have experienced what I had at Spring Valley. The freedom, clothing allowance, spending money, and the right to participate in high school activities were things that I had wanted desperately as a teenager. It pleased me immensely that we were providing such a well thought out, compassionate non-punishing program for these girls.

I never mentioned my childhood or Spring Valley to the court or anyone else, including Donnie and Stacy. I did not want the court or my friends to know about my experiences, and I did not want to burden my children with that inexplicable story. They only knew that I lived in Illinois while in grade school and that my parents divorced when I was twelve. They knew my dad had remarried, and I had lived on a dairy farm in Minnesota while a teenager. This was the truth. I just never filled in details.

As a social work intern, I had a caseload of mental patients at Wayne County General Hospital. The patients to whom I was assigned had no freedom to move around the hospital grounds. They were in locked wards. I saw patients during or right after intake and then worked up a social and psychological assessment of each under the guidance of a casework supervisor. As an intern, I worked primarily with short-term patients, and there were hundreds of them. The goal was to determine their problems and how to best resolve them, and to return the patients to the community as soon as possible. It was a good program, and my work was well supervised. Each patient had a psychological evaluation by a clinical psychologist and was assigned a psychiatrist. However, each psychiatrist had hundreds of patients on his case load, so medication, as opposed to talking, was the primary form of treatment. I suspect the total patient population was well over a thousand in 1964.

On my very first day of seeing patients, Mr. Tinsley, my supervisor, took me to the fourth floor to meet a patient. I was very nervous as we passed through the locked cage-like facility where the nurses and patients were. Mr. Tinsley introduced me to a man about fifty years old. Just an average-looking man dressed in trousers, shirt, and shoes. I shook his hand and smiled at him and said I was glad to meet him.

He smiled back and asked, "Where are you from?"

I said, "I am from Ann Arbor."

"What are you doing here? Are you with the FBI?"

"No, I am a social worker."

"You said you were from Ann Arbor. You do not belong here. You are a spy for the FBI." And he went ballistic. He accused me of spying on him and listening to his thoughts. I didn't know what to do. The guy was getting physically threatening. I looked at Mr. Tinsley with pleading eyes. He just smiled and took over the conversation and quieted the man down. Soon a nurse came and led the patient away quietly talking to him in a soothing voice.

That was my first experience on the ward. Mr. Tinsley got a big charge out of my handling of my first patient. He explained that the man was a paranoid schizophrenic, and I needed to respond in simpler terms, knowing that he was very suspicious and could be combative. When he asked where I was from, I should have said that I was a social worker and my office was downstairs. I learned something that day, and I continued to learn much for the next year as I worked at the hospital with Mr. Tinsley as my supervisor.

There were several other student social workers on staff in the psychiatric unit. Most were from Wayne State University in Detroit. There were three of us from the University of Michigan. I was the only one to make it through the program of the Michigan students. We were exposed to a lot of things, like patient evaluations, which are important. A patient would be brought into a large room and seated at a table. In the room were the patient's psychiatrist, psychologist, social worker, and floor nurse. Several others who were in training for their respective specialty would be observing. The patient was interviewed by the psychiatrist and after about twenty minutes, the patient would leave the room. Then the caseworker would give his evaluation of the patient, followed by the psychologist, and the floor nurse. These evaluations would include previously gathered information from the client. We then engaged in an open discussion of a treatment plan, prognosis, and an approximate date for the patient to leave the hospital. It was all quite professional. I was impressed.

Most of the patients admitted to the hospital were schizophrenic, manic depressive, depressed, or anxiety-ridden to an extreme. There was always a significant precipitating factor that brought them to the psychiatric unit, such as an assault, homelessness, a suicide attempt, bizarre behavior at home or in public, and so forth.

I soon learned from other staff that one could tell the psychotic patients who were housed in the several out buildings because the medication for schizophrenics caused their skin to look sunburned. Sure enough, as we often walked over to the main hospital for lunch that fall through the large hospital grounds area, I learned to tell patient from staff by their sunburns.

The primary method of treating patients was medication. The social workers did most of the talk therapy. Psychiatrists prescribed the medications and psychologists did the testing. However, the hospital was using shock therapy for severely depressed patients, and students were given opportunities to watch this. I found this method of treatment barbaric and only watched it a couple of times. It was disturbing and inhumane.

I learned much working with the patients and staff at the hospital, and I consider it one of the best experiences of my social work career. I had never realized there were so many people suffering from severe mental illness. And this was only part of that population. Our hospital served only Wayne County, Michigan. There were also psychiatric patients at Detroit General Hospital. Ypsilanti State Hospital was about twenty miles away and had thousands of patients.

One day I was assigned a female patient about forty-five years old. She looked "normal" and was quite attractive. Her complaint to me was that she had swallowed a tape recorder, and it was playing messages to her. I queried her as to how she had swallowed it, because a tape recorder was quite large. She couldn't remember how she had swallowed it, but she had. And unfortunately for her, the machine was playing back unpleasant messages using obscene language. All of it was derogatory toward her. My efforts to convince her that she could not have swallowed a tape recorder and to help her understand that the messages were coming from her own mind failed. Medication did not deter the incessant machine. According to her hospital psychiatrist, the unfortunate woman was suffering from an advanced stage of syphilis. I could do nothing to help her except to hope that medication eased her misery over time.

The hospital could be depressing. It was frustrating to see so many patients with horrendous problems that I couldn't alleviate. Problems came in bunches for our patients. Mental illness, poverty, evictions, homelessness, unemployment, physical impairments, illness, and uncaring family and relatives were the typical clusters surrounding a patient. Wealthy people went to a different type of treatment facility for mental health problems. We didn't see those patients at Wayne County General. We treated the poor and the low-paid working classes.

The group home was far less depressing but equally challenging. Our girls for the most part were typical teenagers. None of them were psychotic. As a result Lorraine and I felt comfortable having them live with us and our two young children. Every night we all ate dinner together at our large dining room table. Dinner time was a highlight of the day. It was the time when all ten of us sat down together doing something fun and social: eating. Lorraine loved to cook, and the girls and the rest of us loved to eat. The conversations, for the most part, were not stilted. We succeeded in keeping the dinner time chatter good natured and appropriate. We were secular, you could pray silently to yourself if you wanted before meals, but prayer was not denied, encouraged, or required. But attendance at dinner *was* required unless you had a good excuse.

The court staff, the girls, and our family all got along and worked amazingly well together. The first year went by very quickly. We learned during the course of this year that Lorraine and I needed a regular break from the demands of our responsibility of caring for the girls, our own children, and my work. We took one evening a week for Lorraine and I to go out by ourselves. Sometimes we took Donnie and Stacy, and sometimes we hired a baby sitter. We usually had some time on Saturday or Sunday to do something with our children while the girls were out doing their thing. It was also part of the program to take off one weekend a month. On these weekends, Lorraine and I and the kids would leave the home completely. Usually we went to a hotel, since we had no family in the area. We also took a summer vacation of two weeks, when we left the Ann Arbor area completely. These vacations generally took us back to Minnesota to visit with family. We were paid well enough by the court that we could hire relief parents and babysitters during our absences. All relief parents were interviewed and approved by the court.

We nurtured close relationships with Lorraine's brother Gordy and with my brother Larry and their families. We stayed in touch with Aunt Rachel and her family, and with my Grandma Blomme. During visits to western Minnesota, I would always stop in and see my dad, Mary and their two children, plus Mary's children who still lived at the house. These visits were generally brief. Their house was not a comfortable place for me emotionally.

I finished my field placement at Wayne County General during late summer of 1965 and started a new internship at the end of August for my second year of graduate school. My new field placement was as family caseworker and administrative aide with Catholic Social Services (CSS) in Ann Arbor. It was an ideal placement for several reasons. First, I didn't have to commute to the Detroit area everyday. Second, I gained experience working with middle-class individuals and families. Third, I gained some insight in how a family service agency functions and obtains funding. I had a double major in casework and administration, so this fit perfectly. In addition, I was now closer to the group home, in case Lorraine or the kids needed me during the day.

Marguerite Parrish was the director of CSS, and she was an experienced and able person. Her staff of social workers were accredited with at least a master's in social work degrees, so I had excellent supervision. CSS had a consulting psychiatrist and psychologist too. We provided individual and family counseling, group counseling, foster care, and adoption services. Our funding came from area United Funds and the Catholic Church. We served anybody regardless of religious preference and charged them according to their ability to pay. A person with little financial means paid nothing for our services. Those who could afford to pay were charged on a sliding scale. There was no interference with our program from the Catholic Church. The program functioned as if it were secular.

My caseload consisted of a variety of clients. Some were teenaged boys with problems of truancy and theft. Others were married couples with relationship problems, and some were low-income multi-problem families. I also represented CSS to the United Fund budgeting committees of the smaller towns in our area in an effort to gain their financial support.

I continued working for CSS after graduating from the university in 1966 with a master's in social work. I did marriage counseling, individual counseling, group therapy, and worked as an administrative aide to Ms. Parrish for the next two years while I earned recognition from the Association of Certified Social Workers. During that time I was exposed to many of the problems that people from all social classes face when they contact a social service agency. Even with my work experience, my family background, and all I had seen in the Army and after, I was still often surprised.

I learned that there were some people who had very different ways of pleasing themselves sexually. One married professor enjoyed watching his wife have sex with other men in their own home. He would recruit sexual partners for her, bring them home, and then watch them have sex with his wife. Other men were extremely jealous if their wives gave any hint of being friendly to another man. Some folks paid no attention to their marriage vows when it came to extra marital affairs, and others were completely destroyed by affairs. Rich people's children could be thieves as well as those of the poor. Multi-problem families came in all colors and religions. But the most difficult to work with and help were multi-problem poor families. And like at Wayne County General the patients just kept on coming.

While I was chalking up a lot of experience at the hospital and CSS, Lorraine and I were chalking up a lot of experience as group home parents. Day-to-day living with the girls and our children was generally routine. But there were times that were extraordinary, and we couldn't predict when something out of the ordinary would occur.

Fights between the girls could break out in a bedroom or in the recreation room. These were usually tough physical attacks on each other complete with slapping, slugging, hair pulling, scratching, and cursing. Sometimes a knife or broken bottle would be involved. Fortunately we never had a stabbing or a successful attack with a broken bottle. Generally I was around in the evening when such skirmishes would occur, and I could intervene and stop the fight. However one night in the recreation room a fight broke out between a white girl and a black girl. It was particularly nasty, and the black girl broke off the bottom of a soda pop bottle and was intent on disemboweling the white girl. Ferocious yelling and cursing and name calling accompanied the melee, which of course caught my attention. I rushed downstairs to find the girls circling one another; the one with the broken bottle waiting for the best moment to attack. I told the girl to put the bottle down. I talked calmly to them in attempt to persuade them that no good could come from this fight and that they needed to stop and stop now. They were both crying and extremely angry. I was sure blood would soon be spurting out of someone, and then miraculously one of the other black girls stepped between the two combatants and told her friend with the bottle to attack her if she wanted to kill someone. That did it; the white girl backed off, the black girl with the bottle backed off, and the one who stepped in the middle took the bottle and threw it to the floor smashing it. The fight was over.

There were many suicide attempts or gestures by the girls. We called them gestures because they were efforts to get attention and often opportunities for the caseworkers to help the girl through some of the things that were making her anxious, frightened, or depressed. Frequently, a girl would swallow a whole bottle of aspirin when Lorraine or I were in the house, and she or one of the other girls would come and tell us what had happened. We grew accustomed to these gestures, but we took every incident seriously. So the first thing we'd do was call an ambulance and have the girl taken to the hospital. The hospital would pump the girl's stomach, then observe her and sometimes keep her overnight. Then we would bring the girl back home when she was out of danger. We never lost a girl to suicide. We had wrist cutting too. But all attempts were in the gesture category.

However one of our girls was a frequent user of Quaaludes, a drug popular in the 1960s for its sedative, euphoric effect. She was an intelligent, pretty sixteen-year-old with a nice family background. But she attracted boys like a magnet, and they were usually not the best type of young men. One weekend she went to her parents for a weekend pass. Over this weekend she was apparently using Quaaludes and drinking beer at the same time. She was with some of her friends, and when she lost consciousness they got scared and took her to the hospital. The very pretty young girl who could have had such a bright future died that night. We were saddened beyond belief by her death. It was a terrible shock to us and the other girls.

Beer, marijuana, Quaaludes, and airplane glue were our biggest drug problems in those first years. We tried to discourage using alcohol. We did not pay a lot of attention to marijuana, but we paid a lot of attention to Quaaludes and glue sniffing. They were both extremely dangerous. When the bedrooms or the recreation room was extremely quite at night or on the weekends, we checked for glue sniffling. Actually we generally could smell the glue, and that would take us to their rooms to investigate. There we would find one, two or three girls sitting around a paper bag with glue squeezed out of the tube on the inside of the bag. If we got there early enough they were just acting weird with dilated pupils. If we were late, they would be nearly unconscious, and we would rush them off to the emergency room.

We had acquired a large St. Bernard dog and an Old English sheepdog, both of which were female. They provided good companionship for all of us and a little extra income from puppy sales for Lorraine and I. We never forgot our days of being dollar desperate. The dogs were friendly but also offered us a barking warning when someone was trying to enter the house or were on the property doing something unusual.

The girls living with us were boy magnets, and boys over the years tried every conceivable means of getting into the house and the girls' bedrooms at night. This would generally occur after lights out at ten o'clock. The boys were inventive and bold. One night two or three boys found an extension ladder and placed it up to a second floor window. The dogs heard them, so we let the St. Bernard, who was furiously barking, out the front door. The dog raced around to the west side of the house just as the boys were apparently beginning to climb the ladder. They heard the dog coming jumped off the ladder and started running towards Seventh Street with the dog hot on their heels. I don't know how far they ran down Seventh, but I heard the dog barking as she chased them in the distance.

The girls soon learned to sneak the boys in when relief parents were in the house by having them climb over the garage roof and onto a second floor deck into the girls' bathroom. If Lorraine and I got home before the boys had gone, as soon as they heard us coming they would open the upstairs ceiling attic door and the boys would climb into the attic until we were asleep. Then they would come down, make out, and exit without our knowing that they had even been there. We would find out later, when someone would either brag about what they had done or snitch.

One night according to the girls, two boys came up over the garage roof and jumped over to the roof above our den, a distance of about four feet. From the den roof they climbed through our bedroom window, crawled across the foot of our bed, went out our bedroom door, down the hall and into the girls' rooms—all without waking us up. We were often very tired by the time we went to bed, and I believe we could sleep through most anything.

Problems would come up at school. Some of the kids got the bright idea they could shake down more timid girls for money in the bathrooms at Pioneer High. They would hang out in the bathroom, and when a likely victim came in they would shake her down for money with the threat of giving her a beating if she refused. It worked for a while until the school got wise to it and suspended the girls. At these times, the girls involved would be removed from the group home and sent back to detention until the court felt they could return to us or be placed in a more restricted setting.

One night three young men came to the house and wanted to come in and visit the girls. We didn't let just anybody visit. We needed to know who they were and whom they wanted to visit. They also needed to make prior arrangements; you couldn't just walk up to the house and visit the girls. I answered the door about nine o'clock in the evening and turned the boys away because I did not know who they were and their attitude was bad. They cursed at me as they walked away. A couple hours later they came back. They had fortified their courage with some liquor. I told them I was sorry but they could not come in. I stepped out on the front step to give them this bad news. One of them attempted to push me aside and enter. I became immediately protective of the house and hit him with my fist so hard in the face that he fell in some bushes on the side of the front steps. One of the other young men jumped on me, and we began to wrestle and punch one another in the front yard. I yelled for Lorraine to call the police. I continued to wrestle and punch this guy, and the other two took off running as soon as they heard the police sirens and saw the flashing blue lights coming up West Huron. Then the guy I was fighting took off running. The police gave pursuit and captured them. The next day the police called and thanked me for helping them apprehend three suspected criminals, one of whom was wanted for suspicion of murder.

Lorraine and I talked about how dangerous that night had become for our family and the girls. We decided to arm ourselves with shotguns in case someone really violent did get in the house. We bought two shotguns for the stated purpose of pheasant and duck hunting. But the real reason was in case we needed them to protect the family.

I bought Donnie a really nice bike. One day a kid came by the house and stole it. The neighbor's boy, a friend of Donnie's, saw who stole it and told us. So I called the police and told them who took Donnie's bike. Many of the officers knew me by this time, so they took me along with them and drove up the street several blocks to Jackson Avenue. We found the home of the boy who had stolen the bike. The police were familiar with this family and asked if they had acquired a certain bike. The people said no. But the police looked in back of the house, and sure enough Donnie's bike was there. The police scolded the family, and we loaded the bike into the trunk of the squad car and proceeded out to Jackson Avenue. Just about that time they received a radio call that a stolen car was heading towards the intersection of Dexter Road and Jackson Avenue, where they fed into West Huron.

We sped to a road block that was being set up by several squad cars, including ours. The two policemen in the car told me to stay in the back seat and keep my head down. They jumped out of the car and placed themselves behind the passenger side of the hood and drew their guns. The stolen car sped down Dexter Road towards the blockade. A police car with flashing lights was in hot pursuit, its siren wailing. The stolen vehicle screeched to a halt before hitting the Dexter Road blockade. In a moment all the police officers using their squad cars as shields were aiming their weapons toward the stolen vehicle. An officer on a loudspeaker ordered the driver to exit the car with their hands up. I looked through the window of the car and saw it was a white female driving the stolen car, and she was just setting there. She probably was scared to death that she was going to be shot. I thought the police may shoot her.

After several more warnings the young woman exited the car with her hands up. To my surprise, the person standing there crying with her arms in the air with all the loaded guns pointing at her was one of the girls from our home who had recently runaway. I told the officers this. The police soon had her handcuffed and in a squad car and off they went. They commented that I seemed to know a lot of people on the wrong side of the law. I was amazed that the police used so much firepower against a driver of a stolen car. There must have been at least eight loaded handguns pointing at our girl.

Lorraine told me one day that she was frightened by a girl who had recently been placed in the house. Lorraine said she had been standing at the top of the stairs when this girl came from her bedroom and stood next to her. "I felt like she wanted to push me down the stairs," Lorraine said.

I said that I doubted she would do that. The court wouldn't have placed her with us if she was dangerous. I tried to reassure her but told her to just not turn her back to the girl if she could avoid it.

A few days later the girl ran away. A day or so after that, an elderly woman working behind the reception desk at the Christian Science Reading Room was beaten and robbed. Within days she died of her injuries. A few days later we learned that our former resident was charged for beating and robbing the lady at the Christian Science Reading Room. The girl never came back to our home. Lorraine had developed an extraordinary sense about the girls. She could tell who was to be trusted and who may be dangerous.

There were so many incidents that we became immune to a variety of things. Somehow we just learned to take them in stride. These incidents did not make me nervous or frightened, just wiser and more observant of the people around me, no matter where I was. I don't think Lorraine became alarmed either. She had learned to use her intuition and trust it. I guess we became professional group-home parents.

One weekend we hired a court-approved couple to supervise while we took off with Donnie and Stacy. When we returned, one of the upstairs front windows was broken and the bricks around it were covered with smoke residue. While we were gone some of the girls piled their three mattresses in the middle of the east bedroom and set fire to them. The relief parents called the fire department. The fire trucks came screaming down the street with their lights flashing. The firemen immediately stormed the house ran upstairs and broke down the locked bedroom door with their axes. They quickly put out the fire but not before it had done extensive damage. The fire department also did extensive damage with their trusty axes. The three girls from that bedroom were removed from the house and sent back to the detention facility. It took about a month to make the necessary repairs to the house to put it back in livable order. And three more girls were placed with us.

CHAPTER 28

DOING GOOD AND HAVING FUN

In 1968, Martin Luther King Jr. was assassinated in April, and Robert Kennedy was killed in June. There were riots in the streets of Chicago at the Democratic National Convention, and there were demonstration on the University of Michigan campus. Detroit was burning and rioting. These were turbulent and troubled times. There was a struggle for integration on all levels of society throughout the nation. There was a national war on poverty and a bitter military war in Vietnam. In Ann Arbor, the Welfare Rights Organization was trying to flex its muscle along with the Black Economic Development League, along with the anti-war movement. Someone discovered a covert FBI office in Ann Arbor and blew it up. I became active in the local Democratic Party, was elected precinct captain, and our group home became precinct headquarters for the fall election.

I think it was at about this time that the party asked me to run for city council from the fifth ward. I was honored by their efforts to persuade me to run, but I felt I had my hands full already with the group home and my day job. I also wondered if I could handle the city councilman job. I would have liked to have run for public office. But frankly, I had some fear of being elected. It was a fear left over from my childhood and the Thompson farm. I continued to have a fear that I'd lose my self-control while speaking in public. Although I had spoken in public many times and always had done a good job, this irrational fear that I might make a fool of myself remained. But my ego never let me down and I was, by previous experience, an able public speaker. Nonetheless, lingering self-doubt continued.

I got into the thick of the national problems as they manifested themselves in our area. Many of the local realtors were angry that the city was attempting to get a public housing program started. Many Ann Arbor residents wanted a public housing high rise to be built in the black neighborhood on the northwest side of town. The city wanted to build scattered-site public housing throughout Ann Arbor. This plan called for small groups of public housing units in several different neighborhoods, including the more affluent ones. I supported this program too. It seemed like a better plan than to build a multi-story public housing building in one neighborhood. There was also opposition to the public housing idea on any terms. And the process of deciding and building dragged out. A group of realtors took advantage of this situation and formed an organization to buy older houses, renovate them, and rent these houses to low-income people. They created a private sector approach to provide housing for the poor instead of a public one. Their organization was called Ann Arbor Independent Housing (AAIH). It sought a comfortable umbrella organization to demonstrate their benevolence for the poor among the Protestant church community of the city. They won their refuge in the Washtenaw County Council of Churches, an organization made up of churches throughout the county, but mostly in Ann Arbor.

AAIH and the church council soon learned that there were a multitude of problems with the plan to move families into the few homes they were providing. The families were poor, often living on public assistance, and had few resources. They were unemployed or underemployed. They often needed furniture, transportation, medical and mental health care, and they frequently had children who were delinquent. I knew a lot of the families from my work at Catholic Social Services and the group home.

There was a need for a social worker and perhaps a social service department within the Council of Churches to help these families. Some of the realtors and church leaders had heard of me. They came to me and offered me the job. They offered me a good salary and a lot of leeway to set up a program. I knew it was a hot bed of trouble. Many people hated the fact that AAIH was trying to block the community's public housing effort and many felt the churches should not offer an umbrella of Christian decency for their efforts. I thought it was an opportunity to enlist all the resources of the Protestant community to aid in understanding and providing services for the poor who were in need. I took the job. I made CSS mad by leaving them, but I was ready to move on to this challenge and try my hand at what I thought to be a noble effort within the Christian community. The Catholics had a good program going, but nobody was effectively helping poor multi-problem families.

Our life as a family was also separate from the group home. Lorraine, Donnie, Stacy and I were learning to cope with the group home, my work, and live a good life at the same time. Donnie was a Cub Scout and in Indian Guides. Stacy was a Girl Scout and Lorraine was a leader. I was a scout leader too and served as the PTA president at Bach school for a year. Donnie played little league baseball. They both learned to play musical instruments. There were many children of their age in the neighborhood, so they had plenty of kids to play with after school and in the summer. We began providing for our kids everything we thought good parents should. We got electric train sets, Hot Wheels, and Strombecker cars and tracks. We built rockets and gasoline-powered model airplanes. There were Barbie dolls and bicycles, tennis and golf lessons. We spent a lot of time with them. We tried to do for them what our parents had not done for us.

In 1967, I had become interested in car racing. We bought a new front wheel drive '67 Saab V4 for $2700. Then I bought a '64 front wheel drive Monte Carlo Saab for racing. It had a three cylinder, two cycle engine with a carburetor on each cylinder. It accelerated like a slingshot. I joined the Sports Car Club of America and began entering various racing events. Some were small rally type races, some were closed-course obstacle races, and others were closed course road races. But my favorite was ice racing. I loved racing cars on lake ice. I started entering the Monte Carlo in events throughout the winters of 1967 and 1968. I tried to go to every race within a hundred miles. Lorraine entered many of them with the 1967 Saab. On race weekends we would bundle up our kids and drive off for the race. We would find a motel room and settle in for a weekend of fun. Lorraine entered the all-women Powder Puff classes, and I would enter the men's classes. I soon learned what it took to win at ice racing. I found that I could best compete with oversized snow tires that I had chewed up on a tractionizer, which shredded the tread to gain traction on the ice. Most racers did this because metal studs were illegal.

The ice racing tracks were laid out in a large oval pattern. The way to win was to go all out from the starting flag. When the starter dropped the flag, I put the gas pedal to the floor and kept it there. I could get that little "three banger" up to a 100 miles per hour on the straight away. I cramped the steering wheel hard as I approached the sweeping curved turns at the ends of the oval and let the rear end slide around as I skidded sideways toward the next straightaway. I kept the gas pedal to the floorboard throughout the sideways slide, and when I reached the other side straightaway, the little Saab bit into the ice, gained traction and took off as if it were fire from a sling shot. What a car! There were many races and many wins and some losses. It was so much fun. Often during these times of winter fun, I remembered my winter activities on weekends as a teenager back on the farm. Then I had loaded horse, cow, pig, and chicken shit on to a large horse drawn sled, drove the team of horses with the loaded sled into the field beyond the grove, and threw the shit off with a manure fork onto an ever increasing large stack of frozen shit.

During mid-winter 1968, Lorraine and I entered the Lake City, Michigan ice race, she in the Powder Puff and me in every class with the Monte Carlo. I drove that machine like a man possessed. I won the fastest time of the day on the oval track. I won my heats against the other cars in my class and qualified for the final championship race. The last race involved the three fastest cars from each heat in a final competition, which I believe consisted of twelve cars. This race was about ten laps around the large oval with all twelve cars attempting to end up first across the finish line. My machine and I were one that day. I left the starting line like I had been shot out of a cannon. I raced to the front of the pack and down the first straightaway into the curve with the pedal to metal all the way. I slid sideways around the curve, never letting up on the gas. I used the hand break when I needed a little braking as I approached the next straight away, and down I sped over 100 miles per hour. It was a blast. I kept the lead the entire race. It was the best race I had ever driven, and I won all the marbles. I won first place in the 1968 Lake City Wheel to Wheel Ice Race and got a nice big trophy and a lot of respect from the other drivers at the trophy banquet. Lorraine did very well in the 67 Saab V4. She came in first in the Powder Puff Derby.

During the summer I started racing road race courses, but it was not nearly as much fun. The hard dry surface closed track was not the Saab's strength. It liked lake ice, and so did I. I burned out several clutches in the summer of 1968, and it just became too expensive. I tried the Michigan Press-on Regardless Rally Race that spring but had to drop out when my navigator became car sick.

Around the same time, Lorraine and I took our first-ever family trip with Donnie and Stacy. Usually we took trips to visit our relatives back in Minnesota and stayed with them to save expenses. But now we took a long trip for pleasure. We finally had enough money to buy things that were fun and take trips to enjoy them.

We bought a new 1969 Ford three-quarter-ton pickup and a camper to fit on it. We had already acquired a sixteen-foot Thompson boat with a ninety-horsepower outboard motor. We hired a couple for a month to run the group home for us. We drove off with all are machinery plus a Hodaka dirt bike fastened in hangers on the front bumper of the pickup and the kids' bicycles in the bed of the boat. We were headed to Washington State and British Columbia.

We were a big rig with the motorcycle, pickup camper, and trailing boat. The four of us sat happily in the front seat of the pickup as we headed west on I-94. We drove the first several hundred miles without incident. We were near Atkinson, Illinois, on the expressway when the tongue of the boat trailer snapped and the remainder of the tongue, attached to the boat trailer, dropped onto the freeway. The boat and trailer began to zigzag. As I looked back, the tongue was dragging on the concrete shooting up tremendous sparks. The whole thing was literally wagging our pickup truck. Fortunately I had fastened safety chains from the trailer to the truck bumper, and that was why we were still connected to the wildly careening boat trailer. I was able to pull over and examine the damage. It was not that bad. We needed to find a welder to put the trailer tongue back together. We limped slowly into Atkinson and found a welding shop. He soon had us fixed up, and we were on the way. Lorraine was very concerned by this time. She hadn't wanted me to tow the boat and bring the motorcycle along. So she got on me pretty good about dragging all that "junk" with us. But I was stubborn and insisted on all the junk. We went to Minnesota, stopped and saw Lorraine's folks and brother, my brother and Grandma Blomme, and then headed west to the Black Hills of South Dakota.

We did the tourist thing at Wall Drug Store in Wall, South Dakota. We found Mount Rushmore and stayed in the area a couple of days. Donnie and I took the Hodaka and roamed the surrounding off-road areas where we might find buffalo. We found huge herds. They did not seem in the mood to cause us harm so we had fun cruising around observing them grazing leisurely on the grassy hills near Mount Rushmore.

Then we had to cross the Big Horn Mountains. No one had told us about this mountain range. With our big rig, it was a scary ride up, down, and over these mountains. When I saw the mountains looming in front of us, I looked at the map for a way to avoid them. There was none.

The road over the mountains was only two lanes, and it seemed very narrow to me, often without guard rails on the curves. The kids had been up in the cab overhang of the camper enjoying the view from high above the truck's windshield. As the mountains got steeper and the ravines deeper, to the point of being terrifying, we received a call on the intercom. The kids were frightened. They wanted to get out of the camper and into the front seat of the pickup with us. I don't blame them; it was scary driving that big rig with the mountain to one side and a drop of hundreds of feet on the other. I uttered a lot of "Oh, shit" sounds as I came around sharp turns and caught a glimpse of the valley floor seemingly a thousand feet below.

Fortunately, nothing broke on our rig, and we survived the Big Horns. Can you imagine what would have happened if the boat trailer tongue would have snapped and broken and the boat began to zigzag on that road with no guard rail? The boat was attached to the truck by two loose fitting safety chains to the bumper. These loose chains allowed the boat to zigzag but stay attached to the truck. We probably would have been dragged over the side by the careening boat. Lorraine was right. We should have left the boat at home.

We kept moving west and arrived at Yellowstone around the end of June. We found a campground in the park and proceeded to do all the tourist things. We saw a lot of bears, elk, and moose. One night a bear visited our camper and the ice chest we had hung by a rope in a tree. The bears were very able, and they smacked our ice chest to the ground, opened it and stole our meat. We saw Old Faithful and the Geyser Basin, Yellow Stone Falls, and toured the lake with our boat before we moved on through the four inches of snow that fell during our last night there. We headed northwest.

By this time, Lorraine was getting tired of the camper. She had figured out this was not a vacation for her. There were dirty dishes and dirty clothes, beds that needed to be made and meals to prepare. She decided she liked the Holiday Inn much better and urged us to keep that in mind, or we would regret it. I had already noticed a gradual withdrawal of affection, and the kids and I were feeling the heat of her discontent. She began hurling verbal barbs at us with increasing accuracy. We took heed of what she said and soon were staying in motels and eating out most of the time. Lorraine became a happier "camper," as did the rest of us.

We drove to Spokane and then north into British Columbia. After a seem-ingly short drive east, we were in the Canadian Rockies. These mountains were truly awesome. They were enormous and snow capped. We watched mountain goats, agile beyond belief, scale near vertical mountain cliffs. They and their babies must have suction cups for hooves. They moved with no fear of falling over the most difficult vertical terrain I had ever seen. We stopped in Banff and Lake Louise. We went trail riding on some gentle horses and later took our boat out on a nearby lake. It was the first part of July and the weather was very chilly.

We moved east with all of our rig parts still intact; no more breakdowns. We arrived in Calgary just in time to take in the Calgary Stampede. We were impressed with Calgary; it was a large and lovely city in 1969. It had the largest indoor shopping mall I had ever seen. And they had the Husky Tower, a space needle with a revolving restaurant on top. Of course, we had to eat a meal in the restaurant. From Calgary, we drove east across a vast Canadian plain toward Winnipeg, Manitoba.

Winnipeg is about four hundred miles north of Minneota and nothing like what I had imagined. I thought it would be a primitive frontier town being so far north. I was wrong. It was a beautiful modern city with lovely building and trees. East of Winnipeg, we found Kenora, a small town in the Lake of the

Woods region. We located a campground and stayed for three days. Donnie and I hired a guide, and we took our boat into the lake region. We were soon treated to fantastic walleye fishing. In the evening, the guide cooked the fish, which we thoroughly enjoyed.

There were float planes offering an aerial view of the region. Lorraine and Stacy didn't want to do this, so Donnie and I did. We found a pilot who made deliveries to people living on this wilderness called Lake of the Woods. We went with him one day as he delivered food and equipment to various homes on seemingly several different lakes. The lake region is immense; I could not tell one lake from another. But we enjoyed the several water take offs and landings as well as the view from the air. I told Donnie I was going to take flight training when we returned to Ann Arbor and learn to fly a small plane too. I believe he said, "Good idea, Dad."

Soon we were on our way again. We went south through International Falls and Ely toward Duluth, where we went east through Superior, Wisconsin, and headed for Escanaba, Michigan, and finally the Mackinac Bridge and Mackinac Island. We ate the fudge, saw the Grand Hotel, and a reenactment of the battle for Mackinac. By then we were ready to go home.

We had been gone a month and the group home was still standing.

In 1969 I took up two new interests: dirt bikes and learning to fly. I began flight training that fall with Gordon Aviation at the Ann Arbor Airport. As a child, I had wanted to be a fighter pilot when I grew up. But because I couldn't see the school blackboard from my front row seat without glasses, that was hardly likely. I cruised through my flight training with hardly an incident, other than getting lost several times on my solo flights around southeastern Michigan. Everything on the ground seemed to look the same from the cockpit. There were no road signs in the sky, so I had to learn to recognize landmarks from the air. Two good ones were Lake Erie and the Chrysler Proving Grounds near Chelsea. A technique I soon acquired without being coached was to swoop down on a small town and read the water tower. This was a very effective method to pin-point my location. My cross-country solo flights were often an adventure.

One morning near the end of my training, I took a solo flight to Fort Wayne and South Bend, Indiana. I needed to land my plane at both airports and get my student flight book signed to prove I had reached my destinations. The morning was cold, it was late fall and somewhat overcast. On the way to Fort Wayne, I noticed a few snow flurries, and the guy who signed my book in Fort Wayne warned me that I might run into some snow squalls on my way to South Bend. Soon after leaving Fort Wayne I climbed to about 3000 feet and proceeded west into ever-increasing snow squalls that soon became a storm. I was unable to see the ground below. I could see only a few yards in front of the plane or above it. It felt like I was flying in a milk bottle. I knew I was in trouble. I was trained for visual flight, not to fly by my instruments. I needed to look out the windows and get my references from the ground to know which way was up and which way was down. Soon I was not sure. I said to myself, "Don't panic or you will crash for sure. Stay focused, use your instruments, call South Bend, and ask for help."

I told South Bend tower that I was a student pilot caught in a snow squall, and I was becoming disoriented. In a nice quiet voice, the tower man asked me my location. I told him I thought I was about sixty-five miles southeast of South Bend. After a moment he said he had a radar fix on me and to take a particular heading and elevation. He told me to concentrate on my instruments and trust them. I put all my faith in my instruments and flew that little plane in the direction and at the altitudes he asked for. He talked calmly to me all the way to the South Bend, instructing me to reduce my altitude and change my heading until I could see the numbers on the end of the runway. I made a successful landing. His voice became more stern as he instructed me where to park my plane and to come to an airport office upon exiting the plane. I thought I was going to get my butt chewed. Instead he complimented me on my flight skills and having the good sense to call for help when I needed it. He signed my book, and when the weather settled I flew back to Ann Arbor. I learned something about myself that day. I could perform when I was frightened and under pressure and save my own life. Maybe I learned that at the Thompson farm at Spring Valley.

The job I had taken in 1968 with AAIH and the Council of Churches kept me busy for the next five years. I transitioned from affiliation with AAIH to the director of a newly created social service department within the council very quickly. I encouraged this. I did not want to be associated with AAIH's private attempt to provide housing for poor people. I supported scattered-site public housing. My staff was made up of students from the university's School of Social Work. Sometimes I would have one student and sometimes three. None of them were paid. Over time I also built of a corps of volunteers to help me.

I saw a lot of poverty and problems during those years. The churches now had a place to send those who came to them for help. They sent them to me in bunches. We had no resources to begin with other than AAIH's few houses. My primary method of helping those referred to me was advocacy. I tried to persuade government agencies to help my clients. It was not an easy task. The agencies were often unwilling to give up resources. The clients sent to me were multiple-problem families and individuals. They were generally some combination of homeless, poor, unable to pay rent, facing eviction, evicted, hungry, unemployed, underemployed, poorly educated, and emotionally or mentally ill. Through the Washtenaw County Social Services Department, the federal government provided what were called the categorical aids—aid to dependent children (ADC), aid to the disabled, and aid to the blind. The county provided a direct relief program. The programs that fit most of my clients were ADC or direct relief. Many had been on one or both programs previously but had been kicked off for some reason. The direct relief program was set up to help people if their needs became desperate and they were ineligible for any categorical aids. But the county turned down most requests. They did not like to give out local taxpayer money.

It took some time to get our city's public housing going. In the beginning we had a difficult time finding housing for people who needed it. People with a poor record of paying rent and little income had no chance to obtain housing in the private sector. No one would rent to them.

One my students or I interviewed every client referred to us to determine how we could help. If we learned that the client's problems may be eased by the ADC program or direct relief, we went with the client to try and persuade the agency bureaucrats to provide the help. This generally was quite effective. But on occasion it was necessary to refuse to leave the agency's office until help was given. We staged many sit-ins, and I usually called the local radio station and informed them that we were "sitting in" and why. This type of action brought a big headache for the office, so they would usually try to resolve the problem quickly. In other cases, it would seem more prudent to request a hearing before the social services board, which controlled the direct relief program. The help was always in the form of money or vouchers for food or housing. Sometimes we used these tactics on the public housing commission. As President Johnson's poverty program took effect in Ann Arbor, we used attorneys from a legal aid clinic. This generally was effective, especially with the county.

One day Jesus Christ came to the office for help with food and housing. My secretary told me he was in the waiting room. I walked out and there was a man in his early thirties, slender, about six feet tall with long dark slightly wavy hair and a beard several inches long. His face was quite handsome with deep-set dark eyes. His clothing was ragged and needed washing. I invited him into my office and sat him close to me so I could look him over real well.

I thought, "Well maybe he is Christ. How could I tell for sure if he was Jesus?" I studied his face and asked him his name. He told me in a steady voice that he was Jesus Christ, that he was born in Bethlehem, and his mother's name was Mary. As he explained his background it was clear that he was intelligent and articulate. I spoke with Jesus for about forty-five minutes. I asked him if he could perform a small miracle for me. Maybe he could do something to prove he was Jesus. He said he did not do those things to prove who he was. I could either accept who he was or not.

I learned that he needed some food and would like to find a place to stay for a night or two. Jesus said he had been referred to my office by the Ann Arbor Police Department and that he had spent a night or so in the city jail. I asked him if he had ever been a patient in a mental hospital. He said he had been at Ypsilanti State Hospital for several months. He said they had kept him there because they thought he was crazy, and they did not believe he was Christ.

I had some discretionary money, and I was impressed enough with this man to arrange for him to stay downtown at the Earle Hotel for a few nights. I gave him money for food. I told him that he was very convincing as Jesus Christ, but unless he wanted to end up in jail or the state hospital again, he shouldn't tell people he was Jesus. He should keep that to himself. I said most people expected Jesus to return with more fanfare. Maybe walk around a few feet off the ground in the surrounding sky and perform a miracle or two. And unless he wished to do that he should remain quiet about his identity. He acknowledged my opinion and my advice, took my money, thanked me, and left the office. I never saw or heard from him again.

After he left my office I wondered if Christ really came down to earth and walked on our streets claiming to be the Son of God whether we would recognize him and treat him well. No, I thought, most likely would we put him in a state hospital or jail. I thought if Christ did come to earth he had better create some impressive miracles quickly or we would pen him up and put him on Thorazine for sure.

I had many similar clients referred to me, but never another Christ.

I believed a major part of my job was to educate church people about the needs of the poor in Washtenaw County and to show how difficult it was for poor people to have their needs met by existing public and private programs. This took me to nearly all the churches to speak on these problems, either as a guest speaker during church on Sunday morning, or to interested church groups and organizations during the week. I was amazed by the number of church people who would not accept the fact that there were great numbers of poor and needy people in the county. If they did accept it, many maintained it was the poor person's fault for being poor and in need, and neither they nor the church had any responsibility to alleviate hardship the poor had brought on themselves. The favorite cop out was the harangue about ADC mothers' irresponsibility and promiscuous sexual behavior. However, there were many who felt strongly that it was a Christian's duty to help those in need. Often during my talks, heated debates began between the two factions. But I don't think these debates did much to change the plight of multi-problem poor people and families.

I began to see the churches as fine social organizations that brought people together for social and spiritual needs but not very useful for resolving the problems of my clients. Every case needed a new effort using the same procedures over and over. We were not establishing precedents or changing policy. I was addressing one case at a time, and it was the same fight with the powers for each client. I began to see the problems my clients faced were only resolvable in the long term by a change in the nation's attitude about the causes and prevention of poverty. I agreed with the 1970 Koerner Report, which said we were moving toward two Americas, the rich and an ever increasing number of poor. I have noticed over the years that we are still moving in that direction. Studies and reports seem to change little.

I often wondered how it could be that our nation, founded on Judeo-Christian ideals, had not brought about a more tolerant and helpful society for those who were suffering among us. Christ had said, "What you do unto the least of these, you do unto me."

I was hearing, "God helps those who help themselves" as the official national and local policy.

Meanwhile, back at the group home, the county health department was harassing us for having a cat litter box in the house for our two cats. They believed the litter box was unsightly and unsanitary and perhaps could cause some kind of disease risk for the girls. The obvious solution was to get rid of the cats. But the girls loved the cats, as well as the dogs, and so did my children. Lorraine and I discussed with the health department our desire to keep the cats, and they gave us some time to find an acceptable solution. It seemed to us that the health department was picking on a problem they could have ignored with little consequence. Nonetheless, we needed to get them off our back.

I set about resolving the cat litter box problem with a vengeance. My first effort was to put the litter pan inside a corrugated board beer case. I cut a hole in one end for the cat's entrance and egress. It wasn't long before the cats pee had soaked the beer case. Next I made a plywood box with a removable lid, put a hole in the end of it and painted the interior of the box with waterproof marine enamel. I then put the litter pan inside, but the cat pee soon peeled the paint and the box began to stink horribly as the plywood became soaked with cat urine. This was a tough problem; cat urine is strong stuff. I wondered if I could make the whole box out of plastic. Maybe that would work.

One of our group home girls had a boyfriend, a nice young man. I often visited with him as he waited for his girlfriend to come downstairs. On this particular day I was telling him about the struggle to save our cats from the health department and my need to make an enclosed plastic cat litter box. He said, "I think my dad could help you make a plastic box."

He said his dad was in the plastic business and could weld plastic. I had never heard of welding plastic. I got in touch with his dad and soon I was making a welded up plastic litter box with a lid in his dad's warehouse. It took all day to make, but it looked good. I bought a six-inch hole saw, and put a hole in one end. I firmly believed I had come up with a good solution to the pee problem.

When I got home, I put the cat litter directly in the box, placed the lid on and stepped back. The cats came to check out the new facility immediately. They went in their new toilet and did their thing. After a few weeks it was obvious that this was the solution. I began to think that a lot of people would like to have one of these. Perhaps I could make them and sell them through pet shops. The only problem was it took all day to just make one.

While I was working on this idea, Lorraine and I became the proud parents of a second baby girl. We named her Erin. Erin was a big hit with the girls and Donnie and Stacy. I think our kids were wondering how this happened. Mom and Dad were so old! Now there were eleven of us, two cats and two dogs. We needed a bigger house.

We had been doing well financially. All our loans were paid off, and we began shopping for a bigger house. Fortunately the house at 709 West Huron came up for sale. It was a large brick mansion in excellent condition half a block away. It had been built in 1861 like a fortress. It was known as Martha Washington House and was a landmark house of historical significance. It had twelve rooms on the two main floors and four bathrooms. The basement walk out level had four large bedrooms and two bathrooms plus a community kitchen. It was a gorgeous home. We bought it and all eleven of us plus our pets moved there in December 1971.

By this time I was making a few cat litter boxes and selling them through a local pet supply distributor. The litter container consisted of a deep plastic box with a hole in one end and a wooden lid. I cut the round 6-inch holes with my trusty hole saw. I made wooden lids and covered them with Formica. They looked nice, and I sold quiet a few of them locally. I had an idea however for a better designed litter box in my head, and I set about the task of finding someone to make it a reality. I found a plastic rotation molder in Tecumseh, Michigan. They told me they could manufacture my litter box, but I needed to have a pattern maker create a wooden pattern of my design, and from that, have an aluminum mold made to run on their machines.

I followed their advice and by early 1972, I had four aluminum molds to run on the machines of Jiffy Plastics. I named my invention Kitti Potti and applied for a copyright and patent. While this was going on, a Pitney Bowes representative came around trying to sell me a mailing machine. I wasn't sure I needed one, but I showed him my Kitti Potti invention. I had a real two-piece all-plastic cat litter box with the Kitti Potti name, logo and Haugen Products, Inc. embossed right into the plastic top. My idea came to life. He was very impressed. He said he had never seen anything like it before. I told him there never had been any thing like it before.

"I think this is a natural product for mail order," he said.

"I don't know," I said. "Mail order houses always seemed to me like shady operations. I don't think I want to go in that direction."

"Oh no, many are very ethical and reliable, I think your product will sell like hot cakes, you will make a fortune."

I liked the sound of that and we talked about the mail order business for awhile. I leased a Pitney Bowes machine from him that day. I took his advice and placed ads in *Cats Magazine* and *Family Circle* to come out in September 1972. *Cats* was aimed at people who already had cats. *Family Circle* would reach a larger audience as a very popular nationally circulated magazine available at any supermarket.

CHAPTER 29

THE KITTI POTTI YEARS

Magazines usually come out earlier than you would think. The September issues of *Cats* and *Family Circle* were in their readers' hands in mid to late August. The orders for Kitti Pottis started in August with a trickle, a few letters a day. Within a week they were coming in bunches. Hundreds of letters came to our mailbox during September; each one contained an order for one or more Kitti Pottis and a check. The guy from Pitney Bowes was right! Apparently Kitti Potti was a natural for mail order sales. Maybe it was possible to make a fortune with this invention.

Fortunately I had hired an ad agency to design and place my ads in these two magazines, and they had talked me into running them for three months in each magazine. Each new issue in the succeeding months brought forth a burst of new orders. Soon we rented a large post office box.

I was very stubborn about my idea for a better cat litter box. I obsessively insisted on making it a reality. I took seven thousand dollars of our savings and invested it in the wooden pattern and the aluminum molds to make the Kitti Potti a tangible product. My wife said that I was nuts. I thought she was nuts for not sharing my obsession and enthusiasm. I tried to get some of my friends to invest in the project. None of them wanted to. They too, felt that something had gone awry in my brain. Most tried to discourage me, none thought it was a good investment for them. Kitti Potti was mine, all mine. But of course, the money that came in was Lorraine's too because we were married, and it was our savings I had used. But we didn't have to share any profits or repay any loans.

The money we were receiving belonged to us. I thought, "Oh my God, we are going to be rich." I felt like I had won the lottery. What a feeling! I had been right. My obsession was paying off big time.

I was shocked by the number of orders and how fast they came in. I was absolutely pleased with myself. Actually, I was a pain to my wife for several weeks. I gloated over my success. I reminded her frequently that she had doubted me and had given me a bad time for spending our money foolishly. It was my own stubborn persistence to see my project become a reality that was paying off now, and I was enjoying it.

Apparently a cat owner could just look at a picture of a Kitti Potti and know their cat would use it. The darn thing was so simple it sold itself. I have to admit the engineering was clever. What I had invented really was just a two-piece plastic box with a purpose. Any urine sprayed on the inside walls of this container would simply drain off and fall into the litter. The box was a nice looking, practical private toilet for cats. I was sure that cats everywhere would appreciate the privacy a Kitti Potti could provide them. What cat wants to go to the toilet while others are watching?

At this point in time, I was still working for the Council of Churches and running the group home while selling and shipping Kitti Pottis. I was very busy, and all was going very well until the spring of 1973. Then I started to feel sick. I thought maybe I was working too hard, and it was causing my stomach to misbehave. I had some tests and learned I had a large polyp in my colon that needed to be removed by abdominal surgery. They removed the polyp and about six inches of colon. When I learned how much of my colon the surgeon had removed, I objected. I told the surgeon he had taken too much. I still had more than I needed, he said, and it was fortuitous that I had gotten sick, or I would have probably been dead in about a year. He told me most people at my age of thirty-nine never notice symptoms until it is too late. The polyp becomes cancerous, metastasizes, and it is all over. Fortunately, the polyp was precancerous when they removed it; and like he said, I probably had too much colon anyway. I lucked out. The recovery was difficult and slow.

While I was recuperating I decided to resign from my job at the Council of Churches. I was no longer interested in practicing social work for the council.

I was interested in staying alive. I wanted to just focus on the Kitti Potti business and build it. That did not mean I had lost my empathy for the people I had been working with. I had not. I was still concerned for them, and I followed the lives of many of them over the succeeding years.

But it was time to focus on something else. I started placing more ads in more magazines, like *Better Homes and Gardens*, *House Beautiful*, *Redbook*, *Dog Fancy*, *Cat Fancy*, the *New York Times Magazine*, and others. These ads brought hundreds of orders.

During the late summer, the group home was burglarized one night while we were sleeping. Shortly after that, we decided it was time to discontinue our participation with the court. We had been operating the home for about nine years. Donnie was fifteen, Stacey fourteen, and we had three-year-old Erin. It was time to leave. Our older kids were too close in age to the girls. We were tired, burned out, and getting paranoid. Too many kids had come to our home with friends with criminal records. We were concerned.

The court willingly accepted our decision to quit. They understood our reasons. So in October 1973, after nine years and two months, we concluded our career as group-home parents. We had done the very best we could for approximately two hundred girls who had been under our care. I often have wondered how each one turned out and if their stay with us made a difference in the long run. Over the years we kept track of many of the girls. In the short term, most of them were doing well. Long term, I don't know.

How quickly our family shrunk that October. By November there was just the five of us living in the main two floors of Martha Washington, our own sturdy brick mansion. We rented the four units on the lower basement level to women, usually graduate students. It was up to Kitti Potti now to keep us financially healthy. And I took my own health to mind, gut and heart. I began a personal campaign to make myself healthier. I had grown my five-foot-nine-inch self to a 190-pound fat person by doing a lot of eating, sitting, and listening to other people's problems. Those days were over for me. I began a regimen of dieting, motocross racing, and running.

Donnie was fifteen and very interested in motocross. I had captured his interest in motorcycles with the Hodaka that we had carted halfway across

North America and used to herd buffalo in the area around Mount Rushmore. Since then, I had gone through a Bultaco and Czech bike called a CZ, but just to do trail riding. Motocross racing was an entirely different sport. Donnie was ready, he bought himself a 125cc CZ identical to mine, and we began practicing motocross together. Before long we were into the 125cc-class Yamaha YZs, the Yamaha Monoshock, and the Honda Elsinore. We began competing in local races at a course near the Milan Drag Strip just outside of Detroit.

These races were grueling, body punishing endurance events. They drew competitors from the entire southeastern part of Michigan. Usually there were as many as forty bikes entered in each heat. There were several elimination heats in each contest. The heats lasted a predetermined twenty to forty minutes, with a final winner's heat to crown the day's champion. In each heat and in the final race, all forty competitors lined their bikes up abreast of one another with their engines racing in a growling crescendo. The undulating growling sound was like that of a bunch of strange powerful beasts. This metaphor is literally quite true. All the bikes burst off the line at the drop of a starting cord and raced towards a corner where an opening of about six feet allowed entrance on to the main motocross track. This corner was called the "hole." The young and bold roared across the 100 yards of wide flat toward the hole at speeds of sixty miles per hour or more. Bikes and riders often crashed into each other in the pursuit of a good hole shot. Other bikes raced right over the top of downed bikes and bikers or attempted to go around. It was a rough and dangerous sport, but much fun. Donnie raced for the good hole shots and to take the lead. I raced at a pace to survive the hole shot. He usually finished in the top five, and I finished in the middle of the pack. Two heats of twenty minutes or more, each "going all out" on a motocross bike, requires strength, skill, endurance and daring. You do not sit down on a motocross bike. You stand on the pegs so you can shift your weight and maneuver the bike into the turns and over the bumps and jumps.

The fat more or less melted off me over the course of a few months of running, racing, and practicing. I went back down to about 160 pounds, and I felt great. The quality of my life was improving rapidly. Motocross gave me an opportunity to spend a lot of time with my son. We were doing something wild and crazy in racing motocross. My teenage son loved it, and so did I.

I started my running effort slowly. I had too. I did not have the lung or leg power to make it up the West Huron Street hill from the bottom end to the top, a distance of about two blocks. My ability increased over time, and I was soon running around the block. Then I started running a longer distance. I ran from the house south to Pioneer High School and back, about two miles. Within a few months of running nearly every day, I was able to run about a seven-minute mile. I started to compete in local 10k races and then the Dexter-to-Ann Arbor fifteen mile races. I could do those at about an eight minutes per mile. I didn't know I could run that fast.

I soon learned that strenuous physical activity was really good for my mind and body. Running distance melted away tension. It felt good to run. And it felt so good to come home and take a hot shower. I felt like a new man after a good run and a hot shower. I was able to get the runner's high others talked about, and running became addictive for me.

Compared to the group home, the Council of Churches, and CSS, building Kitti Potti into a viable business was easy. It was much less stressful than anything else I had done. I kept flexible hours. I worked whenever I needed to. I had a lot of free time to do my racing, running, and many other things. And the money! Everyday the mailbox was stuffed with envelopes containing checks. Nearly everyday when lunchtime rolled around, we left the office together. Lorraine and I put Erin on the back of one of our bicycles and the three of us would pedal off to lunch somewhere. It was a very nice way to live. I had no idea life could be so easy-going and good. Why hadn't my dad and mom made a life like this for my brother and I?

On the advice of my friend and lawyer, Pat Conner, I formed the business into a sub-chapter S corporation called Haugen Products Inc. We rapidly added products suggested by pet owners I met at cat shows and in the letters from customers. People were full of good advice and willingly offered it. I think everybody likes to see a person succeed at what they attempt. Their desire to give me advice on how to run my business seemed to be a compulsive need. So I politely listened.

Someone told me you should make garbage bag liners to fit the Kitti Potti. People could put the liner in the bottom box, pour the kitty litter into the liner, and place the top over the bottom piece to hold the liner in place. With liners, the cat owner disposed of the soiled litter by just twisting a tie on to the bag and dropping it in the garbage can. They would not need to get their hands near the soiled litter. We soon sold literally tons of liners.

The corrugated-board box salesman told us we should keep the names and addresses of all our customers as they would become a valuable mailing list. We started doing as he suggested and placed the names into a computer.

Before long, we had a catalogue with about one hundred cat items. Then we added dog items. Soon we had a complete line of cat and dog products. We began mailing catalogues to our customers twice a year, and we placed one in each Kitti Potti we shipped. I found listening to the people was all I needed to do to make my business successful. The salespeople who called on our customers and on us became our product advisors.

Cat owners loved the Kitti Potti. They invited us to cat shows to show it off as soon as folks began to hear about this new contraption and began to call me "the Kitti Potti man." The more bold ones called me "the king of cat shit." I suppose I was. They often wanted me to autograph their newly purchased Kitti Potti. I think people were fascinated that such an average looking guy had come up with such a winning product. Many people said, "It's such a simple idea. I don't know why I didn't think of that!" I also don't know why someone else hadn't thought of it before.

It was early in 1975 when we bought 717 West Huron, a large house with five apartments next door. A few months later we bought another house on the east side of Ann Arbor. We moved to our new residence and turned Martha Washington in to a rooming house for women. We had fifteen rental rooms, two common kitchens and five and one-half bathrooms in that house. We moved our office into the lower floor at 717 and used the garages on both properties to store, box and ship our pet products. We now had nineteen units to rent out as a source of income. It was an insurance policy, so to speak, if Haugen Products withered or was no longer a money tree.

By mid-1975 we were selling Kitti Pottis to Sears Roebuck in the United States for their catalogues and to Sears Simpson in Canada. We were also selling to Macy's and Gimbel's in New York City. Unbelievable! I had secured patent rights in the United States, Canada, England, France, and Germany. I had acquired a distributor in Hagen, West Germany, for the European market, and he was ordering Kitti Pottis by the ocean freight container.

The skinny neglected long-haired waif from Spring Valley High School was building a small empire. It did my ego a world of good. I did not need therapy now. The business was my therapist. I wished the people from Spring Valley who had stood up an applauded me at my graduation could see me now. I wondered if Lorna was learning of my success. I often thought of her, but I never saw her when we went back to Minneota.

There were many people in Ann Arbor and perhaps across the nation who believed social workers were "bleeding hearts" for the poor and down trodden, not capable of real men's work in the market place of capitalism. These do-gooders caused their taxes to go up. Many conservative people maintained that poor and black people only needed to pull themselves up by their bootstraps and join the middle class. They saw mental illness as weakness; with willpower, afflicted people could just get over it. I resented their take on social workers like myself. I took great satisfaction in the fact that many local Republicans were taking note of my business success.

The family went to England in October 1975 to visit friends and vacation. I was pleased beyond words to see Kitti Pottis for sale in the pet department at Harrods department store in London. I couldn't believe that Harrods was selling Kitti Pottis.

During my childhood, we never had enough money. I had started to work setting pins at the bowling alley in Kewanee when I was nine. I had worked like a slave on the farm at Spring Valley. Neither Dad nor the Thompsons ever willingly gave me any money for my labor. I struggled while living in Minneota, Marshall, and Minneapolis, never earning quite enough to keep up with the bills. I had sold baby chicks, Culligan water softeners, and furniture; I unloaded boxcars, cleaned toilets, cracked batteries, sold blood, and never made enough to really get ahead. My college education made the difference. It was only when we moved to Ann Arbor that we started to earn more than we were spending. We had done well with the group home and my work for CSS and the Council of Churches. But now our finances were in a different category. It was so enjoyable to have more than enough money. It was unbelievable to see it come through the mail everyday like magic. It seemed impossible for this to be happening, but it was. Everyday was like Christmas.

It made me giddy and generous! I bought twin Fiat X 1-9 sports cars for Lorraine and me in celebration of her birthday in 1975. I ordered personalized plates for each car, one said "Kitti" and the other said "Potti." Our friends thought our cars were too much fun, and they chided us over who was driving Kitti and who was driving Potti.

The extraordinary sales continued in 1976. We were in a remarkable situation. We owned two houses that were income properties. Our office, storage, and shipping spaces were located on our property, so there was no rent to pay. We had one full-time secretary and a part-time packing and shipping person. Lorraine did much of the bookkeeping. I worked on marketing, and the kids helped with packing and shipping when they could. We had almost no overhead costs.

One day a white-haired man driving a shiny new red Corvette convertible came by to buy a Kitti Potti. He said he wanted to buy one from the man himself. He was amused by our humble facilities, and yet he somehow was aware of how well I had been doing.

"Don't ever change the way your doing business, son," he said. "Keep your overhead low. That's the way to make money. Don't change a thing."

He took his Kitti Potti and drove off, and I never saw him again. Who was that guy? He looked like a white-haired George C. Scott. I came to think of him as a wise old sage, maybe a prophet.

My mother called one day. She had heard from Aunt Rachel that I was doing well. Mom was living in Covington, Kentucky, had remarried, and said she would like to visit and bring her new husband, Tom, along. I said it was fine, but I was thinking "Oh, shit!" I had written her off long ago as irretrievable and had made up my mind that she could not be made into a decent kind of mother.

Mother and Tom showed up a few days later. Tom was a nice old fellow, and my mother was an old lady. I hardly recognized her. I was not sure she was nice, but all of us were on our best behavior, and the visit went well. Mom was particularly taken with little Erin, who was as cute as a button. My older kids politely ignored my mother. They really didn't know her. Mom asked us to visit them in Kentucky, and we promised we would.

We did visit them in a month or so. It was the beginning of a series of trips to Kentucky with Erin. Lorraine had the notion that I should try to make up with my mother, but I was hesitant. I didn't trust her. I had not forgotten what she had exposed me to as a child, and I hadn't forgiven her. I had more or less just forgotten about her existence—out of sight, out of mind. I discovered that the more time I spent with her, the more frustrated and angry I became. I wanted to tell her off. She was in denial about her past behavior, and that infuriated me. Absence had made at least my conscious mind forget her; presence now brought back the unresolved sadness and hate.

My life was good without her, but Lorraine felt I needed to work things out. I insisted I didn't need her in my life; she was nothing but trouble. Lorraine argued that I should try to resolve our issues; I would be better off for at least trying to make peace with her.

We visited Mom and Tom many times over the next couple of years. Mom and I had many opportunities to be alone on these visits. On every one of these occasions, I wanted to take her to task. I was angry at her. Once when we were sitting alone in her kitchen, the words just came blurting out of my mouth.

"Why did you take me with you when you had sex in the back seat of cars with your boyfriends?" I asked her.

She looked at me like I had struck her with a bolt of lightening.

"Why did you make me go to sleep in the front seat while you were fucking them in the back seat?"

She was stunned. "Why did you take me to Lake Benton while you shacked up with Mr. D? Why did make me lie for you?"

The shock on her face disappeared. She became furious with my questions and repeatedly called me a liar and troublemaker. She asked me why I was punishing her with these accusations.

"Mom, you know you did those things." I repeated over and over. "You made me lie for you to Dad by threatening me and bribing me."

She attempted to deny everything. But I could see her cracking. I kept after her, and she finally admitted her behavior.

"Yes, I did those things," she said. "They were terrible things to do. I have been suffering for them ever since."

"How?" I asked.

She said she had been physically ill almost everyday since she left Lawrence and me. I asked her why she did those things, why she left us, and she said she didn't know. "I must have been crazy during those years."

We talked for a while longer more quietly. Her admission helped a lot. But I still wasn't satisfied. She wasn't crying. I wanted real crying, remorse, apologies, and maybe blood. There was none of that. Mom had hardened herself. It was not easy to read what was going on inside her head by her face.

Over time, because of that single confrontation, I began to accept her as a real person, a flawed one, but a person, my biological mother. I had long ago taken her sister Rachel as my real mother, and I was not about to substitute Rachel for Mom. That attitude helped me have a decent relationship with Mom until she died many years later.

In 1976, Lorraine, the children, our lawyer, and I went to Germany to meet our distributor and to vacation. The distributor was doing a good job for us. We were well entertained for a few days in the Hagen area, and then we drove to Baden Baden, Munich, Garmisch, Innsbruck, and Bavaria. I was surprised by how beautiful Germany was. Southern Germany is gorgeous. Twenty years after the war, the scars were no longer visible. Only our sobering visit to Dachau reminded us of the terrible atrocities committed by the Germans in World War II. I wondered if our distributor had taken part in any of those mass executions of the Jews. He was of the right age to have been in the war.

I went to a Roman Catholic church in a Bavarian city, and I noticed they had a memorial to German soldiers killed in World War II from the parish. How odd, I thought. We had the same kind of memorials in the States for our World War II dead. Did God take sides in that war, or was he on both sides? I was taught as a child God was on our side.

The tall ships were in New York harbor on July 4, 1976. That day, Lorraine and I were in Michigan with friends on Lake Superior aboard a large ferry. Our friend Art Spang had rented it for the cruise. Art and his wife had moved to Copper Harbor a year or so before. I wondered why they had moved there.

It must have been six hundred miles north, and all their friends lived in Ann Arbor. It seemed so stupid to leave your friends and live in the wilderness with the waves of Lake Superior lapping up on your back deck. I could never leave my friends. I needed to stay with them.

When Donnie went off to college in September 1976, I quit motocross and started playing racquetball. I usually played with my friends. When I was good enough, I joined a league. I kept on running and did some biking. I had become a physical fitness nut. But I was doing a good job of staying healthy. My entire family was now into cross country and downhill skiing too. Being my own boss and not having to work at a nine-to-five job allowed us to do so many things.

Lorraine and I and the kids had developed a routine over the last few years of going to Florida for at least a couple of weeks in the winter, to Minnesota in the summer, and to Lake Michigan at Glen Arbor when ever we could get away.

All of us went to Glen Arbor during the summer of 1977 for a short vacation following my birthday. When we returned home we found our house had been burglarized. Someone had broken a basement window and entered the house. They stole all the electronics, like the stereos and TVs. They stole our two Fiat X 1-9 sports cars. People had come into our house and just took what they wanted, and to add insult to injury they vandalized the house. We were beginning to worry that our days in the group home had made us too familiar to a criminal element. They knew where we lived.

Otherwise, 1977 was a good year for us. I think total sales for Haugen Products were $400,000. Sears was buying about $100,000 per year for their catalogues. The U.S. Department of Commerce invited Haugen Products to Paris for a trade exposition in the summer of 1977. We were honored by the invitation and accepted. We did the show with our European distributor. Afterward, Lorraine and I rented a car and drove to Belgium. We visited St. Laurens, the little village where my grandmother was born. Stacy went off to college that year at Eastern Michigan University. It was just Erin, Lorraine, and me at home now.

That year also brought the first Kitti Potti rip off. I had expected it sooner. The world, I had learned from others, had no respect for patents. Companies would copy your products with no guilt or compensation. They more or less said "sue us." It was the American way. We were lucky to have had five years with no competition.

This competitor was soon joined by another. To avoid design patent infringement, they altered the design slightly by changing the shape of the entrance hole and the way the top fit over the bottom. I had also been granted a utility patent for another Kitti Potti, the spray-proof model. No one ever tried to copy that model. The copycat products were inferior to the Kitti Potti, but they sold for less money. They were made by the injection molding process, a less expensive method.

To keep our sales volume up, I thought I needed to expand the business. In 1979 I decided to rent a large warehouse on the south side of Ann Arbor. I opened a pet shop and used the rest of the large facility for storage and shipping. We rented out our office at 717 West Huron as an apartment and moved the entire operation to Platt Road. We increased our overhead by leasing the building by several thousand dollars per month. But I thought we could make it up by selling our line of pet products locally and by adding, fish, birds, lizards, snakes, pet food, aquariums, dog grooming, and so forth. We even got a state permit to have two monkeys as a store attraction.

To run the retail store, I had to hire more employees. That created more overhead. Then another shock came. Sears Roebuck decided to sell one our competitor's litter boxes in their upcoming catalogues because they were less expensive. That knocked out $100,000 of income per year. Fortunately our mail order and distributor/dealer sales remained good.

I needed to pay much more attention to the business now. We started pony rides for the kids on Saturdays to bring in families with kids to our pet shop. We mailed out fliers to the appropriate zip codes. I hired a savvy pet store manager. We hung in there in 1979. Sales overall were good. But now it took about $20,000 a month in sales to more or less break even with modest salaries for Lorraine and I. More copycat litter boxes showed up on the market in 1980.

Not only were the competitors beginning to cut into our total national and international sales, but our new location was presenting a problem I had not anticipated. We were getting burglarized. During the first burglary, they only broke the cash register and stole a little cash. The next time they broke the register and didn't find cash. However, they stole our monkeys, Macaws and parrots, and they vandalized the place. This burglary was followed by even more burglaries. The police offered little protection. We were in a bad location and began to worry that we would be robbed at gunpoint. Someone might get killed. We decided to always have two people in the store at any one time and to close by six o'clock each night. No more night store hours.

I thought of the white-haired man in the shiny red corvette who had driven over to see "the man" and buy a Kitti Potti. "Keep your overhead low," he had advised. "Don't change a thing."

I was beginning to wish I had listened to him.

We had been going to Florida in March for the last couple of years. The winter 1981 we stayed a month on Marco Island. On the way back we stopped in Atlanta and visited some friends, as we had the year before. The Volkerts had been our next door neighbors in Ann Arbor and had now bought a lovely house at a reasonable price and were doing very well. Real estate was much cheaper in Atlanta than in Ann Arbor. We had looked a little bit the year before, and we liked what we saw. Atlanta is hard to resist in the spring. It's seductive with all the trees and flowers. While we were there we visited Roswell and looked at a fine home in a new subdivision.

Before we had arrived back in Ann Arbor, Lorraine and I decided we would give up our lease on the warehouse and discontinue the pet shop. It was too dangerous for us to continue. We feared someone might get hurt. We would think about offering Haugen Products for sale as well. We were fed up with the competition, and we were considering moving away from Ann Arbor. We had been burglarized too often. Maybe next they would kidnap Erin. A great number of people knew we had done very well in business. We could sell our houses and buy in Roswell, Georgia. If we didn't like it there we could leave. We could always come back to Ann Arbor if we wanted.

Within a few months we had built a house in Roswell. We sold our rental properties and our residence at considerable profits. They had been extremely good investments. I sold Haugen Products to Animal Veterinary Products in July 1981, a competitor of ours in the mail order business.

DON HAUGEN

We moved to our new home in Georgia in mid-August. I was forty-seven years old; Lorraine was forty-two, and Erin was ten. We had enough money to last a long time before we needed to worry. Interest rates were 18 percent or better. One could live quite well just on interest. The Michigan economy was crippled and staggering. The auto industry was in poor shape. The whole economy of southeastern Michigan was in a slump, like the rest of the country at that time.

Lorraine and I had secured our future. We had sold the business at just the right time, before all the large-company competition rendered Kitti Potti essentially worthless on the market. We had made ourselves safer and would not need to worry further about crime against any of us or our property. We built a beautiful new home in a nice neighborhood with a golf course, tennis courts and swimming pool.

It had been twenty years and a couple of months since I had started as a freshman at the University of Minnesota, seventeen years since we moved to Ann Arbor and started the group home, and almost nine years since I first ran an ad in a magazine offering a Kitti Potti for sale. We had gone from rags to riches during those years in Ann Arbor.

I walked away from the Thompson farm in the darkness of a cold and foggy September morning in 1952. In my wildest dreams I never imagined I would be so fortunate in the years that lay ahead of me.

CHAPTER 30

GEORGIA

The morning after we moved into our new house, I woke up with a very uncomfortable feeling. I felt like crying. Tears just trickled down my face as I sat on the edge of the bed. A terrible realization was settling in: I had sold my creation, all my patents and copyrights, and Haugen Products, which we had built from scratch. I felt like I had sold away almost everything dear to me. I told Lorraine what I was thinking and feeling over morning coffee. She understood and also felt the loss. I knew I had done something else too. I had always said that I would never move away from my friends, but I did. Lorraine moved away from her friends too. We both realized what we had done. We had sold the company, our real estate holdings, and moved for perfectly rational reasons. Nonetheless, we were feeling the loss and hurting.

Some friends had preceded us to the Atlanta area: Joel Vandermale and his new wife, and the Volkert family. We had known both families for many years while they lived in Ann Arbor. We had visited the Volkerts in Atlanta the past two years on our return trips from Florida. Each year we stopped around the end of March or the first of April. In the spring, Atlanta adorns itself lavishly with a multitude of flowering plants, bushes and trees. It is seductively warm, sunny, and pleasing to the senses compared to Ann Arbor, which is still cold and grey in early April. This seductive quality among other things is what led us to choose Atlanta as our new place to live.

Doret Volkert was a happy high-energy person. She and her husband, Henry, were children in Germany during World War II. Although we were not German, they introduced us to Atlanta's German community. We went to German Club with them. They were very popular members. Henry often played the accordion, and he and Doret sang German songs while people danced. It was a lively fun-loving group of people, and the Volkerts were at its core.

Within what now seems to have been only a few months, lovely, vivacious, friendly Doret was diagnosed with breast cancer. She died very soon. It was so very difficult to understand how such an energetic and happy person could die so quickly. She had far too much life force in her to be taken so fast. It was unfair and horribly sad.

We had known Joel Vandermale since he was in college. He and his wife had been group-home relief parents offering a break or taking care of the girls when we needed to be elsewhere for a night. We often played tennis together and went out to dinner. Joel and I started running together. He always wanted to beat me in races. He was a serious competitor. One afternoon he called me and said he had just finished the Boston marathon. He challenged me to run the next one with him. He took up flying because he envied the fact that I had a pilot's license. When he earned his graduate degree in hospital administration, he became the youngest hospital administrator of a major hospital in Michigan. He was a very able young man.

This is a very strange world of inexplicable fate. Handsome, energetic, and able Joel Vandermale was killed when the plane he was piloting crashed only a couple of miles from our house. I think he was going to fly low over our house and dip his wings to say, "Hi, it's me." He had learned to fly in part because I had. He had recently bought a plane and was using it in business. On the morning of his death, Joel was on his way to South Carolina. There was no reason for him to be near our house when he crashed if he was going to South Carolina.

Lorraine and I attended his funeral in Decatur. I remember standing in the parking lot outside the church after the funeral service with Lorraine. We were in each others arms, crying uncontrollably. Lorraine and I held each other and cried together for a very long time. How could such an energetic, enthusiastic young man be dead? It too seemed so unfair. He left a young wife and infant son.

I have learned in so many ways that death is impartial, unfair, and random in its choice of victims. This sinks painfully into my conscious mind when energetic dear friends die unexpectedly much before their time.

Donnie and Stacy were with us the summer of 1981 until college classes began again for them in Michigan. Erin started the fifth grade in a nearby elementary school. Lorraine and I missed the older kids as soon as they were gone, and we were lonesome for our friends in Ann Arbor too. So we traveled frequently to Michigan. At first we began looking for business opportunities. We found nothing that interested us. We looked at farms and country acreages near Ann Arbor and Chelsea. Nothing seemed quite right.

What we really wanted was to move right back into our old house and take over where we had left off with Haugen Products. But neither was possible. Life moves on. The choices you make have consequences. Some decisions you make are final and irreversible, and you must accept what you have done. That was our condition. The choices we had made were irreversible. We accepted our situation and began the process of adjusting.

The man who built our house had gotten himself into financial trouble. He had built a few "spec" houses, and they were not selling. Interest on these house loans was bankrupting him as he waited for buyers. He had a customer who wanted to build a house, but he didn't have the credit for a loan to get started. I had become friendly with the builder, so I felt secure in financing the start up building costs. He and I built a very large and lovely house for the man and his family. But that was it. The housing market dried up. It was too risky to build spec houses.

I got a real estate license, thinking I might get into sales. I quickly found out this was not something I liked. It was boring, and sales were tough to come by in the slow market. I played a lot of golf, and I did a lot of running. When I wasn't golfing or running, I was making things out of clay. I was a person who needed constant activity.

I enjoyed playing with clay and I found myself migrating toward what I liked to do instead of working at a paying job. Of course, I didn't need a paying job. But I had this irrational feeling that always made me think I needed to be earning money. I felt guilty otherwise.

Since childhood, I had sculpted small figures and heads with a pocketknife with relative ease. And for some reason it relaxed and pleased me to make faces and figures with clay. It was much easier than carving with a knife. So I kept playing in the clay doing what I liked for a while.

Grandma Blomme died in June 1982, and I went back to Minnesota for the funeral. She had lived to be ninety-four years old. Hundreds of her family and friends attended the services and reception. I was able to see all of my aunts, uncles, cousins, and my mother. It was a sad time and yet joyous as all the family had a chance to visit.

My mother was living in Minneota. I had helped her move there after Tom had died shortly before Grandma's death. He had been fairly wealthy, so now Mom had money. She showed it off with nice clothes and flashy jewelry. She bought a house right in front of the Icelandic Lutheran Church that my nephew had remodeled. It was only a few blocks from my dad and Larry.

What odd creatures we are in this world. My brother and I had hated Mom. Now she was living only a few blocks from Lawrence and Dad in the same town where we had all started out as a family. Perhaps we have a tendency to return to where we were born; maybe it is some sort of human homing migration pattern. I actually helped Mom by arranging for her to move all her household goods to her new home in Minneota. And I drove her to Minnesota in her car from Kentucky.

Her name was partially back up on the toilet-room wall. I had reconstituted her to some extent. But she made it difficult. By the time of Grandma's funeral, she had already involved herself with younger local man by the time of Grandma's funeral. Not my Dad, and that irritated me no end.

As I mentioned, Dad lived only a few blocks from Mom. His wife Mary had passed away too. Dad thought he would reunite with Mom, and the two of them tried it at Mom's house for a couple of weeks. I was all in favor of that. But it didn't work. She kicked him out. She said he was dirty and had a dirty mind. He was eighty-one years old. He went back to his tumbledown little house.

A few years later I went with my mom to visit two friends of hers. It was a dinner invitation. Mom brought her young boyfriend. After dinner they turned on the TV, stuck in a porno movie, and began watching it. I was shocked and embarrassed. I wondered what the hell was wrong with these people. She made me furious. Did she not have any common sense? Mom was about seventy-five years old. I was not going to watch a porno movie with my mom and her boy-friend. I told them I was not going to watch this kind of crap with my mother, and I left.

Dad's name appeared again on the toilet wall, but largely because I felt sorry for him. He never had the good sense to just forget my mother. I asked him about that. He just stood there in front of me with watery eyes, and after a long moment he said, "I still love her." I believe he did. And I guess I loved my dad. It was just so hard to have a meaningful relationship with him. He didn't talk. Maybe the truth is I wanted him to love me, but I never felt that he did.

Larry's name was only partially on the wall again too. The long separation while I was on the farm at Spring Valley created an emotional distance between us that we were never able to bridge. My Army duty, college, and Ann Arbor had ensured that not only the emotional distance would remain between us, but a geographical one too. I had visited him and his family many times over the years, but he was unable to reciprocate. Larry had gone partially blind and was unable to drive, and he didn't like to travel. He had suffered some kind of spon-taneous hemorrhaging of the retina in both eyes. He was unable to work, and his large family was on the borderline of poverty. He was frequently frustrated and at times drank to excess. His situation and my success probably pushed us even further apart. I was the one with the education and the money, and I believe that hurt him.

How strange it is the way things work out. Certainly God never planned out all these dysfunctional relationships. They are the consequences of choices we and others have made that become so very painful to ourselves.

I saw Lorna on this visit. I went to the post office where she was the post-master and asked her to have coffee. We sat in Minneota's Corner Café and talked about our lives, hers with Dick and mine with Lorraine. We perhaps mentioned how it may have been if our romance had ended up in a marriage. She was so beautiful, so lovely. My God, I really could hardly keep from sweeping her up into my arms and kissing her. But I didn't. I kept my urges and feel-ings in check. I carried on a reasonable, polite adult married-man conversation with her. My love for her had not gone away. I had just kept it under wraps. I had been going about life letting her choices and their consequences play out. I had made my choices and those resulting consequences were playing out. I never knew until years later that as we sat talking, she had wished that I would take her in my arms.

Donnie came home to Atlanta in the summer of 1982. He got a summer job, and when he wasn't working we played a lot of golf. As the summer progressed we both decided that we would like an adventure. We chose to walk the Appalachian Trail, a trail that is about 2200 miles long. The trek should be started in early spring in North Georgia if you were going to make it to Maine by late autumn. Donnie took the fall semester off at college, and we walked a portion of the trail. We took our Labrador Retriever Bingo along. We started in Churchtown, Pennsylvania, near Harrisburg, and walked south. We intended to walk as far as we could before the weather turned cold and bad. We bought all the equipment and maps we needed. We got ourselves into condition by running and walking hills with full packs.

In September, Lorraine and Erin took us to Churchtown and dropped us off. Soon the girls and their car disappeared down the road, and Donnie and I were left standing with hundreds of miles to walk before we reached Georgia.

The trail was rocky in Pennsylvania, and by the end of the second day we had a lot of foot blisters. We found that the expensive leather hiking boots we had bought were murderous on our feet. Our feet would slip forward in our shoes walking downhill on the mountain trails and in a short time blisters formed. The bottoms of our feet were soon covered in moleskin. Within a week, we threw our leather boots away and wore the running shoes we carried in our packs. Running shoes were just the trick for easing the pain of sore feet and eliminating blisters.

The first two weeks nearly killed us. The mountains were steep, the packs were heavy, the ground was hard, and we were soft. But by the end of two weeks are feet were much better and we had hardened considerably. The frequent rain kept us wet or damp for much of the time. We washed our sweat and/or rain soaked clothes in streams and dried them on our backpacks as we walked. If the sun didn't shine the clothes stayed wet. We cooked our freeze-dried food over a little gas stove with water we took from springs. At night we crawled in our sleeping bags and either slept in the open or in our small two-man tent. Bingo insisted on sleeping in the tent with us.

We walked down through Harpers Ferry, West Virginia, and continued south through the Shenandoah National Park toward Waynesboro, Virginia. By this time, we were well toughened to the trail. We were able to walk fifteen to twenty miles a day without difficulty. Shenandoah is a beautiful park about one hundred miles long. It is quite easy as far hiking goes, and deer often raised their heads to watch us walk by. Bingo enjoyed chasing the deer, so we had to keep him on a leash much of the time. Bingo caused us considerable discomfort early on in the park after he chased a skunk. The skunk peed on him and the odor was enough to make you vomit. We tried to wash the stench off of him with spring water and mud, but to no avail. We would not allow him to sleep in the tent, and he spent most nights pushed up against the outside of the tent whining over being rejected.

In addition to the stench of our dog, the problem we were finding is that hiking the trail gets boring. The trail follows the highest ridges of the Appalachians and fairly often one finds great vistas of valleys and distant mountains. But much of what you see is the dirt, rocks, and tree roots in front of your feet. Watching where you place you feet is necessary to avoid falling. Injury on the trail is a something you want to avoid. It is difficult to get help. We would go for two or three days without seeing another person. When we did slow down or stop to take in the view, we saw trees, branches, and leaves followed by more trees, branches and leaves. But the leaves were turning to autumn colors, and they were spectacular when the sun brightened them. Then occasionally there was the reward of a breathtaking vista uninterrupted by trees, branches, and leaves.

We left the trail in Waynesboro and sent Bingo home with Lorraine and Erin. We got a ride down to the north end of the Great Smokey Mountain National Park, where we began the most difficult hiking of the trip. The Smokies were awesomely beautiful and more rugged. There were steep long accents and rugged stumble inducing descents. They were a challenge that stretched over a distance of about one hundred miles to the Fontana dam on the south end.

The climb from Newfound Gap to Klingman's Dome, the highest point in the park, was memorable. It started out as a relatively easy seven-mile hike and turned into a hand-and-knees climb as we reached the summit in a cold drizzle that turned to freezing rain. At the summit it was extremely cold, and ice was forming on everything. We pitched our tent and went to the public restrooms in attempt to warm up. There were no heaters. We were very wet, and we feared that hypothermia might set in overnight. Fortunately a guy came into the restroom and saw our hopeless efforts to get warm. He offered us a ride down to Cherokee, North Carolina, where there was a motel. We took the offer.

The motel was next to a McDonald's. We spent two nights in the motel warming up and eating burgers and fries. I learned here to always carry a credit card while camping. We chose to go back up to the Dome by hitchhiking. Once we arrived on top, we found the campsite we had abandoned, packed up the gear we had left and headed south. It took about a week to walk the entire length of the park. We saw a couple of bears and lots of wild hogs. Lorraine picked us up near the dam, and we returned home. It had been a good experience. We had hiked the trail for an adventure. We tested our durability and easily passed the test. We could have walked the entire two thousand miles if we had wanted to. It is amazing that a person can walk such a great distance escaping the sights and sounds of civilization for the most part.

My knees held up well on the trail. But when I returned home, my usual routine of running to relieve physical and mental stress was failing me. In 1983 I developed a severe problem in my left knee. I stopped running for long periods to let the swelling go down. Finally I had knee surgery. The recovery was slow and left me highly frustrated. I stayed depressed until I could start running again.

While on the trail, I thought about what I would like to do with the rest of my life. I made up my mind that I was going to try and become a professional sculptor. That is, I was going to try and earn a living by selling sculpture. I told Lorraine and the kids what I was going to do, and they said to go for it. They had confidence in me, or maybe they were just being nice.

I thought I was a good sculptor. But how did I stack up against other sculptors? I needed to find out. Late that autumn, I took a sculpture class at in

Atlanta. My teacher was Teena Stern Watson. She was about five feet six inches tall, with deep-set dark brown eyes, prominent cheekbones, and dark brown curly hair. To my eyes she seemed skinny. Perhaps she worked too hard and didn't eat enough. The first day I met her, she was dressed in a loose-fitting print dress. She didn't appear to have much of a figure, but she carried herself as if she had been a ballerina. I noticed she drove an old model Honda Civic. Perhaps she was poor, maybe an ADC mother with a bunch of kids and no husband. But she seemed to know what she was doing.

I liked her as a teacher, and I felt I could talk to her about my interest in sculpture. I brought some samples of my work one day late in the session, and after class she looked at them. She was impressed by my skill with clay and invited me to join her next class.

I followed Teena to her next teaching assignment. She started teaching at the Abernathy Art Center, and I took the winter session. Teena and I became friends during this session. I think it was because of our common interest in figurative sculpture and our similar skill levels. We found ourselves talking after class about where to buy clay, tools, armatures, and about sculpture in general.

I learned in the course of a few months that Teena was not on ADC. She was married to Jack Watson, who had been President Jimmy Carter's chief of staff. The old car she drove was out of choice, as were the plain, loose-fitting dresses. She had been a professional dancer and still took dancing classes. Her skinny body was by choice too.

Soon Jack, Teena, Lorraine, and I were going out to dinner together and dining at each other's homes. During the day Teena and I often worked at her studio, where we would share a professional model. Sometimes she would come to the studio I had created in my house, and we would work there with a shared model. We often got into arguments because Teena didn't want me to make the same gesture that she was making of the model. Well, it was pretty hard to make the model change gestures, so we each could make a different looking sculpture in a session of a couple of hours. But we did. We were scrappy with each other and arrogant in regard to our respective skills. She thought she was better than me. I thought I was better than her. Yet we enjoyed working with each other.

In June 1984, Teena and I went to the New York Academy of Art for a two-week session on building the life-size figure in clay. We stayed at the Quaker Friends House in Greenwich Village. Our relationship was purely platonic. We each had a spouse, and as far as I knew both marriages were reasonably happy. Our common interest was sculpture, and we were both obsessed with improving our own skills.

The academy was not prepared for the many students that enrolled in their summer session. As a result, the school had none of the supplies needed available in the building. Each of us was given a list of materials we would need to build our sculpture. We needed to go to lower Manhattan and find them. We had to buy lumber, plywood, and wheels to build platforms for life-size clay figures, which would end up weighing at least two hundred pounds. We had to purchase clay in the area and get it up to the fourth floor of the academy.

Clay comes in fifty pound boxes. There were many buildings being remodeled in the area. They had large Dumpsters near these sites. We went "Dumpster diving" to find plumbing pipe, electrical conduit, and wire to make the skeletal structure for our figures. Teena was an agile Dumpster diver. She felt no shame in digging in the trash for the good stuff. In fact, she enjoyed it. Once we accumulated a bunch of pipe, conduit, and wire, we had to carry it to the building and up to the academy. With the necessary materials on hand I made the platforms for us, and we each constructed our armatures. Armatures are the structures that serve as an internal framework or skeleton while modeling a sculpture. For these we used galvanized pipe, conduit, copper tubing, wire, or whatever we could to make a stable armature on which to hang clay. It took about three days to make the preparation, and then we began the work of applying the clay to the armatures. The trick was to apply the clay in such a manner that the finished piece would look like the model. Teena and I successfully completed our sculptures in the two weeks. Most of the others did not.

Our professional model had an amusing and unusual way of relieving the kinks in his body after holding a pose for a half hour or so. This behavior intrigued the ladies in the class. During his breaks he hung upside down in the nude with the aid of inversion boots. This was a most unusual sight to behold, and the ladies wasted little time in finding the humor of the unusual positions his genitalia would assume. Their comments were loud, often derogatory, and funny. I am surprised the guy continued to relax in this manner during his breaks, considering the female abuse leveled at him, which he surely overheard.

I learned a lot about Teena during these two weeks. She was born and raised in a beautiful Atlanta neighborhood. Her house had central heating, indoor plumbing with hot and cold running water, plus a garage for two cars. She was her high school's homecoming queen and a cheerleader. Teena went to college in Pittsburgh, Pennsylvania where she earned a Bachelor of Science degree in retailing and fashion design. Her father, during his healthy years was the vice president of the Atlanta Gas and Light Company and later became the President of Scripto, Incorporated. Her mother taught dance and from the age of three Teena began training with her mother to become a ballerina. Teena spent much of her early adult life as a professional dancer, at first in Ballet and then in Modern Dance.

I did not have the love, comforts and security that Teena experienced in her childhood home. And, I missed out on the parental encouragement and financial underpinning that a set of caring parents can provide too. Fate! Ah …fickle Fate!

Teena and I had come from very different worlds. But we enjoyed each other's company and shared a common passion for sculpture and art.

At the academy, I realized I did have a special talent. I was faster and better than any other student enrolled. I was headed in the right direction. I began working more enthusiastically on my creations and started casting my better pieces in bronze. I applied for a job at Abernathy Art Center in Atlanta and began teaching sculpture in the fall.

I was experiencing knee problems with my right knee now, and running any distance was out of the question. I started playing league racquetball and taking aerobic classes. And although these activities gave me a good workout, I was frustrated because I continued to have reoccurring knee problems. I just couldn't get my frustrations out of my system anymore, and I was often irritated.

I was also troubled by the manner in which we had become accustomed to living. Financially, I thought we should only live on interest and whatever I was earning. We shouldn't be spending principal. I suggested that maybe Lorraine should get a job. I often also complained that I was not receiving enough affection from Lorraine. I don't know what I expected; we had been married for twenty-seven years. But I wanted something more.

Now Lorraine and I had enjoyed a fiery romantic time prior to and during our marriage. Then the children came. Lorraine became a mother, and I was a dad. Our life became oriented around raising the children, getting my college education, and work. Then there was the group home and Kitti Potti. And by that time, more than two decades had passed. Over those twenty-five years romance kind of faded, and our relationship morphed into something else. Over time, we began to look like each other. We began to think and talk like each other. We could finish each other's sentences. We could go to dinner together alone and hardly utter a word. It wasn't necessary. We knew everything about each other and the way each of us thought and talked. Have you ever noticed an older married couple in a restaurant having dinner alone together? They seldom speak to each other. If an older couple is alone, eating and talking, look for wedding rings. They are probably not married.

I wrote a poem many years ago for Lorraine.

'57 Chevrolet

do you remember
   that autumn day
      a generation or more ago
         the salmon colored chevrolet
            the handsome young men in hunting clothes
            porter groves and joe dero's

we followed you, you made such a fuss
   we were talking dumb and making passes
      finally you parked and rode with us
         days later i picked you up after classes

i thought you were so very pretty
   i wanted you to choose me from the rest
      you did, itty bitty mitty
         but i think you liked the '57 chevy best

you looked like barbara stanwyck
   you sounded like her too
      the cold you had did the trick
      and i fell in love with you

our's was a fiery affair from the start
   you'd go to school, and i'd be cool all day
      at night, we'd drink beer and talk smart
      then make love in the '57 chevrolet

you were a wondrous sensuous joy to me
  i loved to feel your naked heated skin
    your starch billowy crinoline
      your nubiant swollen breasts
        your curly prickly pubic nest
          a wondrous sensuous toy for me
            to touch
              and smell
              and feel
              and see

And so it was, but was no more. Our older children were finished with college and beginning to take their place in the work world. Stacy became an English teacher and Donnie took a job in the hazardous waste business. He had always liked to make smoky stink bombs and blow things up.

Aunt Rachel called me one day in 1985. I was so pleased to get her call. I was surprised though, because she usually wrote letters instead of calling.

"Donnie," she said, "I called you because I wanted to tell you how much I love you. I have always loved you as if you were my own child. I am so sorry I did not come for you while you were at Spring Valley."

She continued, "The doctors here have told me that I am going to die tomorrow or the next day, and I wanted to make sure I told you I loved you before I die."

I was shocked and couldn't believe what she was saying. I thought for sure there must be some mistake. Her voice was so strong.

"Where are you?" I asked.

She said she was at McKinnon Hospital in Sioux Falls. I asked, "Are you sure you are going to die in a day or two? You sound so strong. You don't sound sick."

She told me that she was sure and that she was calling those who had been important in her life to say goodbye. I believed her, and my emotions began to tumble forth through my body and brain. Tears were steaming down my face, and I began sobbing. She told me not to cry. I tried to stop. I told her how much I loved her and how much she had meant to me during my life. She kept her composure throughout the call. And then she said goodbye. I didn't keep my composure. I sobbed for hours.

Rachel died two days later. I went back home to Minneota and was absolutely numb throughout the whole funeral. My psyche would not allow me to feel all the pain of her death. It has poured out of me several times since then as I have tried to talk about her. I have never been able to tell people about her phone call without the tears beginning to flow. Her death was a terrible experience for me. I loved my Aunt Rachel. She was really my mother.

I believe it was that same year that I went to Minnesota by myself for some reason that I can't recall. Maybe it was just to visit Larry. I learned from my brother that Lorna was divorced. I stopped by the post office to see her. She was happy to see me. I asked her if we could spend any time together. She said we could spend the next three days together, and so we did. We did nothing to be ashamed of. We went to dinner, took walks together, sat and talked, hugged and kissed and resisted all temptations to have sex. The passion was still there. So we just behaved ourselves. I learned from her that she had a serious boyfriend, and although he was out of the country, she thought they might marry when he returned.

I returned to Minnesota with Lorraine to visit later that summer. Midge was home, and she and Lorna were looking for a house in Minneota for Lorna and her future husband. I even went with Lorraine, Lorna, and Midge to look at the new house. I cannot tell you how much this visit hurt. I had been so moved by the situation and my affection for Lorna that I wrote two poems and sent them to her a short time later. One was called "The Wind."

The Wind

Recently, on this very land you now stand upon,
   a man came.
He came from afar, in search of himself
   to the land that was once his own.

The church, tall, wooden and white stood empty and alone.
   uninviting, discomforting, cold.

The man went to his mother's house.
   He said, "please mother, touch me, feel me, hold me in
      your arms and tell me who I am.

His mother said, "I wish it would rain, the farmers need rain."
   The man turned and walked away, as he did, he heard his mother say:
   "and the wind,
      the wind,
         it blows here, everyday,"

The man went to his father's house
   He said, "please father, touch me, feel me, hold me in
      your arms and tell me who I am.
         His father said, "I wish it would stop raining. We have had too much
         rain."

The man turned and walked away, and as he did, he heard his father say:
   "and the wind,
      the wind,
         it blows here every day."

The man went to his brother's house.
   He said, "please brother, touch me, feel me, hold me in

your arms and tell me who I am.

His brother said, "whiskey is my friend, without it, I don't know who I am."

The man turned and walked away, and as he did, he heard his brother say
"and the wind,
the wind,
it blows here every day."

The man went to the house of the tall and lovely young woman,
now a lady, he had loved so dearly in his youth.

The lady said, "I am glad you came. I wanted to see you again. We can be together for three days."
On the first day, the man said,
"I want to touch you, feel you, hold you in my arms, I need to find out who I am."
The lady said,
"you can not touch me, feel me, or hold me in your arms, I don't know who you are."

On the second day, the lady said,
"I want to be with you. I am glad you came. We can be together."
The man said
"I want to touch you, feel you, hold you in my arms. I need to find out who I am."
The lady said,
"you can not touch me feel me, or hold me in your arms, I don't know who you are."

On the third day, the lady said,
"I am so glad you came. I wanted to be with you. We can be together."

The man said

"I want to touch you, feel you, hold you in my arms. I need to find out who I am."

The tall, white, wooden church stood silently on the windswept prairie. God has failed to touch it, feel it, or hold it in his arms.

The man said

"I must go now."

He walked to the tall and lovely woman, now seated. The man bent down to kiss her lips. As he did, he felt her lips grab passionately at his own, once, twice, and then apart.

In that fleeting moment passion lit the church. God's embrace was everywhere. There were trees, bushes, flowers, and there were people. The people took the emptiness and made it into joy. They kissed and hugged, laughed and played and filled the church with song.

Then as quickly as their lips had touched, they parted. All vanished as quickly as it came. The man turned and walked away, and as he did, he thought he heard her say,

"and the wind,
   the wind,
      the relentless wind,
         it blows here everyday."

To me, from my experience, those lonely-looking white wooden Protestant churches on the Minnesota prairie appeared so cold and empty on the outside that only a saint would dare venture in. They seemed starved for the loving compassionate embrace of the Father. They symbolized one whole stoic side of my family. And I felt like I needed a father's embrace.

I never saw Lorna again until 2004. And then by coincidence, she noticed me crossing the street in Minnesota. I was walking with my wife and my brother. She shouted my name. I looked and there she was. She was with her two grown daughters. As we walked closer I could tell Lorna was happy to see me by the big smile on her face. Her big hug confirmed it. For a long moment, I wished everyone would disappear so we could be alone. They didn't and, after a few pleasantries, we went on our separate ways

CHAPTER 31

FINDING MYSELF

How do you find yourself, anyway? I did not say to myself, "Well, it is time for me to go out and find myself." But unknowingly, that was the journey I was beginning. I was in some trouble emotionally. I had not seen a therapist since Dr. Hauck back in 1960. I was frustrated and unhappy. I did not think I was getting enough attention or affection. I felt like I had no more magic to perform. I wasn't doing another Kitti Potti thing. I wasn't making another fortune. Too many people were depending on me for everything, and I had no more to give.

Lorraine was a dear and honest person, and we talked about my feelings. She didn't know what to do for me. We both thought it was that old ugly childhood coming back to haunt me. We had heard many times over the years that people like me who were abused and neglected as children and adolescents often could never get enough affection. They were insatiable in their appetite. Maybe I was like that. It was time for me to dig around in that childhood again and try to free myself from it. It was time.

I found a clinical psychologist and began weekly therapy. I did not like going through all that old and painful stuff, but I did. Actually, I had an amazing ability to recall things. I wrote down memories as they came to me, and then even more memory came into my awareness. It was at this time that the foundation for this memoir was laid. I continued in therapy for several months. Therapy was not making me feel less anxious. I thought I needed a pill to make me feel happy. I knew about Valium, and I wanted some. But a psychologist cannot prescribe medication. I saw a medical doctor and got some Valium, and it was a wonder drug. It made me feel great. Anxiety melted away. The only problem was that my doctor didn't think I should stay on it. It was habit forming and addictive. I didn't believe that story, and I thought it was stupid to refuse future prescriptions because Valium was miraculous. But I did not get on Valium.

I continued with my sculpture. I was showing my work at major local shows and enjoying slow but steady success. I continued teaching and working with Teena. On several occasions Teena, Lorraine, and I would go to sculpture workshops in Scottsdale, Arizona. Some of the best sculptors in the world came there to teach one- or two-week courses in figurative sculpture.

Teena got a divorce in 1987. I had advised her against it, but I guess she knew her own life better than I did.

I had surgery on my right knee, and the doctor advised me never to run any distance races again. I should ride a bicycle instead, he said. I rode the hell out of that bike going thirty or forty miles a day three or four times a week. I played league racquetball as soon as I could again. I needed a lot of physical expenditure of energy to feel good. It was my Valium.

I noticed that Teena was going out with new male friends, and I discovered I didn't like it. I was jealous. I had formed more than a friendship with her. When she walked in front of me I began to notice her shapely legs. I noticed her cute little butt, and her strong body. I paid attention to every nuance of her finely sculpted beautiful face.

Maybe we live too long. The same spouse for thirty years may be more than you can expect from most people. Maybe all romance dims with the passing years. Perhaps that is why we are becoming a population of serial monogamists. Is it because of boredom? Whatever the reason, Teena was exciting to me, and she was stirring something in me that had been dormant. And it was definitely sexual.

In June 1989, I competed in the James Wilbur Johnson International figure-sculpting contest in Baltimore, Maryland. This contest invited the best sculptors from around the world to a five-day competition. Sculptors were chosen based on pictures of their previous work.

Lorraine did not want me to go to Baltimore to compete if I was accepted. She knew that my relationship to Teena had grown into something more than friendship. I had made up my mind that if I was accepted I was going. I thought I was good, and I wanted to prove it.

I was accepted and, as fate would have it, so was Teena. We went separately to the competition, but of course we met there.

There were approximately thirty sculptors invited to compete from those who applied. We competed against each other sculpting the same model in a single gesture or pose. We were placed in a large room with the model and a monitor. We could not leave the room during the sculpting sessions except for breaks. We could not help each other. At the end of the fifth day, three internationally known sculptors judged our individual sculptures. They called off the honorable mention pieces and then the third, second, and first place winners. Teena won an honorable mention award. My name wasn't called out until the very last. I had won first place at the 1989 James Wilbur Johnson International Figure Sculpture Competition. It was a great honor and a tremendous boost to my flagging ego. I was indeed good at what I was doing.

I had been calling home to talk with Lorraine and Erin while I was competing in Baltimore. Each phone call with Lorraine was an argument. She was very upset with me for going to Baltimore with Teena. I began to think this was a juncture in my life where I had to make a choice. My relationship with Teena was enjoyable, and I was doing really well with my sculpture. My marriage had become boring, and Lorraine wanted Teena to exit from my world forever. I needed to make a choice. I chose Teena. I knew there would be bad consequences, and there were.

When I returned to Atlanta, I didn't go home. I went to a hotel. In time, I rented an apartment, bought some furniture and moved in. Lorraine was heartbroken. I felt terrible for her. We went to marriage counseling for several months, but it didn't resolve our situation. I was in love with Teena.

Erin and Stacy were heartbroken. They didn't want their parents to divorce. I understood their anger and sadness. I had felt the same way when my parents divorced. Donnie seemed to accept the situation much better than the girls.

About this same time I was chosen by the Atlanta Committee for the Olympic Games to make a sculpture that would be given to each of the eighty-eight delegates in Tokyo when they presented to the IOC. Those delegates chose

Atlanta as the home for the 1996 summer games, and my small sculpture, "The Olympic Dream Child," became a popular souvenir.

Erin started as freshman at the University of Georgia in the fall of 1989. I spent the next four years in that apartment by myself. Teena remained in the home where she and Jack had lived. I frequently went to movies or had dinner with Erin and Lorraine. I tried to get over to the University of Georgia every couple of weeks to have dinner with Erin. I took care of her college expenses. Within a year Lorraine found a boyfriend, and Teena continued to be my girl-friend. But she didn't stop dating other men because, as she said, I was still married to Lorraine. Teena's dating other men often made me angry. I thought we had made a commitment to each other.

I was often lonely. I wondered at times why I had moved out of what was for a great a number of years a perfectly good marriage. I took a lot of criticism from friends in Atlanta, Minnesota, and Michigan. My mother, of all people, was furious with me. One of my friends in Ann Arbor was so angry with me she said, "As far as I am concerned, I will never acknowledge your existence again. You are dead to me from now on." I have neither seen nor spoken to her since, and I am pleased for that.

People do not like to see marriages break up. They choose sides. They administer verbal punishment to the side they believe is wrong and verbal emotional support for the side that was wronged. I was among the former group. It would have been much easier for me to just move back home to Lorraine, but I didn't. In time, Lorraine and I were divorced, and Teena and I were married.

I was kind of a mess until my marriage to Teena. I was anxious and started to have panic attacks. My anxiety didn't stop me from continuing my work or teaching, but I did feel I needed some professional help. I swallowed my pride and found a competent psychiatrist. I found him easy to talk to, and I was on my way to better health. I was finding myself.

While I was in therapy, for some reason I began visiting places where I had spent my childhood. I wasn't instructed by my therapist to take these trips, I just wanted to. Teena went with me. My visits to my past were usually part of other trips, like visiting Teena's sister near St. Louis.

I went to Cambridge, Illinois, and found the Catholic church we attended when I was six years old. I went south of town and found the Eddie Roman farm, where we first lived when we moved to Illinois. I found the place where my first-grade one room country school once stood. We went by the huge old cemetery next to the forest where my brother and I played. I remember the monsters we created out of the trees at night, and the adventurous sled rides we took over the snow-dodging trees. The house with the big "red-bellied stove" was gone. We went to Bishop Hill and had lunch. We did all of this on bicycles in the soft warm breezes of summer.

We went to Galva, where I made my first communion. The farm we lived on where my Mom washed our clothes with the gasoline-powered washing machine was gone. But the railroad tracks were still there. We went to Kewanee, the city we moved to when I was nine years old and left soon after my twelfth birthday. There I visited Helmer Street and Dewey Avenue, streets we had lived on and Chautauqua Park where I had played. The YMCA and the Catholic church were still standing. We visited Vine Street. I couldn't find 219 South Vine, the house where I had written "Mom, Dad, Lawrence, and Me" on the toilet-room wall. We went to Atkinson and found Rachel's old farm and the Green River. I was finding myself in these places. These places of my memory did exist in reality.

When we went on one of our annual visits to Minnesota to visit my brother in Minneota, Teena and I drove south from the Minneapolis airport to Spring Valley. We rode all over the town of on our bikes. We rode by the old high school and out to the Thompson farm. It had deteriorated badly. The beautiful groves, the white picket fence, the gingerbread stucco house, and the big red barn were gone. Only the stubby little silo remained. I was saddened by the way it looked. To my mind, it appeared as if something horrible had happened here. It had. My hands trembled. I have gone by the farm many times since then, and it has become less painful to look at. I have found a way to make the entire area pleasant to me. Every year I spend a few days in autumn playing golf with Teena at the Maple Valley Golf Course, a short distance north of Spring Valley. I have been taking the pain out of my adolescence and redefining Spring Valley for myself, with a pleasant present-day reality.

At the same time, I was becoming acquainted with relatives I had never met before but had found them on the Internet. I had been searching for genealogical history of my grandparents on both sides. I had responded to a woman's posting about relatives of the Viker family of Norway. I e-mailed that I was a relative of that family. Before long another relative from Fargo wrote to me. She was unaware of the first woman's posting and my response. In short order, the three of us brought the extended Haugen family into perspective over the Internet. I learned of my Haugen family genealogy dating back to the time of Christ, an impossible-to-imagine occurrence. On my great grandmother Viker's side, I was a descendant of the ancient kings of Norway. That was a surprise. These relatives were not all gentle. They included Eric the Bloodaxe and Harold the Fairhaired. The Haugen family was the one of which I was a part, and I could be proud of that. I was indeed finding myself.

A short time later Teena and I went to Norway. We located the Viker family farm and the Viker Church. They are located north of Honefos, about ten miles on the west side of Lake Sperling. A small river flows out of the lake to Honefos, where a lovely fountain spews water high into the air from the middle of the river. We rented bikes and toured the area. We rode to the Norehov Church, where Elling and Gunhilde signed out on the church register in April 1853. The beautiful white wooden church still stands in a shady grove near a large orchard. We returned to Oslo for our departure, leaving a couple of days to visit the Viegland Sculpture Gardens, a truly remarkable place for two crazy sculptors to visit.

These were all mini-vacations interspersed within our time devoted to our work as sculptors. As time went on, I cast all my work in bronze, and I was selling it. Teena was doing well with her work too. We were each getting commissions for life-size pieces. Sometime in 1990, Teena had suggested we collaborate and work on the large pieces together. I was not sure of that idea. Her argument was that no one else was doing collaborative work, and it would bring out the best of both of our talents. We each had a different opinion as to what our individual strengths were. I believed I was the best at everything. She believed she was best at choosing gestures and designing clothes, and I was the best at faces and hands.

I was concerned we would each lose our individual identity in these joint efforts. Nonetheless, we made a collaborative piece for the Cerebral Palsy Foundation. It was an effort born out of fighting like you could hardly imagine. Teena thought she knew how the gesture should be set. I thought I knew best. I could do the faces and hands better than her. I reminded her who won the International Sculpture Competition. She refused to accept defeat with that argument. We had terrible verbal battles. The fun was in making up. We always made up, and we always ended up with a really fine sculpture.

We did the same for our next sculpture, a life-size bronze for Rabun Gap Nachoochie School. We sculpted George Woodruff of Coca Cola's Woodruff family. He was well-known in Georgia as a generous philanthropist. As we planned the gesture and the armature, we got into terrible arguments. We got in to even more arguments as we began applying the clay to make the figure and put his clothes on. Despite our verbal battles, we always arrived at a consensus, and the end result was an excellent piece of sculpture. The face of the George Woodruff sculpture is one of my favorites. I take great pride in the fact that I created that face with my hands.

One of the next projects was a public demonstration in downtown Chattanooga, where we sculpted a life-size skateboarder. The public watched us as we worked and argued. We turned out a fine sculpture that is now located at the River Gallery complex in Chattanooga.

We began doing demonstrations for groups of artists. We did three of them for the Atlanta Artists Guild. I would choose a person from the audience and have him or her come up on stage. I would start from scratch with two twenty-five pound bags of clay and a head armature. Teena loved to talk, and she talked to the audience about sculpture while I would sculpt the person's portrait in about an hour. People were amazed by what we could do. They would ask me how I could sculpt such a good likeness in such a short time. I would tell them I don't know. I just look at the person, and my fingers put the clay on the armature in such a manner that it ends up looking like the person. The image comes in through my eyes and goes out through my fingers into the clay portrait. I would tell them I had magic fingers. People would laugh and often say, "We believe you."

We did this over and over for groups in the Southeast. We were an excellent dog and pony show. Sometimes we sculpted each others portraits in about an hour or so in front of an audience. We would make each other's face and head real at first, and then we would begin to exaggerate features like a really big nose, big ears, or big mouth. People laughed at our antics and marveled at our skill with clay. We enjoyed performing.

We always took our bicycles and tennis racquets along on out-of-town trips, and we toured the towns and countryside when we were not working. Today we take our bicycles and our golf clubs.

I continued to take some commissions for life-size pieces and portraits on my own. Our collaborative efforts were not hurting us individually; if anything we were becoming better known. More and more commission opportunities were offered to us, most of them from competitions in which we competed with other artists for a job. We presented our ideas for the sculpture along with a small clay study of our ideas. The customer was usually an organization, which would then choose the sculptor. We became very good at presenting our ideas.

One of the competitions we won was for the Faces of War Memorial in Roswell, Georgia, a fine memorial to veterans, especially those of the Vietnam war. It consists of some fifty faces of U.S. servicemen, as well as Vietnamese men, women, and children. Some are screaming, some are barking out orders, some are quiet, some are wounded, some are dead or dying, some are crying. The faces have the common feature of all appearing paranoid. The eyes, if they are open, are turned dramatically to the side to see what is coming at them. A life-size American soldier walks out of this background of faces into the future represented by a little girl twirling around in a swishing nightgown as she takes the hand of the soldier. A fine layer of water flows over the faces to indicate tears and cleansing. It is a very moving sculpture. Every year about four thousand people celebrate Memorial Day there. I am very proud of this work.

Faces of War was a collaborative effort. Teena and I fought over every detail of every face and figure in the sculpture. People who worked at the Old Mill in Roswell while we were building it there can testify to that. But out of our conflicting views, we created a consensus cast in bronze that became extraordinary work of art. The sculpture brings tears to my eyes when I visit it.

Teena and I have created a great number of public life-size bronze sculptures since 1989. There are many that stand out in my mind. We created an Angel of Redemption for Cedar Lane Cemetery in Milledgeville, which contains thousands of people who died while patients at the mental hospital there and whose bodies were unclaimed. We created a large over life-size bronze angel with his left arm and open hand extended down towards the graves, and his right arm and open hand extended upward toward heaven. It is a fitting and moving sculpture that can bring tears to your eyes.

We were awarded a commission by the state of Georgia to create a memorial to the mule and the tenant farmer. This sculpture is located at the Georgia Agri-center in Perry. It is a slightly over life-size bronze of a black tenant farmer plowing with a mule. Little Jimmy Carter is walking along side the farmer carrying a bucket of drinking water. The sculpture was inspired in part by President Carter's book *An Hour Before Sunrise*. President Carter came out and dedicated this sculpture one sunny October day in 2003. In his speech he paid tribute to the black tenant farmer and his mule as the backbone of Georgia agriculture from the late 1860s to about 1950.

I am particularly proud of our life-size sculpture of William and Virginia Rose Clemens, located in the Clemens Gardens, St. Cloud Minnesota, my home state. It pleases me that we were chosen from many competitors to create this very special bronze depicting Virginia in a wheelchair and her husband, William pushing her through the rose gardens she loved.

I have enjoyed incredible success as a sculptor, far beyond what I ever could have expected. I have created many publicly displayed bronze portraits of people in the Southeast United States. Several of them are in the Shepherd Center in Atlanta. But for the most part they are scattered throughout the region. I have done portrait busts of many of Atlanta's philanthropists and the region's rich and famous, and a great number of private bronze busts for others who are not so famous but treasured.

In our collaborative efforts, Teena and I have had the same good fortune. I dare say we have created more bronze public life-size sculpture in Georgia than any sculptors ever. They will remain as our legacy long after we are gone, and I am proud of these achievements. I have worked hard at what I enjoy.

It was not all work however. We took many vacations together in Europe and in the United States. We have been to the great art centers of Europe and ogled the works of the old master sculptors and painters. We have traveled to the West to view western-style sculpture. We have traveled the eastern states to view the works of great artists from Brook Green Gardens to Washington D.C., the museums of New York, and the Maine studios of St. Gaudens. As we ogled and admired, we took our bicycles along and pedaled from place to place. We pedaled all over Washington D.C. and from there to Harper's Ferry. We have toured every Shaker community in the country and a good number of the Amish communities.

Amish communities are excellent places for bicycling. We particularly enjoyed the Amish area of Lancaster County, Pennsylvania, where we have bicycled many times. Our last trip was the only time I have ever witnessed anything close to a miracle.

Teena and I and two of our friends, Kathy and Tom, were riding our bikes near Intercourse, Pennsylvania. We had lunch there and planned to ride over to Paradise. They have great names for towns in Pennsylvania. We were east of Intercourse riding on a secondary road enjoying the Amish farm places and cropland. It was a lazy ride on a lovely summer day. Kathy was in the lead as we came up to a larger road and a stop sign. There was a solid grove of trees on the right and open field to the left, and up in front beyond the busier highway was another open field.

The road we were riding on dead ended into that highway. We had to turn right or left. Kathy stopped went out onto the highway and turned left. I stopped looked to my right. I noticed we were on a rise, and to the right I heard the sound of a speeding automobile. I couldn't see anything so I proceeded to follow Kathy across the highway to the right-hand side and pedaled slowly behind her. I looked back to see where Teena was. She was at the stop sign and Tom was a long way behind her. She pulled out onto the road following us just as I saw the speeding car come up over the rise and into view. The old car was going very fast, and bearing down on Teena. Teena was crossing the highway but still in the middle of the road when the driver must have seen her and immediately jammed her foot on to the brakes. The tires squealed and the car began to zig zag across the road.

The driver had been going way too fast and the car was out of control. I screamed at Teena to get into the ditch. I screamed and screamed. She seemed to pay no attention. It was obvious the car was going to overtake her and run right over her. Teena and her bike went into the ditch and fell over in front of a large utility pole. I screamed for her to run but she couldn't get up. Kathy and I ran from the shoulder and into the field behind the large utility pole to avoid being hit. The speeding car did not slow down; out of control it headed straight for Teena, who was struggling to get up. The car was going to run right over the top of her and smash her against the utility pole. Then a miracle happened. The car's front ended lifted into the air. The entire vehicle became airborne and hovered several feet above Teena. Its back wheels were spinning furiously but were off the ground. I ran over to Teena and pulled her out from under the vehicle, now several feet above our heads. I took her into the field and held her tight with both arms. The car had hit the utility pole guy-wire and ran right up it, the entire length of the car. The engine was still roaring and the rear wheels still spinning. I was squeezing Teena so tightly she squirmed from my grasp. She didn't understand what had happened or realize she had just escaped death by some miracle. I did though, and I continued to hug her. I was so happy that my wife, friend, and soul mate was spared a certain inexplicable fate from out of nowhere on a sunny afternoon.

We haven't been back to Intercourse or Paradise since.

I wrote this poem for Teena some time ago.

The Dancer

I saw you dancing,
  dancing in space
    high above the floor

you saw me,
  stopped
    and stood,
      heels together
        toes apart
          your hands behind your back

I looked deep into
  your dark brown eyes
    and saw into
    your soul

you giggled
  turned
    and danced away,
      in space,
        high above the floor

I can feel you dancing now,
  dancing upon my heart,
    blowing kisses into the wind,
      leaving footprints
        upon my soul

  My good friend and wife is my constant companion these days as we travel, play, and work on our mutual joy,. We have been living and working together since 1989. If you ever see us at a restaurant eating together, you will notice wedding rings and animated conversation.

EPILOGUE

What happened to Mom, Dad, Lawrence, and me over time?

I wrote "Mom" on the toilet-room wall so many years ago. When I crossed off her name, I never realized what a prophetic a gesture it was. Mom really was gone forever. When she left, our family was broken. The efforts I made to heal the wounds she had caused during my childhood were for the most part unsuccessful. The choices she made and their consequences have lasted a lifetime. I don't know why she behaved the way she did. Despite my best efforts to understand her ancestors and their experiences, there seems to be no logical explanation for my mother's behavior. She had come from a good family. She married three times, the first and last time in the Roman Catholic Church. How she managed that is beyond my understanding of Catholicism. I know she had her previous marriages annulled before she married Tom, but I have no idea how she arranged the annulments. She died in 1992 at the age of eighty-one. She was buried in Minneota's Saint Edward's Catholic Cemetery. She had taken my brother and me out of her will a few weeks before her death, inflicting one last painful rejection of us.

Dad lived from 1901 to 2000. He was a sturdy Norwegian. He never suffered from any serious illness. He had so much stress in his life, I have not come close to describing it all. Yet his health seemed to be unaffected and impervious to stress. I never understood him. I never learned why he did not stand up for himself or me at Spring Valley. He had come from a fine family and his ancestors before him were of fine Norwegian stock.

When I was a child, I kept my mother's secret sexual life from him. I never told him her secrets. I have come to believe that he knew I was my mother's accomplice in deceit. I recall Dad as being thoughtful and kind toward me, at times, when I was a small child. But by the time I was about eight or nine, he had lost his ability to love and care for me, and perhaps for anyone. I really don't know why. Perhaps my mother had just crushed his ego; maybe he was already a defeated man. By the time I was in the fifth grade, he no longer acted like a father to me. I loved him and wanted him to love me. But he never became loving or caring toward me. He remained emotionally distant through Spring Valley and my adult life. The only thing he changed was his religious affiliation. After Spring Valley, he went back to the Lutheran church of his childhood. His funeral service was in the Hope Lutheran Church, where he had been baptized. He is buried at the Lutheran Cemetery near Minneota. I cried at his funeral. He never left a will.

Lawrence lived in Minneota. He and his wife raised eight children. They now have about thirty grandchildren and five great grandchildren. Larry's life had its share of strife, but his later years were comfortable. His children and grandchildren remain for the most part in Minnesota. Our parents divorce caused Lawrence and me to be separated, which created a barrier between us that we could never quite undo. Lawrence had just turned fifteen and I had just turned twelve at the time of the divorce. He was through puberty, and I hadn't even started. He quit school; I continued. He went to a different part of the country; I ended up at Spring Valley. We were separated for six years, until I was just over eighteen. We grew to have very different personalities during the Spring Valley years, and an intellectual and emotional barrier developed between us. We became strangers and very different from each other. I go to Minnesota every year to visit him and his family because I love my brother. But even though it has been nearly six decades since Spring Valley, Larry always asked me, "What the hell really happened there? Why didn't the ol' man stand up for himself? Why didn't you do something?"

I always gave him the same answer, "I don't really know." It's easier than trying to explain.

Larry died unexpectedly and suddenly on April 27, 2010. I miss him.

In my imagination, my name is still on the toilet-room wall. I not only survived, I thrived once I escaped the consequences of my parents' choices and could finally make my own. But it has taken me a long time to work through the emotional damage they all inflicted on me. I am still working on it.

Today, when I try to figure out why people behave as they do, I keep some criteria for evaluation in mind: family background, environment, choices, consequences, and fate. The family you are born into is crucial. Your parents give you the genes and create the environment of your infancy and youth. During the first eighteen years or so of your life, your parents' choices have consequences for you. By the end of adolescence, you are making choices that determine your future and living with the consequences of your parents' choices. I add in a factor I call inexplicable and unpredictable fate. Fate can be deadly.

Some people think predicting behavior is difficult. However, it is not hard to predict a probable behavior pattern if you know some or all of these criteria. Once a pattern of behavior is established, a person tends to behave in a similar manner from then on. The old axiom about a leopard not changing its spots is an appropriate metaphor. Once you knew her, my mom's behavior was predictable. She most likely would remain narcissistic and promiscuous. My dad's behavior was predictable too. He would most likely remain emotionally distant and unable to assert himself. Using this method of thinking, even fate is predictable to some extent. Elling and Martha's fates were characterized by troublesome and hurtful relationships. Their behavior affected everyone who became emotionally close to them. One could predict that their children's fates would be bleak, at best.

It would be nice if you could trade in your flawed, dysfunctional parents for a set of really good ones. What if you could simply pray quietly or scream at the top of your voice to God? "Hey, look at me over here! Please help me! Something is very wrong! You made a mistake. These people are killing my very soul. I need to be out of here. I want out!" And a miracle occurs, and by the grace of God, you are out of there. You get a new and better set of parents. Well, that scenario will never happen. From my experience, there is no divine intervention. Unfortunately, you are stuck, and you are on your own.

So how did I escape a fate that would, in all likelihood, be bleak?

People who have recently become familiar with my story ask, "How did you survive? How did you turn out so well? Why didn't you turn out to be a criminal, a murderer, serial killer, or end up in an institution of some kind?" I tell them I just kept coping with whatever came up as best I could. Sometimes I just hung on to my sanity by a thread. At times, I accepted my miserable fate, and sometimes I fought it. Mostly, I think I acted on a strong will to survive. I could have killed the Thompsons or some of the kids at school. I had the reasons and the urges, but I feared the temptations, and had enough sense to realize I would only end up dead or in an institution. So I just kept repressing my anger.

At first, it was difficult to keep my sadness and anger contained. But I kept people in my mind that I wanted to please, like my mother, Aunt Rachel, and my brother, even if they were nowhere to be found. They existed in my memory, and I believed I mattered to them. This worked, until reality set in later. I had a tremendous struggle with my feelings of anger and abandonment while in the Army and afterwards. I alternated between wanting to prove I was a good person and not giving a damn. It was not until I met Lorraine that I began trying to be a good person. My relationship with Lorraine changed my life. She loved me. I knew it, and I felt it. Her love made all the difference. I had someone real and tangible who cared about me. I had my wife, and soon I had my children. Their love inspired me to make good choices and the consequences were good.

And I had Lorna. I always kept her in my mind. She was my muse. I wanted to prove to her that I would "amount to something." I altered fate, and it has been kind to me as an adult.

I have been asked if my experience affected my belief in God. Yes it did. I wanted God to intervene in my young life so many times and change my future. The miserable fate of my young life played out despite my best and most earnest prayers.

I like the concept of a God that intervenes to ease suffering and make the world a better place. But I haven't experienced it in my own life. My Protestant and Catholic relatives could not stand one another. Some of my Lutheran relatives could not tolerate me. Their intolerance caused me considerable emotional pain. I see this same kind of intolerance play out on the national and international stage. Organized religion, in my opinion, is intolerant.

Today I am religious in my own way. I pray to a God who in my mind is friendly, kind and forgiving. My God has no religious affiliation. He is an inexplicable force and energy.

Unfortunately, based on my experience and my observation of the world, I do not believe God intervenes to alleviate suffering. He does not stop rapes, murders, wars, genocides, diseases or catastrophes of any kind. I have no answer as to why a benevolent Father would not intervene on the side of good for his children. It is my opinion that no one really knows the answer to the question. I know some will say God does intervene, and frequently offer proof, but the proof is generally very subjective, questionable, and in the world of reality seems delusional.

I have taken you on a trip through my memories. It helped me put my life in perspective. I marvel at my own tenacity through childhood, Spring Valley, and the rest of the trip. In some ways it has been a miraculous journey. Maybe God did step into my life and change things for me; if so I was unaware. I know that a very personal love did come from Lorraine for me and it was a powerful healing medicine.

Lorraine lived in the large house we built together back in 1981 until she passed away in 2008 after a heroic battle against cancer. She never married again. She was the director of an art center in Sandy Springs, where Teena teaches and I began teaching sculpture. Lorraine and I remained good friends until her death.

Lorna lives with her professor and poet husband, John, in Minnesota. She is a published author of short stories. We enjoy a friendship and communication once again. Teena and I visited Lorna and John last autumn.

Donnie has given me four grandchildren whom I enjoy and adore. We see them often.

Stacy teaches high school English. She has not married.

Erin is married and lives nearby. She is a writer and works in fashion. I see her all the time.

My children are college educated and making their way in this world of choices, consequences, and fate. They are taking part in this fantastic, beautiful, yet strange, wonderful, and inexplicable world.

Made in the USA
Lexington, KY
25 August 2010